# SECURITY FORCES
# IN AFRICAN STATES

# SECURITY FORCES
# IN AFRICAN STATES

## Cases and Assessment

EDITED BY

## Paul Shemella and Nicholas Tomb

**Rapid Communications in Conflict and Security (RCCS) Series**
General Editor: Geoffrey R.H. Burn

## CAMBRIA
### PRESS

Amherst, New York

*Front cover image.* An Ethiopian soldier rests his gun during a break from patrol,
4th September 2014. AMISOM Photo / Ilyas A. Abukar

Requests for permission should be directed to
permissions@cambriapress.com, or mailed to:
Cambria Press
100 Corporate Parkway, Suite 128
Amherst, New York 14226

Library of Congress Cataloging-in-Publication Data

Names: Shemella, Paul, 1950- editor. | Tomb, Nicholas, editor.

Title: Security forces in African states : cases and assessment /
edited by Paul Shemella and Nicholas Tomb.

Description: Amherst, New York : Cambria Press, [2017] |
Series: Cambria rapid communications in conflict and security |
Includes bibliographical references and index.

Identifiers: LCCN 2016054840 | ISBN 9781604979817 (alk. paper)

Subjects: LCSH: Civil-military relations--Africa--Case studies.
| Africa--Armed Forces--Case studies. | Law enforcement--
Africa--Case studies. | Human security--Africa--Case studies.

Classification: LCC JQ1873.5.C58 S43 2017 |
DDC 355.0096--dc23
LC record available at https://lccn.loc.gov/2016054840

# TABLE OF CONTENTS

# List of Tables

# SECURITY FORCES
# IN AFRICAN STATES

CHAPTER 1

# THE LARGER CONTEXT

*Paul Shemella*

It is well known that most African polities suffer from the conditions brought about by weak or bad governance: poverty, illiteracy, political instability, and often conflict.[1] Less well known is the degree to which the mismanagement of security forces has contributed to these outcomes. In this realm, issues of roles and missions loom large. As a general rule, armed forces are focused on providing what is known as *traditional security* through deterrence and defense, while law enforcement organizations anchor the government's efforts to create a climate of *human security* throughout the society.[2] Armed forces can be used to help governments improve human security along the difficult road to prosperity, literacy, political stability, and domestic tranquility. But that is not the primary role of armies and navies. As central as security is to social well-being, good governance is largely an exercise in making distinctions between these two broad types of security, and then applying armed forces, law enforcement, and intelligence resources appropriately (in coordination with the rest of the government). Too often, the military leg of this triad —driven by fearful or misguided politicians—actually serves to diminish human security. Perhaps the most essential element of governing well is making security forces part of the solution rather than part of the problem.

The African institutional landscape features a routine convergence of roles and missions for law enforcement and armed forces elements. Consequently, in this volume, we will include national-level law enforcement personnel under the rubric *military*. When we speak of *civil-military relations*, we are describing relationships among nonmilitary citizens (including government officials) and national police, gendarmerie, maritime law enforcement, intelligence, and other security institutions— well as the armed forces. Our experience with teaching this subject in the developing world convinces us that clear distinctions between the armed forces and law enforcement rarely exist outside the Western liberal democratic bubble.[3] The case studies herein will evaluate, within a more comprehensive analysis, whether the capacities of law enforcement forces are *adequate*, and if the capacities of armed forces are *necessary*. This book is, more than anything else, an examination of African governance through a broadened civil-military relations lens. Good governance overall goes far beyond the cultivation of high capacity (but deliberately constrained) security institutions. It is impossible without them.

For a long time, scholars have searched for answers to the question *Why are some countries poor and others not?* and have settled on four basic theories: bad geography, culture, ignorance, and bad institutions.[4] Poverty may result from all of these factors, but we believe that dysfunctional institutions are a major part of the problem. Dysfunctional *security* institutions tend to wield even more influence than the others because they are better resourced, ubiquitous, armed, and often political.[5] This leads us to examine the related questions of how a family of security institutions can be reformed and constrained. Management and control mechanisms vary from government to government, but certain principles—rooting out corruption, for example—are universal.[6] Africa, with a plethora of poor countries, is perhaps the best place to test these ideas.

Paul Collier has written that countries wracked by poverty are the victims of four possible "traps" that keep their economies from growing fast enough to escape: the conflict trap, the natural resources trap, the trap of being landlocked, and the trap of bad governance.[7] Avoiding or exiting the conflict trap is difficult if national-level security institutions have too much power relative to the civilians who are supposed to control them (or if civilian leaders have coopted the armed forces for their personal agendas). Bad governance is the most critical of the four; escaping this trap provides the key to unlocking all the others. Often standing in the way are comparatively powerful *armed forces* unbalancing the web of government institutions needed to drive good governance and produce total security. In the extreme, with ample evidence from African history, armed forces can decide to take on the role of governance themselves.[8]

All human beings wish to be governed well, but what do we really mean by *good governance*? As expected, the definitions available vary with the perspective of the organizations attempting to answer this question. However, a survey of the most important of those organizations reveals two common pillars: lack of violence and good civil-military relations.[9] Good governance is both a precondition and a product of human security. No individual citizen living in fear is secure; no society living with systemic sources of fear can be described as well governed. But human security is also the alleviation of want. Fear and want are mutually reinforcing; fear is an obstacle to satisfying want, and people without enough to eat are constantly afraid. Resisting invasion requires different tools and strategies than preventing hunger, but in both cases it is ordinary people who should benefit from the actions of their security forces. Indeed, the fundamental value of any nation's military must be that soldiers are willing to sacrifice—even themselves—for their fellow citizens. Security institutions, properly trained and resourced, are on the critical path to governing well, especially when they work closely with the rest of the government.

Since our teaching programs are necessarily short, The Center for Civil-Military Relations needed an analytical tool that could be introduced and understood within a few days. We did not find such a tool, so we decided to develop our own assessment framework.[10] Beyond brevity, the value of such a framework would be to send a student home with something practical that he or she could apply quickly and without further assistance. Our framework focuses on the security sector, but its reach goes beyond that. Lasting improvements will not come from the efforts of security forces alone; they derive from broad-based, inter-institutional, and long-term government programs.

The front-end assessment for this approach should begin with an evaluation of how well security institutions are designed, governed and operated within the institutional mix—a complex task that resists formulaic approaches (because each government—and the society it serves—is unique). Chapter 2 will introduce the framework, and the case studies that follow will use it as a diagnostic resource (the case studies, in turn, will have informed the assessment framework). The concluding chapter will link the experiences of our selected governments back to the tools, and to each other. We believe this framework can be used to assess security governance and capacity in any African government.[11]

In order to set the context within which our series of assessments will proceed, it would be useful to consider what governance across the African continent actually looks like—a spectrum of possible outcomes for the region. Merilee Grindle has published a typology of government regimes around the world, organized according to the following short descriptions of how power is exercised:

1. collapsed states
2. personal rule
3. minimally institutionalized states

4. institutionalized noncompetitive states
5. institutionalized competitive states[12]

The listing suggests a path to security and prosperity for any state, regardless of where it starts out, but it also suggests how a highly institutionalized state can regress. Africa offers examples of each category, as well as the potential for transition. The expected recovery timeline may be long for "collapsed states" like Somalia and the Central African Republic, but the experiences of Rwanda, Uganda, and others illustrate surprisingly swift movement in the right direction. Mali and Zimbabwe remind us that momentum in the wrong direction can also develop quickly. We will show that the emergence of nonpartisan and high-capacity security institutions can generate momentum towards good governance.

Our case studies draw from this spectrum of political systems while assessing the governance and capacity of security forces—and the implications of these arrangements for governance overall. There is much bad news here, but there is also reason to expect continued improvement in many of the cases, if only because some of them start from such a low base. In chapter 3, Nicholas Tomb examines security issues in the Democratic Republic of Congo, a country lying somewhere on either side of personal rule ("minimally institutionalized state" or "collapsed state"). Rife with corruption and vast ungovernable spaces, this side of the Congo River—in the very heart of Africa—is a good place to begin testing the value of the framework.

Since independence, West Africa has been the stage for the most military coups on the continent.[13] We thought a larger number of cases from that region might help the reader understand why. In chapter 4, Thomas Bruneau analyzes Guinea-Bissau, a thoroughly corrupted waypoint for cocaine shipments from South America bound for Europe. In chapter 5, Paul Clarke takes us to neighboring Guinea and its very different security sector challenges. In chapter 6, Cristiana Matei discusses Mali, perhaps the best recent example of bad civil-military relations and security forces dysfunction. In chapter 7, Madoua Teko-Folly takes a look at the less well-known security problems of Togo, a state that has never gotten out from under personal rule. In chapter 8, rounding out our West Africa examples, Thomas Mockaitis examines the very complex case of Nigeria.

In chapter 9, Lawrence Cline analyzes the security forces of Kenya, an institutionalized and marginally competitive state and shows us how a reasonably well-developed government can falter badly. With chapter 10, Bruce Sweeney, a former US Defense Attaché in Addis Ababa, will examine neighboring Ethiopia, the only African country (other than Liberia) that has not been colonized by Europeans. The Ethiopia case demonstrates better than most how difficult it can be to deliver both traditional security and human security at the same time. In chapter 11 Christopher Jasparro discusses the counterintuitive case of Chad, a country long besieged with internal and external threats but militarily and politically stronger than might be expected—at least in the near future.

North Africa is different than the rest of the continent, but when one examines the issue of security governance it is not *that* different. Chapter 12 is an examination of Tunisia's security forces. Lawrence Cline examines the institutional development of armed forces, police forces, and intelligence agencies in the only government to survive the Arab Spring with a more democratic political system. Tunisia, though still riddled with security problems, could become a laboratory for what might be possible in a democratic society on the fringe of the Arab world, and perhaps a model for much of North Africa and the Sahel. That said, the jury is still out.

The uncontested employment of coercive force is, however, only a starting point. The appropriate capacity of that force—and how it can be controlled democratically—are equally essential issues. Although we have striven to be as comprehensive as possible, one book cannot cover everything and some important countries have had to be omitted. Nevertheless, we hope the cases we have included will provide readers with the motivation and experience to apply our assessment tools to other African countries. In chapter 13, the selected governments have been removed from their individual contexts and plugged back into the tables from chapter 2. In this way, best practices can be shared with the reader and serve as a point of reference for future assessments.

Africa's development is either stuck—or it is in overdrive—depending on which of the continent's fifty-four countries one is examining.[14] More broadly, the question that arises is whether the African glass is half empty or half full. The issues for us to examine here include whether or not a particular country is moving toward an institutionalized competitive political system, how security forces can contribute to this outcome, and which best practices might have wider application. With the chapters that follow, we aim to help the reader understand these questions and gain insight into the way ahead.

## NOTES

1. For one of the best sources on why Africans suffer from these afflictions see Greg Mills, *Why Africa is Poor: And What Africans Can Do About It* (Johannesburg, South Africa: Penguin Books, 2010). Mills' argument that Africans themselves must fix these problems inspires the assessment framework developed in this text.
2. Former UN Secretary-General, Kofi Annan (perhaps borrowing from Franklin Delano Roosevelt) defines human security as "...freedom from fear and freedom from want." The full text of his definition can be found at http://www.gdrc.org/sustdev/husec/Definitions.pdf.
3. David Chuter and Florence Gaub, *Understanding African Armies* (Paris: The European Union Institute for Security Studies, April 2016), 12.
4. For a good summary of these arguments, see Francis Fukuyama, *Political Order and Political Decay: From the Industrial Revolution to the Globalization of Democracy*, (New York: Farrar, Straus and Giroux, 2014), 227–241.
5. In this volume, the term *security institutions* will include armed forces, law enforcement institutions, and intelligence organizations. The three are often referred to collectively as the *security sector*.
6. All governments suffer from the disease of corruption. Even the NATO alliance is attempting to drive corruption down to the lowest possible level. For any government dealing seriously with this issue, the NATO program is worth studying. See Todor Tagarev, *Building Integrity and Reducing Corruption in Defence: A Compendium of Best Practices* (Geneva: The Geneva Center for Democratic Control of Armed Forces, 2010).
7. Paul Collier, *The Bottom Billion* (Oxford: Oxford University Press, 2007), 17–75.
8. Despite the conventional wisdom of outsiders, African populations tend to reject military rule. For a discussion of these attitudes, statistics, and reforms see Chuter and Gaub, *Understanding African Armies*, 31.
9. Merilee Grindle, "Good Enough Governance Revisited," *Development Policy Review*, 2007, 25(5), 556–557.
10. The Western donor community does not lack security assessment tools, but they tend to be overly complicated and difficult to implement.
11. Governance is reflected in policies and strategies. Capacity, both administrative and operational, is the ability to execute policies and strategies.
12. Grindle, "Good Enough Governance Revisited," 564.

13. Chuter and Gaub, *Understanding African Armies*, 25.
14. For an exhaustive but readable history of modern Africa, which provides the context needed to understand the possible direction the continent might be heading, see Martin Meredith, *The Fate of Africa: A History of the Continent Since Independence* (New York: Public Affairs, 2011).

CHAPTER 2

# TOOLS FOR ASSESSMENT
# OF SECURITY

## LEVEL 1 AND LEVEL 2

*Paul Shemella*

Only governments can provide what social scientists call *public goods*, a series of services and conditions that benefit all the citizens of a society without regard for status or wealth. Examples include clean air and water, environmental protection, a legal system, public health, transportation infrastructure, private property rights, and contract enforcement. But public goods also include national defense, public safety and maritime security, conditions necessary for individuals, families and communities to thrive.[1] Developing countries cannot develop further without security; developed countries cannot *stay* developed without security.

As it matures, a government does not need to hold a monopoly on very many things, but it must, if it wishes to govern well, maintain control of all coercive force. At the same time, governments must decide how best to *use* coercive force, both domestically and internationally; then put in place the policies, structures, and processes needed to achieve its desired outcomes. This chapter will introduce a handful of tools for assessing the governance and capacity of security institutions. Collectively, the tools comprise a basic framework (what we call "Level 1") as well as a more detailed assessment framework (what we call "Level 2"). Subsequent chapters will examine the security forces of individual African countries through both analytical lenses.

## National Brands

Governments use security forces in two basic ways: internally and externally. In fully democratic countries, the internal use of force is exercised by police institutions—but armed forces are sometimes called upon to assist (riot control and disaster relief are just two examples). Legal frameworks and operational mechanisms for this sharing of roles prevent backsliding into a reliance on the use of soldiers for law enforcement functions. The ways in which governments use their armed forces tells us a lot about how well they govern, as well as how they want their own citizens and other governments to view them. Table 1 lists six categories of governments, sorted according to the way they use armed forces (as opposed to police and other government institutions).

Minimally institutionalized states tend to use armed forces for domestic roles more often than those states that are highly institutionalized. Some African governments have threats and resources sufficient to delineate security roles more clearly, casting themselves as warfighters or defenders (and governments with enough resources can decide to fill multiple roles). Many others, however, must settle for a regular mixing of armed forces with police forces in order to maintain internal security. These countries, often the focus of Western security sector reform (SSR) assistance, seek more resources along with the institutional transformation necessary to rebrand themselves ("fireman" countries are normally farther along this path than "policeman" countries). The transition from one category to another thus depends on good policies (governance), operational capability over time (capacity), and a clear articulation of how security forces will be used.[2]

A growing number of African governments—some profiled in this volume—have chosen to dedicate a portion of their armed forces to peacekeeping missions outside the country, thus beginning the process of rebranding their nations. Going in the other direction are "troublemaker" governments that allow their armed forces either to assume power themselves, or to exert overwhelming influence on use-of-force decisions by civilian leadership. Large armies without legitimate external roles not only waste public resources; they become politicized. Whether deliberate or not, the way in which governments use armed forces leaves them with a national brand that other governments must consider as they make their own bilateral and regional policy choices. National brands —reinforced by the daily performance of security forces—also provide incentives or disincentives for citizens to support their own governments, a crucial precondition for good governance overall.[3]

## SECURITY THREATS AND SOCIETAL RISK

Evaluating the governance and capacity of security forces in African countries begins with an understanding of threats and proceeds through an examination of risk. Threats at the state level (often called *traditional security*) are well understood: the imposition of another government's will (sometimes in the form of outright invasion), large-scale terrorism or guerrilla activity, support for the internal opponents of a sitting regime, or the violation of maritime borders and air space. At the same time, African citizens face a long list of *human security* threats (the responses to which compete for the same government resources) that leave them fearful and hungry. Without human security, there can be no traditional security; without traditional security, there can be no human security. So, how can government resources be distributed in the most effective ways to counter these threats? Table 2 is a generic, non-exhaustive threat matrix that establishes a conceptual basis for the generation (or reform) of security forces in Africa.

If threats are the basis for generating security forces, the evaluation of *risk* is a necessary interim stepping stone. Risk can be defined according to the following simple formula:

$$\text{Risk} = (\text{Threat} + \text{Vulnerability}) - \text{Capability}$$

A threat is merely the potential for causing harm. Vulnerability (the susceptibility to that harm) and capability (the means to offset that susceptibility) can be evaluated through a process of risk assessment.[4] One such process uses a panel of experts to consider the country-specific variables of history, vulnerability, maximum threat, and probability.[5] These deliberations would account for a government's successful efforts (already taken) to reduce vulnerability. They would also reveal areas that require more resources and perhaps creative new approaches to enhancing security. The result of risk assessment, then, is a listing of the relative risk associated with each significant threat. That is the next step —and a good baseline—for building security institutions.[6]

## Why Institutions?

Government leaders must develop institutions to express their instruments of national power.[7] Even so-called African "big men" bent on personal rule need a hierarchy of experts to carry out their proposals and actions—a government of ministers and bureaucrats building institutional capacity. In the early stages of transition, nominal democracies often begin with charismatic individuals who bring personal networks of family and friends into the political elite. From this foundation, fragile at best, new institutions must be created (or re-created) for a spectrum of public purposes. It will take some time (and a lot of work) for these institutions to become self-sustaining and merit-based. It will also take time for the executive—with its reliance on security forces—to engineer a dynamic balance among security, legislative, judicial, and civil society institutions.[8] The blueprint for this transition is normally laid out in a carefully drafted white paper on defense and security that forms the basis of formal roles and expected missions.

How does a government build the right institutions, making sure they are big enough—but not *too* big? The first and most important ingredient is good leadership. The leader must design (or redesign) the institution and infuse it with a command climate that encourages people at all levels to work together, as well as with other institutions.[9] Given the right authorities and incentives, individuals within the institution contribute ideas and take action horizontally. Viewing the governance of security institutions through a human security lens reminds us that good governance at the national level is an interagency enterprise. For that, institutions require complementarity and reciprocity; they must be dependent on each other *and* willing to act as a team. Institutions with just enough resources to fulfill their assigned roles can complement partner institutions without seeking to supplant them. The ultimate goal—very difficult in practice—is to develop trust between institutions. Team building across the spectrum of government is just as important as building capacity within a single institution. The only institution that counts is, in fact, the government itself.

If security institutions, especially armed forces, soak up too much of the national budget, there will not be enough money left to develop the others. Within the family of security institutions, it is usually the armed forces—most powerful to begin with—that end up with the lion's share of resources. The strict enforcement of security institutional roles (and the withholding of unnecessary resources) can help governments develop sustained capacity in *all* their institutions. The political environment is constantly changing, and the institutions that respond must change with it. Government institutions are, in this sense, similar to Schumpeter's businesses; they can be created, re-created, or destroyed altogether.[10] Security institutions, as the oldest and most conservative, resist the control that is a precondition for such changes. They also have the guns. That brings us back to Plato's question on *who guards the guardians?*[11]

## DEMOCRATIC CONTROL OF SECURITY INSTITUTIONS

Just as important as building structures to control security institutions is designing a system of implementing that control. The broader question, then, is how exactly does a government guard the *guardians?*[12] In the middle stages of transition, young democracies (if they work at all) are fragile. At this point, security institutions can either stop progress in its tracks through partisanship (and, perhaps, *coup d'etat*) or they can facilitate further transition by adopting the role of honest broker between the government and its citizens. The honest broker role, however, can engender a self-image of organizational (and even moral) superiority that also freezes the transition—with or without a coup. Security forces with the power and motivation to take over the government "to protect it" from antidemocratic forces do not contribute to its growth or stability. Ultimately—and with the right human chemistry—a triangle of creative tension forms among civil society, security forces, and the government. This balance of power, known as *civil-military relations*, stands to benefit all three groups as they work together to provide both traditional and human security.[13]

Democracy developed and spread based upon the relationship of three national-level variables: government, rule of law, and *democratic account-ability* where the former is limited by both of the latter (each serving to support the other).[14] At the institutional level, democratic control of security forces can been seen the same way—a triangle with the vertices institutional leadership, rule of law (as it pertains to security forces), and the accountability mechanisms put in place to check the power of the executive. Given that security forces are normally subordinate to more than one ministry (perhaps the first step towards democratic control), laws and accountability mechanisms emerge as multifaceted and compre-hensive, with individual ministers managing the process. However, as

Thomas Bruneau has noted, civilian control of the armed forces is not meaningful if effectiveness and efficiency are lost in the process.[15] The same can be said for security forces as a whole. Democratic control is thus a three-legged stool at two levels—national and institutional.

Governments wishing to structure a system for democratic control of security forces can impose limitations on four institutional characteristics: roles, size, budget, and power.

**Limit roles.** Governments can limit the assigned roles for security institutions by restricting them to technical projects, say building infrastructure, preventing cyber attacks, or investigating crimes. Without stated roles, security forces almost inevitably take on *implied* roles; in some cases they simply do what they want. This institutional sloppiness works both ways; governments without strong and reliable *nonsecurity* institutions often use security forces as a general reservoir of manpower and expertise.

**Limit size.** "Downsizing" is a common way to channel security institutions into forms of behavior that do not threaten governments or the societies they serve. It is easy for Western technical and financial partners to suggest African governments reduce the size of their security forces, but dumping large numbers of trained military personnel on the street with few job prospects is not a recipe for public security or political stability.

**Limit budgets.** Some security institutions are underfunded, but others may be overfunded. Only a budgeting process, based upon risk analysis and opportunity costs, can help government officials determine how to distribute precious resources. But simply reducing the amount of money those institutions receive will not necessarily cause them to restructure themselves in productive ways. Resources must match roles; limiting roles is a precondition for limiting budgets.

**Limit power.** The fourth option is to limit the *power* of security forces, that is, to place legal, political, and practical constraints on what they can actually do. Beginning with the Constitution, all the way to the battlefield or town square, security forces should face a continuous series of constraints that preserve the benefits of their actions while minimizing the consequences. In the absence of constraints, senior security officials, steeped in leadership, can "lean into" politics. Guns plus political savvy is an all-too-common formula for military rule.

Placing limits on the roles, size, budget, and power of security forces as a *sector* of government is not enough, however. Constraints must also be applied to individual security institutions relative to each other. Table 3 suggests basic rules of thumb for all governments to consider when assigning roles (and resources) to security forces. Given the inevitability of overlapping requirements for different security institutions, such a set of rules can help guide governments toward the most rational, effective, and efficient use of their security institutions as a whole.[16]

The foregoing discussion might lead to a deeper understanding of how specific governments use security forces. In an effort to go further, table 4 views the political systems introduced in chapter 1 through a security forces lens. Categorizing African governments according to how security forces are governed, developed, and employed enables all concerned parties to identify what is deficient and how to improve it. Governments that make progress toward democratic control of security forces will inevitably move closer to full democracy. The heart of such an arrangement is a bargain between the executive and the legislature: security forces need resources, while legislatures need information. The *soul* of the arrangement—without which nothing works—is a strong connection between security forces and the public.[17] Transparency, even with regard to intelligence institutions, is the fuel that makes democratic machinery run smoothly.

While recognizing that the critical path towards good governance requires government control of coercive force, that control must be increasingly democratic. The ultimate civilian control can be seen in dictatorships like North Korea and (less extremely) the nominally democratic but authoritarian regimes that govern so many of Africa's transitional states. The challenge of democratic control poses a major dilemma, however, that advanced democracies do not seem to adequately appreciate. Whatever mechanisms new democracies opt to exercise, the control of security forces (and society generally) requires strong leadership. The question that arises, then, is two-fold: *how strong, and for how long?* Some of the most "successful" African governments have been those with strong leaders, "re-elected" for decades (see Cameroon and Rwanda). We think that a transition as difficult as the democratic one may benefit from a period of authoritarian rule, but this is certainly not a prescription for better long-term outcomes. Governments that do not evolve into "institutionalized competitive states" are unlikely to develop the broad, multifaceted control of security forces that is an essential pillar of full democracy.[18]

## A FRAMEWORK FOR ASSESSING SECURITY FORCES: LEVEL 2

The structuring, controlling, and operating of security forces is such a complex series of parallel activities that a comprehensive assessment tool cannot be avoided. The tool should be rigorous enough to guide a thorough examination of security governance but simple enough to be understood by the practitioners who will actually use it. Tables 5–7 constitute a series of tools for assessing the governance and capacity of security forces in a notional government. These tables (Level 2) allow us to examine the policies, structures, and processes for managing security forces as a whole, breaking the sector into its three broad components.

Establishing democratic control at the national level, however, does not automatically result in democratic control within each security institution. Democratic control at the institutional level can be evaluated using a table similar to the national-level tables above. The questions reflect organizational imperatives, but the measurement process is the same. Government officials, working with key personnel in each security institution (and perhaps international technical partners) would generate tables for each of the following security institutions: Army, Navy, Air Force, National Police, Gendarmerie, Coast Guard, National Intelligence Agency, and others as appropriate. Table 8 allows us to evaluate the performance of particular security institutions as they attempt to enhance operational capacity and implement democratic control.

The Likert scale (1–10) for grading the governance and capacity for each desired outcome is somewhat subjective but not trivial.[19] Such a scheme allows those who *know* to convert their judgment into numbers that can be easily understood by those who *decide*. The integrity of the assessment process depends upon having knowledgeable individuals— from within and from outside the government—assign numbers to both sets of indicators listed for each desired outcome. The procedure is most valuable when *groups* of experts share their numbers and attempt to justify them to each other. The results of such working sessions are three-fold. First, the structured discussion yields new insight into specific problems. Second, the governance and capacity measures can be totaled to indicate where additional resources should be applied in order to improve both democratic control and institutional performance. Third, the "major shortfalls" can be identified with some consensus, generating credible proposals and detailed remedial plans to national and institutional leadership. Taken together, Tables 5–8 can reveal what government officials and their civil society organizations need to know as they strive to restructure and reform their security forces.

## CONCLUSION

The tools offered in this chapter can be used in various ways to evaluate how well a selected African government is governing and developing its security force institutions.[20] Within this set of tools also lie the means to assess how well single security institutions are performing their roles and expected missions. One cannot assess the effectiveness of a government at-large without looking in detail at how policies, strategies, bureaucratic structures, and decision-making processes enable security institutions.

At the same time, governments and their security institutions should be examining how their activities can be synchronized with those of neighboring countries. Confronted by the same limitations as under-resourced institutions, poor countries can make security more cost-effective by sharing assets where feasible and coordinating operations.[21] Regional and international peacekeeping efforts facilitate such sharing, while providing the legitimate external roles that often lead to more professional security forces.

The case studies that follow will draw on the analytical tools in this chapter to discuss the efforts of those governments to govern and operate their security forces. The cases have been selected to illustrate a diversity of responses to universal security challenges. In addition to examining the unique aspects of particular countries, each case study will address specifically the following set of questions, derived directly from tables 1 through 4:

- What is the "national brand" of the country as a consequence of the way the government uses its armed forces?
- What are the most significant threats that must be dealt with by the security sector?
- What are the roles of the armed forces and law enforcement forces, and how do they complement one another?
- Into which category of political system does the country fit most accurately? To what degree do security institutions influence the government's political system?
- Does the governance and capacity of the security sector contribute to healthy relationships between security forces and society, as well as good governance overall? If not, why not?
- What are the trends for security sector institutions, and are there measures of effectiveness that can be captured and tracked over time?

The Mali case will be examined not only through the Level 1 assessment questions, but also at Level 2 through the completion of tables 5–7 in the concluding chapter. The continent of Africa is well suited to such a wide-ranging and comprehensive approach. Lessons learned by the governments profiled here, bound together by the Level 1 and Level 2 assessments, can instigate real progress in the transformation of security establishments elsewhere in Africa and beyond.

Table 1. National Branding: How Governments Use Armed Forces.

| 1. Warfighter | Initiate conflict with other states. Prevail militarily. |
|---|---|
| 2. Defender | Repel invasion and obtain assistance from other countries. Defend against transnational threats. |
| 3. Peacekeeper | Organize, train, and deploy armed forces specifically for international peacekeeping missions. |
| 4. Fireman | Use armed forces to perform any domestic mission that other government institutions cannot be trusted to accomplish. |
| 5. Policeman | Use armed forces to enforce laws. Police in support. |
| 6. Troublemaker | Allow armed forces to determine when to use coercive force against other States. |

Table 2. African Security Threats.

|  | External | Internal |
|---|---|---|
| **Traditional** | Invasion | Public Disorder |
|  | Border Violations | Organized Crime |
|  | Bombardment | Political Violence |
|  | Jihadist Terrorism | Tribalism |
| **Human** | Natural disaster | Bad Governance |
|  | Mass Migration | Food Insecurity |
|  | Wildlife Poaching | Health Insecurity |
|  | Climate Change | Corruption |

Note. *Some threats are manifested in multiple categories. Many can be man-made, as well as natural.


Table 3. Thumb Rules for Roles: Armed Forces vs Law Enforcement.

| Armed Forces | War with neighboring States. War with terrorist organizations. Civil war. Peacekeeping operations. Preserving territorial integrity.  Defense of maritime borders and air space. Building critical infrastructure (roads, bridges, dams). |
|---|---|
| Law Enforcement | Public security. Citizen security. Criminal investigations. Protecting critical infrastructure. Cyber security. Security of inland waters. |
| Either or Both | Border security. Counter-narcotics. Counter-terrorism. Riot control. Maritime domain awareness. Disaster relief. Elections security. Civic action. |

## Table 4. Security Forces in Differing Political Systems.

| | |
|---|---|
| 1. Collapsed State | The government, if there is one, does not have exclusive control of coercive force. Competing power centers have their own armies or militias and national political control is contested. State-on-State conflict is less likely, but terrorist organizations can flourish, threatening other States. |
| 2. Personal Rule | Government is run by one powerful individual, assisted by family and friends. Corruption is rampant. Security forces focused on maintaining order and protecting the ruler. Armed forces will engage with neighboring States if necessary to fulfill those roles. |
| 3. Minimally Institutionalized State | Marginally capable and largely corrupt armed forces dominate the security sector; law enforcement and intelligence institutions wrest their rightful roles from the armed forces. The government is weak and may view security forces as a threat to the regime. Non-security institutions must compete for roles and resources. |
| 4. Institutionalized Non-competitive State | Security institutions are well established but share power, influence and funding with non-security institutions. Corruption is systematic. Decision-making is top-down by the same political party for long periods. |
| 5. Institutionalized Competitive State | Ruling teams are changed regularly and non-violently. Corruption is slowly being reduced. Most decision-making is devolved to a balanced web of government institutions. Security forces have clear roles, sufficient resources, and necessary capacity, while remaining under democratic control. |

Table 5a. Level 2 Assessment: Armed Forces.

| Armed Forces | Desired Outcome | Governance Measure (1-10) | Capacity Measure (1-10) | Major Shortfalls |
|---|---|---|---|---|
| 1 | **The armed forces have legal and well-defined external and internal roles.** Without such roles, armed forces, especially armies, can pose a threat to elected civilian leaders by assuming political influence or through direct action against a government with which they disagree. | The extent to which government policies, strategies and laws lead to the desired outcome. | Does the government have the institutional capacity and political will to implement the policies, strategies and laws? | List the most important obstacles blocking the government's attainment of the desired outcome. |
| 2 | **Internal roles are coordinated with law enforcement and intelligence at all levels of strategy.** Internal roles for the armed forces should be minimized, but they are inevitable. In the absence of natural or man-made disaster (where institutional boundaries may break down temporarily) police institutions should have the primary roles for the domestic use of force, while the armed forces should be in support of those efforts. | " | " | " |

Table 5b. Level 2 Assessment: Armed Forces (*cont.*).

| Armed Forces | Desired Outcome | Governance Measure (1-10) | Capacity Measure (1-10) | Major Shortfalls |
|---|---|---|---|---|
| 3 | **Officers of the armed forces and civilian officials are given opportunities to educate each other regarding the proper use of armed forces.** Unless both sides of the traditional civil-military equation are adequately informed, the treatment and employment of soldiers, sailors, and airmen could be mishandled. The spectrum of results could range from inappropriate politicization of the officer corps to military defeat against existential threats. | " | " | " |
| 4 | **Military services reflect the ethnic, gender, and tribal composition of the society at large.** In order to be effective in keeping citizens safe and secure, military institutions should, as much as possible, look like the society they serve. | " | " | " |

Table 5c. Level 2 Assessment: Armed Forces (*cont.*).

| Armed Forces | Desired Outcome | Governance Measure (1-10) | Capacity Measure (1-10) | Major Shortfalls |
|---|---|---|---|---|
| 5 | **There is continuous legislative oversight of armed forces activities.** Those who make the laws must understand armed forces issues, develop a process for considering legislation, and enact laws that will improve all aspects of performance for these institutions. One marker for such requirements is whether or not the legislature has formed a "Defense Committee." | " | " | " |
| 6 | **The armed forces are trusted by all segments of society.** Without that trust there can be no security – traditional or human (especially if armed forces personnel have domestic security roles). It is very important for armed forces institutions to avoid political alliances with civilian leaders so that ordinary citizens understand these institutions are working for *them*. | " | " | " |

Table 5d. Level 2 Assessment: Armed Forces (*cont.*).

| Armed Forces | Desired Outcome | Governance Measure (1-10) | Capacity Measure (1-10) | Major Shortfalls |
|---|---|---|---|---|
| 7 | **Armed forces institutions play no role in the national economy.** Any participation by armed forces in the national economy should be discouraged, and programs to avoid such activities should be implemented as soon as possible. Armed forces institutions with sufficient formal budgets are free to concentrate on defense of the nation; armed forces personnel with adequate salaries do not have the incentive to engage in criminal activities or corruption. | " | " | " |
| 8 | **Decision-making by and about the armed forces is transparent.** Policies should be in place to inform both government officials and ordinary citizens regarding armed forces activities. In order to build trust and confidence, armed forces institutions should establish outreach programs to civil-society organizations and the media sector. | " | " | " |

Table 5e. Level 2 Assessment: Armed Forces (*cont.*).

| Armed Forces | Desired Outcome | Governance Measure (1-10) | Capacity Measure (1-10) | Major Shortfalls |
|---|---|---|---|---|
| 9 | **Private armies and militias do not operate in the country.** These groups of citizens challenge political stability and can easily overwhelm law enforcement institutions, creating a significant internal role for the national army. There can be no tolerance for the exercise of coercive force within the population. Ongoing efforts against criminality can be augmented by public-private security partnerships, and the armed forces can assist police with public order if necessary. | " | " | " |

Table 5f. Level 2 Assessment: Armed Forces (*cont.*).

| Armed Forces | Desired Outcome | Governance Measure (1-10) | Capacity Measure (1-10) | Major Shortfalls |
|---|---|---|---|---|
| 10 | **Civilians exercise effective democratic control of the armed forces.** This condition amounts to the aggregation of the other nine, demonstrating that democratic control is a multi-faceted process sensitive to initial conditions, individual personalities, and ongoing environmental changes. | " | " | " |
| *Total Scores (x/100)* | | **Average the scores for desired outcomes.** | **Average the scores for desired outcomes.** | **Add additional major shortfalls.** |

Table 6a. Level 2 Assessment: Law Enforcement.

| Law Enforce-ment | Desired Outcome | Governance Measure (1-10) | Capacity Measure (1-10) | Major Shortfalls |
|---|---|---|---|---|
| 1 | **The internal roles for law enforcement institutions are legally and clearly defined.** Law enforcement should have the lead role in maintaining citizen security and public order. Ambiguity in the statement of these roles can open the way for armed forces—normally better endowed with resources in the first place—to take the lead. | The extent to which government policies, strategies and laws lead to the desired outcome. | Does the government have the institutional capacity and political will to implement the policies, strategies and laws? | List the most important obstacles blocking the government's attainment of the desired outcome. |
| 2 | **There are legal and operational mechanisms for allowing armed forces and intelligence units to support law enforcement institutions.** The separation—and occasional integration—of soldiers and policemen can lead to rational resource distribution, increased public trust, and better governance overall. | " | " | " |
| 3 | **Law enforcement institutions maintain partnerships with commercial security companies.** Commercial businesses can secure their infrastructure with private security forces, but only the government can provide security over a wide area. While guarding against co-optation by powerful private interests, governments can rely on these partnerships to reduce the burden on their own institutions. | " | " | " |

Table 6b. Level 2 Assessment: Law Enforcement (*cont.*).

| Law Enforce -ment | Desired Outcome | Governance Measure (1-10) | Capacity Measure (1-10) | Major Shortfalls |
|---|---|---|---|---|
| 4 | **There is a legal framework for the use of law enforcement at all levels.** Systems of justice consist of three pillars: laws, law enforcement, and punishment for those who violate the law. Criminal threats are constantly changing; laws must be updated and strengthened to keep them useful in prosecuting groups or individuals. | " | " | " |
| 5 | **There is continuous legislative oversight of law enforcement activities.** Beyond acquiring the knowledge needed to make better laws, legislative structures should be maintained to investigate breeches of law enforcement practices. Laws are needed to establish the rules by which society operates, and these laws must apply to law enforcement officials themselves. | " | " | " |
| 6 | **Law enforcement institutions reflect the ethnic, gender, and tribal composition of the society at large.** In order to be effective in keeping citizens safe and secure, law enforcement institutions should, as much as possible, look like the society they serve. Whether they are enforcing laws or soliciting information, police should make all citizens feel like productive members of a collective social enterprise. | " | " | " |

Table 6c. Level 2 Assessment: Law Enforcement (*cont.*).

| Law Enforcement | Desired Outcome | Governance Measure (1-10) | Capacity Measure (1-10) | Major Shortfalls |
|---|---|---|---|---|
| 7 | **Law enforcement personnel are trusted by all segments of society.** In the absence of that trust, a government might be tempted to replace certain law enforcement institutions with elements of the armed forces. This distorts the budget and misallocates precious resources. Lack of trust in police institutions is often linked to corruption that citizens observe every day. | " | " | " |
| 8 | **Law enforcement institutions play no role in the national economy.** In the absence of sufficient funding, law enforcement personnel might not be paid enough to resist bribery, and security institutions could decide to participate in the national economy, formally or informally. | " | " | " |
| 9 | **There is a system of judicial oversight regarding law enforcement activities.** If police themselves are subject to the laws, special structures and processes for punishing those who break them must be in place. Impunity for law enforcement personnel is associated with lack of citizen trust and bad governance. | " | " | " |

Table 6d. Level 2 Assessment: Law Enforcement (*cont.*).

| Law Enforce -ment | *Desired Outcome* | *Governance Measure (1-10)* | *Capacity Measure (1-10)* | *Major Shortfalls* |
|---|---|---|---|---|
| 10 | **Civilians exercise effective democratic control of law enforcement institutions.** There is nothing more detrimental to human security than "rogue" police institutions invading the privacy of citizens and seeking financial or political advantage. *This condition is the culmination of efforts to attain all the Desired Outcomes listed above.* | " | " | " |
| Total Scores (x/100) | | **Average the scores for desired outcomes.** | **Average the scores for desired outcomes.** | **Add additional major shortfalls.** |

Table 7a. Level 2 Assessment: Intelligence.

| Intelligence | Desired Outcome | Governance Measure (1-10) | Capacity Measure (1-10) | Major Shortfalls |
|---|---|---|---|---|
| 1 | **Intelligence institutions and agencies, both civilian and military, have legal and well-defined roles, both internal and external.** As with other security sector elements, roles and resources should be synchronized. Overlapping roles for intelligence institutions are, however, sometimes worth the extra cost, providing additional insight into the most critical national security issues. | The extent to which government policies, strategies and laws lead to the desired outcome. | Does the government have the institutional capacity and political will to implement the policies, strategies and laws? | List the most important obstacles blocking the government's attainment of the desired outcome. |
| 2 | **There are separate oversight mechanisms for armed forces-led intelligence services and civilian-led intelligence services.** Without independent channels of oversight, the necessary diversity of perspective between vastly different intelligence production strains could be lost. | " | " | " |

Table 7b. Level 2 Assessment: Intelligence (*cont.*).

| Intelligence | Desired Outcome | Governance Measure (1-10) | Capacity Measure (1-10) | Major Shortfalls |
|---|---|---|---|---|
| 3 | **There are opportunities for civilian policy makers and intelligence officials to educate one another regarding the intelligence profession.** Only by discussing the most difficult issues face-to-face with those providing intelligence can policy makers be sure they have the best insight to inform national security decision-making. | " | " | " |
| 4 | **There is an effective mechanism for sharing information among all intelligence institutions.** No single institution has a complete national or regional threat picture. Intelligence agencies that share data and analysis avoid the "group think" that can arise in the absence of diverse reporting. Habitual sharing ensures that the overlaps remain reasonable and the gaps are filled. | " | " | " |

Table 7c. Level 2 Assessment: Intelligence (*cont.*).

| Intelligence | Desired Outcome | Governance Measure (1-10) | Capacity Measure (1-10) | Major Shortfalls |
|---|---|---|---|---|
| 5 | **There is a legal framework for all intelligence activities.** Intelligence, like other elements of the security sector, requires an interlocking set of laws upon which to base its operations and administration. | " | " | " |
| 6 | **Intelligence institutions and agencies are subject to executive oversight.** Otherwise, history has demonstrated that those institutions may be tempted to assume responsibilities and conduct operations inconsistent with the legal framework. Although structures are somewhat different in each country, a formal mechanism needs to be in place before intelligence agencies can be considered under control. | " | " | " |

Table 7d. Level 2 Assessment: Intelligence (*cont.*).

| Intelligence | Desired Outcome | Governance Measure (1-10) | Capacity Measure (1-10) | Major Shortfalls |
|---|---|---|---|---|
| 7 | **Intelligence institutions and agencies are subject to legislative oversight.** This normally involves setting up a committee in the legislature with the specific duty to monitor what intelligence agencies are doing, and how they are doing it. Legislative and executive oversight, taken together, can begin to deliver the democratic control of intelligence that is a prerequisite for maintaining security within the bounds of good governance practice. | " | " | " |
| 8 | **There is a mechanism for judicial review of sensitive intelligence activities.** Certain operations are routine, falling clearly within the established legal framework; others may require scrutiny prior to being launched. Judicial review should be available for all intelligence operations and imposed by justice ministries whenever there is reasonable cause. | " | " | " |

Table 7e. Level 2 Assessment: Intelligence (*cont.*).

| Intelligence | Desired Outcome | Governance Measure (1-10) | Capacity Measure (1-10) | Major Shortfalls |
|---|---|---|---|---|
| 9 | **There is a system for periodically declassifying intelligence information.** Intelligence documents are often classified when first written. Unless there is a system for reviewing classification periodically, crucial information that should be known to government officials outside the intelligence sphere (or the public) will remain unavailable. Some documents should remain secret for a long time, but others should be made available as soon as possible. | " | " | " |
| 10 | **Civilians exercise effective democratic control of all intelligence institutions and agencies.** *This outcome is the culmination of the efforts listed above.* There is nothing that inspires fear in a civilian population more than illegal or unsanctioned intelligence operations. | " | " | " |
| *Total Scores (x/100)* | | **Average the scores for desired outcomes.** | **Average the scores for desired outcomes.** | **Add additional major shortfalls.** |

Table 8a. Level 2 Assessment: Institutional Perspective.

| Security Institution | Desired Outcome | Governance Measure (1-10) | Capacity Measure (1-10) | Major Shortfalls |
|---|---|---|---|---|
| 1 | **The institution's leaders understand their assigned roles and have prepared their institutions to execute the missions they expect will be necessary to fulfill those roles.** Roles include both primary and secondary responsibilities that will remain stable over time. The leader must also have a vision for the institution, along with a style of leadership that unites people in the pursuit of that vision. | The degree to which the institution possesses policies, strategies and procedures to achieve the desired outcome. | How much capacity does the institution possess to implement the policies, strategies and procedures? | List the most important obstacles blocking the institution's attainment of the desired outcome. |
| 2 | **The institution has the resources needed to fulfill its roles.** The leaders of resource-deficient institutions are obliged to make the case for more funding. If the government does not have the money, it should remove some roles from the institution. | " | " | " |
| 3 | **There are mechanisms for coordinating the activities of this institution with other institutions.** Unless there is a formal mechanism for coordination and integration, government efforts will be disjointed and resources will be wasted. | " | " | " |

Table 8b. Level 2 Assessment: Institutional Perspective(*cont.*).

| Security Institution | Desired Outcome | Governance Measure (1-10) | Capacity Measure (1-10) | Major Shortfalls |
|---|---|---|---|---|
| 4 | **The institution is integrated into appropriate security strategies at the national, community, and citizen levels.** Only a "whole of government" approach, combining hard and soft power, will contribute to enhancing security in all its forms. | " | " | " |
| 5 | **Personnel have the education, training, and equipment to perform bureaucratic tasks and expected operational missions.** Institutional readiness must be developed from the bottom up as well as from the top down. | " | " | " |
| 6 | **There is a merit-based promotion system in place.** At the same time, ethnic and gender balance should reflect generally the composition of the nation as a whole. Security institutions cannot be effective unless they look and act like the rest of the country. | " | " | " |

Table 8c. Level 2 Assessment: Institutional Perspective (*cont.*).

| Security Institution | Desired Outcome | Governance Measure (1-10) | Capacity Measure (1-10) | Major Shortfalls |
|---|---|---|---|---|
| 7 | **Personnel within the institution are subordinate to the rule of law.** Appropriate punishments for breaking laws are written and well understood. | " | " | " |
| 8 | **Personnel, especially senior leaders, avoid political partisanship.** Unless there is a system of incentives and disincentives to discourage political influence, individuals (or whole institutions) will be tempted to become political actors. | " | " | " |
| 9 | **The institution is fulfilling its assigned roles effectively.** There should be "measures of effectiveness" in place to evaluate whether policies and strategies are working. If those measures indicate failure, the institution must be prepared to make the changes necessary to put itself on the path to success. | " | " | " |
| 10 | **The institution is fulfilling its roles in the most efficient manner possible.** This assessment should take into account whether roles and resources are balanced, and the extent to which corruption impedes the performance of the institution. | " | " | " |
| *Total Scores (x/100)* | | **Average the scores for desired outcomes.** | **Average the scores for desired outcomes.** | **Add additional major shortfalls.** |

## NOTES

1. Defense and security are not the same thing. Defense is the act of preparing to repel a known threat from outside the country (normally the first responsibility of armed forces), while security is a *climate* within which all citizens can thrive. Total security requires effective defense, but defense (and armed forces that produce it) is not enough.
2. Such a transformation assumes there is political will to move beyond the symbiosis that often exists between African leaders and their security chiefs.
3. The need to go beyond branding to "loyalty beyond reason" is an advertising concept that all government leaders would do well to study. See the PBS interview with Kevin Roberts, CEO of *Saatchi and Saatchi Worldwide*, http://www.pbs.org/wgbh/pages/frontline/shows/persuaders/themes/brand.html.
4. The value of these assessment criteria can be increased through mitigation measures taken during the planning phase of disaster response.
5. Due to the complexity of analyzing the four assessment criteria, as well as the need for informed debate, panels of experts are more effective than single-source inputs.
6. For a complete description of risk assessment, see James Petroni, "Risk Assessment," in *Fighting Back: What Governments Can Do About Terrorism*, ed. Paul Shemella (Stanford, CA: Stanford University Press, 2011), 117–130.
7. The list normally includes the following: diplomacy, information, military, economic, financial, intelligence, and law enforcement. What should be added to this list are emergency management, moral factors, and civil society itself.
8. A catalytic event such as revolution or terrorist attack can speed the process, but slow change (frustrating but careful) is the norm.
9. Unless the leadership wishes to maintain a portion of the security forces separate from, and unaccountable to, the rest of the government. Meredith (p. 622) offers Robert Mugabe's "5 Brigade" in Zimbabwe as an example of this.
10. Joseph Schumpeter, *Capitalism, Socialism and Democracy* (New York: Harper, 1975) [orig. pub. 1942].
11. Plato in *The Republic*.

12. Thomas Bruneau and Scott Tollefson, *Who Guards the Guardians and How?* (Austin: University of Texas Press, 2006).
13. As African countries continue the transition to full democracy, the concept of civil-military relations will take on more relevance. The degree to which civil-military relations becomes a pillar of governance is indeed a measure of democratic development.
14. Fukuyama, 405.
15. Thomas Bruneau and Cristina Matei, *The Routledge Handbook of Civil-Military Relations* (London: Routledge, 2013), 26–35.
16. There is a training aspect to successful mutual support among security institutions. Policies, operational procedures, rules of engagement, and even terminology can be different, causing confusion and failure.
17. Joseph Nye has charged the civilian component of government with the challenge of learning as much as they can about military culture and behavior. In his "liberal tradition" of civil-military relations, mutual understanding is paramount. See Larry Diamond and Marc Plattner, *Civil-Military Relations and Democracy* (Baltimore: Johns Hopkins University Press, 1996), 152–153.
18. South Africa may be an exception to this rule. Since the retirement of Nelson Mandela, the ANC has retained power to such an extent that the country can scarcely be labeled "competitive." It is, however, still highly institutionalized, with solid democratic civilian control of security forces.
19. This method of analysis produces more useful discussions among experts than would a scale with simply "high-medium-low" gradations. That is because each participant must pick a number—and then defend it in front of his peers. Numbers, then, lead to deeper thinking, which leads to more useful ideas and, ultimately, better decisions.
20. Although this framework would be useful for Western governments in their efforts to support African government reform, the most significant application would be as a method for African governments to assess *themselves.*
21. African maritime domains are enormous and can be monitored effectively only by pooling national assets. In the same vein, Nigeria needed the assistance of Chad, Niger, and Cameroon to begin rolling back Boko Haram.

Chapter 3

# The Case of the Democratic Republic of Congo

*Nicholas Tomb[1]*

Steeped in mystery and intrigue, the Democratic Republic of the Congo has arguably failed to live up to its potential more than any other country in Africa. Although the territory possesses an abundance of natural resources, a terribly harsh colonial past followed by decades of mismanagement and conflict have impoverished the Congolese people. Starting with King Leopold's Force Publique, continuing with President Mobutu Sese Seko's Division Spéciale Présidentielle, and extending to President Joseph Kabila's Garde Républicaine, the national armed forces have enforced a system of exploitation that has privileged the few at the expense of the many. Beaten into submission generation after generation, the population has grown sadly acquiescent, suffering through years of bad governance and an abusive military that routinely terrorizes the very people that it is supposed to protect.

## BACKGROUND

By the mid-nineteenth century the "scramble for Africa" was gaining force, with European powers racing to claim control of "the dark continent." In an effort to avoid military conflict between the conquering powers, diplomats met in Berlin in November of 1884 to divide the continent. In 1870, approximately 10 percent of Africa was under European control; by 1914 that number had increased to 90 percent, with only Ethiopia (Abyssinia) and Liberia retaining independence. Demonstrating deft diplomacy, King Leopold II of Belgium managed to play the greater European powers of England, France, and Germany against one another by convincing them that open trade in Africa was in the best interest of all countries. Through this policy, he was able to found and make himself the sole owner of some two million square kilometers, known as the Congo Free State.[2]

While ownership of the country was turned over to the Belgian state in 1908, the era of strong personal rule over the country survived national independence in 1965. Mobutu Sese Seko's thirty-two-year reign epitomized the "African Big Man" as the former Army Chief of Staff treated the national treasury as his personal bank account. Cunning, charismatic, and possessing an undeniably sharp intellect, Mobutu inspired mind-boggling stories of legendary excess. While citizens in the resource-rich nation struggled to survive and the international community poured billions of dollars into the country, Mobutu cavalierly chartered Concorde jets and sipped glasses of his signature pink champagne, pitting his military officers against one another and buying off political adversaries.[3]

Supporting Mobutu was a complex web of cronies, allies, family members, and military officers—all of whom were overseeing personal fiefdoms of their own. This widespread corruption undermined what limited state institutions and infrastructure the country had, and as usual, the powerful were enriched at the expense of the weak. Accounts of military commanders selling ammunition to advancing rebel forces, thus undermining the defense of their own soldiers, show just how rampant the corruption had become.[4]

The Great Lakes region of central Africa was in chaos when the First Congo War began in 1996. Millions of refugees who had fled the 1994 genocide in Rwanda were living in squalid camps in eastern Zaire.[5] Entrenched among the refugees were Hutu militias and other armed groups that terrorized the citizenry and used the territory as a staging ground to launch cross-border raids into neighboring countries. By this point, Mobutu's harsh and selfish rule had created enemies in virtually all sectors of Zairian society. The economy was in shambles, and the nation was in a state of general collapse. Mobutu faced enemies everywhere, and eventually his internal and external foes allied against him. When Laurent-Désiré Kabila, with support from Rwanda, Uganda and Angola, led the Alliance of Democratic Forces for the Liberation of Congo across the country to Kinshasa, there was virtually no resistance from what was left of Mobutu's army. The greatest challenge the advancing forces met was the dreadful state of Zaire's crumbling infrastructure.

Declaring himself President, Kabila promised great change, but delivered more of the same. The underlying causes of the First Congo War remained largely in place, and ethnic relations between Hutu and Tutsi in the East remained tense. As Kabila became entangled in these tensions, he turned on his Rwandan and Ugandan allies, and set the stage for the Second Congo War—the deadliest war in modern African history. Hostilities were exacerbated by a complex network of alliances that involved nine African countries and approximately twenty separate armed groups. The war (1998–2003) and its aftermath resulted in over five million deaths, principally through disease and starvation, making it the deadliest worldwide conflict since World War II. Millions more were internally displaced or sought asylum in neighboring countries, creating a humanitarian crisis that persists to this day.

MONUSCO, the largest United Nations Peacekeeping force in the world (with approximately 20,000 uniformed personnel) and its predecessor, MONUC, have been supporting an uneasy peace in the country since 1999. Nowhere is the instability worse than in the eastern part of Congo where ethnic tensions continue to plague the population and where multiple militia groups operate in the vacuum of state authority. The prospects of restoring security and the rule of law are low, due in large part to the illegitimate activities of local authorities, but especially to the ill-disciplined national army that regularly terrorizes local populations. Congo has been called the "worst country in the world to be a woman," with sexual-based violence, torture, and other crimes—often perpetrated by the national armed forces—committed with impunity.[6] Over a decade after the end of the Second Congo War, the country still fails to constitute a unified, functional nation-state; and the majority of its population continues to live in extreme poverty with the UN providing many important services.[7]

In 2001 Laurent Kabila was assassinated by a bodyguard and, by a unanimous vote of his recently appointed parliament, his son Joseph was sworn in to replace him as president. The younger Kabila proved to be a slightly better leader than his father. Slowly, inflation came under control and foreign aid resumed. A peace agreement was signed, establishing ceasefires with Rwanda and Uganda, the withdrawal of all foreign troops from Congolese territory, and the integration of armed groups into a new national army.[8] A law passed on November 12, 2004, formally created the new national Forces Armées de la République Démocratique du Congo (FARDC).[9]

Despite some progress, clear benchmarks for security sector reform (SSR) in the aftermath of the conflict were never put in place, and an effective restructuring of the national armed forces was never implemented. As the International Crisis Group noted in its 2006 report on SSR in the DRC:

> The [peace] process failed adequately to define appropriate principles and mechanisms for forming the various factions into a new and genuinely unified national army. Negotiators sought to keep command structures sufficiently weak that no single faction could control them and so created multiple competing power structures. No comprehensive security sector review was undertaken and thus no systematic effort was made to base the new security services on careful assessment of risks, needs and capabilities.[10]

Joseph Kabila, like other Congolese leaders before him, fears the threat that a strong national army poses, and has intentionally kept the armed forces scattered and weak. In short, as has always been the case in the DRC, the leader never wanted a professional army and never got one.

President Kabila, who will reach the end of his second term in November 2016, is constitutionally barred from running for a third term of office. At the time of this writing, the nation is alive with speculation about his next steps. While Kabila himself has remained strangely quiet about his future plans, his allies in parliament have advanced various schemes for him to retain power. There has been a recent trend across Africa for presidents to amend national constitutions or manipulate definitions to extend their terms in office. Congolese civil society organizations and political opposition groups have voiced their strong opposition to any changes to the Constitution, and have organized multiple protests— sometimes violent—across the country. In January 2015 at least thirty-six protestors were killed in the cities of Kinshasa and Goma when police lost control and called in the Republican Guard for support.[11] While legislation to amend the Constitution to allow a third term in office has been withdrawn, the National Independent Elections Commission recently stated that it has to update its voter rolls before credible elections can take place. There is some legitimacy to this claim (between 5–10 million Congolese have turned eighteen years old since the last elections were held in 2011, thus any elections without updated voter rolls would disenfranchise millions of eligible voters), but many Congolese simply see this as a creative way for Kabila to retain power.

It remains to be seen whether the DRC will achieve the first peaceful political transition in its turbulent history. What is clear, however, is that the state security forces will play an important role in this transition, and that their actions will be a powerful indicator of the strength of security governance and civil-military relations in the DRC.

This brief historical overview of the DRC helps to explain the current deplorable condition of its armed forces. A mass of poorly trained and equipped soldiers and various rebel groups, the FARDC has never been effectively integrated, and loyalties often lie with former commanders rather than with the formal command structure. Corruption, misman-agement, and the failure to provide basic pay has led to an ill-disciplined, unprofessional force that often leaves soldiers little option other than to exploit the citizenry to survive.

## ARMED FORCES

Any analysis of the FARDC is difficult, as it is less one comprehensive force than a series of separate forces with unique roles, missions, and loyalties, often operating independently of civilian control or military command.[12] Further, few details (such as comprehensive defense budgets) are available to give an accurate picture of the overall strength of the armed forces.[13] What data are available do not paint a very pretty picture. The Governance and Capacity Assessment framework (tables 5–8) introduced in chapter 2 provides a simple but constructive way to organize our thinking about state security forces, and forms the basis for the analysis of the security sector conducted in this and subsequent chapters.

The FARDC consists of an army, navy, and air force. Of the three branches, the army is by far the strongest, with approximately 63,000 soldiers. The modest air force consists mostly of old Soviet-era planes, while the navy "is considered to be in a state of near total disarray... unable to police its 37 km coastline."[14] The FARDC nominally operates under the control of the Ministry of Defense and (along with the intelligence services) has the primary responsibility to protect state institutions, the populace and their property, the territorial integrity of the country, and all external security issues. It also fulfills an internal security role, primarily combating indigenous armed groups in the east and enforcing law and order when the police lose control.

The 2006 Constitution of the DRC states that the president of the nation is commander in chief of the armed forces and chair of the High Defense Council.[15] The High Defense Council is composed of the ministers of defense and interior, the national security advisor, the chief of the armed forces, heads of the military branches, and the four vice presidents. The council, chaired by the president, is responsible for making decisions on issues of national security. In its early years, the High Defense Council also consisted of commanders from rebel forces that were integrating into the national army. A 2013 organic law overhauled the structure of the FARDC, with the stated goal of establishing an army that is national, apolitical and republican. Over time, President Kabila has managed to reshuffle the higher echelons of the military, installing his own appointees and thus tightening his control over the FARDC, its structure, command, and operations.[16]

Despite the clear and reasonable balance of powers outlined in the Constitution and national law, in practice, management of the national armed forces is much more concentrated, ad hoc and corrupt. There is very limited civilian oversight of the FARDC or accountability for its soldiers. The country receives an "F" on Transparency International's 2015 Government Defence Anti-Corruption Index, an analysis of seventy-seven indicators that provides a detailed assessment of the integrity of national defense institutions.[17] Similarly, while the Constitution details a process for the promotion of officers in the FARDC—with the minister of defense making recommendations to the president, who in turn nominates officers for promotion to the Parliament—in practice there is a long history in the FARDC's short existence of the president promoting friends, family and ethnic allies to positions of power in the national armed forces.[18]

The Parliament consistently fails to pass laws to better manage the security sector or hold the Ministry of Defense or service branches accountable, provide effective civilian oversight of the security sector, critique budgets or otherwise contribute effectively to defense governance.[19] There is ample evidence that corrupt force commanders regularly use the soldiers under their command for personal profit, collecting payments for "ghost soldiers" and skimming payments from their troops (and their dependents).[20] FARDC units are heavily involved in the national economy, playing an important, illicit role in gold and diamond mining, timber harvests, ivory poaching, weapons smuggling—and anything else that will turn a profit.[21]

It is a well-documented fact that nearly all segments of Congolese society fear and distrust the FARDC.[22]

## THE REPUBLICAN GUARD

Although the state security forces are typically untrained, ill-equipped, and ineffective at implementing their constitutional mandates, one branch stands out as a reasonably professional force: the Republican Guard. Information about the Republican Guard is limited, but it is a force of 10,000–15,000 soldiers that operates outside the regular FARDC command structure, reporting directly to the president. Although its soldiers receive regular pay and enjoy better working conditions than do the regular FARDC troops, allegations of the Republican Guard committing rapes, murders and robberies with impunity are well documented.[23]

While the Republican Guard is headquartered in Kinshasa, President Kabila deploys the force across the country, ostensibly to provide security for presidential visits. In practice, however, soldiers remain in place well after his departure. They can be recognized by their maroon berets and are often present at airports, government offices, and other strategic locations across the DRC. Soldiers of the Republican Guard are frequently called upon to suppress civil unrest when local police forces lose control. During the presidential elections in 2011, the UN reported that Republican Guard soldiers shot at protestors, killing thirty-three of them and wounding eighty-three. Another 265 were arrested, and many reported that they were tortured.[24] The Republican Guard was also called out in 2015 when citizens (violently) took to the streets to protest efforts to amend the constitution to grant the president a third term of office. It is reported that the Republican Guard is the only military force in the DRC that President Kabila trusts.[25]

## LAW ENFORCEMENT

The National Police, the Police Nationale Congolaise (PNC), is constitutionally responsible for public safety; the security of persons and their property; law and order; and the security of senior government officials.[26] Unfortunately, much like its military counterparts in the FARDC, the PNC is riddled with corruption and has encountered many difficulties in fulfilling its constitutional mandates. The Constitution stipulates that the police are apolitical. With jurisdiction over the entire national territory, the police are in the service of the Congolese nation, and no person can use the police for his or her own purposes. The police are theoretically subject to local civilian authority and the minister responsible for home affairs.

In practice, there is little legislative oversight of the PNC, which largely operates at the whim of commanding officers, usually in some form of corrupt rent-seeking activity rather than in support of public security. The PNC numbers around 110,000 officers, who, on average, are paid around US$30 per month. The force, staffed largely by ex-soldiers and former rebels, is poorly trained, lacks basic equipment and is widely seen as more of a threat to the population than a guarantor of its security.[27]

## INTELLIGENCE

Despite the many abuses detailed above, the state institution that does more than any other to subvert the rights of the citizenry, while enforcing the supremacy of the ruling regime, must be the dreaded National Intelligence Agency (known by its French acronym, ANR). Created in early 1997 as an intelligence service for the Alliance of Democratic Forces for the Liberation of Congo, the ANR appropriated the Kinshasa offices of Mobutu's National Intelligence and Protection Service when Laurent Kabila took over the national capital. Despite the change in name, the intelligence services basically played the same oppressive role under Laurent Kabila that they did under Mobutu, a role that has extended into Joseph Kabila's administration as well.

Operating under the direct authority of the president, the ANR is charged with ensuring the country's internal and external security. In practice, this means doing whatever is needed to secure the positions of power that the president and his inner circle enjoy. Operating in total secrecy and under a legal framework that differs from the common criminal law and national legal procedures, the ANR has secret agents spread across the country, in schools, churches, hotels, restaurants, pubs—everywhere—looking for "enemies of the state." According to a source cited by the Doha Centre for Media Freedom, "these guys are told to spy on journalists and opposition politicians, as well as university lecturers who might bad-mouth the regime to the media or write books compromising the regime—these are the people they see as the number-one enemies and threats to the regime."[28]

A November 2015 report by Amnesty International carefully documents the ANR's pattern of abuse. The report, like many before it, paints the picture of a state institution terrorizing its populace in the service of the ruling power, operating beyond its constitutional mandate and repeatedly violating nationally and internationally protected human rights without anyone being held accountable.[29] Typically, the targets of the ANR are journalists, political opposition groups, and human rights campaigners.

## Prospects for Improvement

While the state security forces are sufficiently corrupt and predatory to create a net security loss, some modest progress has been made in the effort to professionalize the force. Some credit for this must be given to the brave Congolese reformers struggling to improve their nation. Credit also goes to donor governments who fund programs aimed at making the security sector more transparent and accountable. The biggest challenge facing these efforts is that the donor governments want a professional force more than Congolese government does. Until this situation is reversed, real progress and reform seems unlikely. A security sector reform advisor hired by the US Embassy in Kinshasa describes efforts to reform the FARDC as taking "five steps forward and four steps back."[30]

Positive steps include the impressive Chain of Payments project. Led by the EU Mission for Security Sector Reform (EUSEC), and its sister organization the Support Programme for Security Sector Reform (PROGRESS) in 2005, the project oversaw the issuance of identification cards to FARDC soldiers. ID cards, coupled with the creation of a centralized salary payment process, resulted in the separation of salary payments from the chain of command, making it harder for senior officers to withhold or skim pay from lower ranked soldiers and reducing the FARDC's manpower count from 190,000 to 120,000 soldiers.[31]

The US Defense Institute for International Legal Studies (DIILS) has also been active in the DRC, helping establish a Uniform Code of Military Justice within the FARDC, as well as mobile military courts, which travel across the country prosecuting cases. In one instance, a hotline set up by a mobile court to collect information about human rights abuses led local residents to report the suspicious behavior of a FARDC soldier, resulting in successful prosecution of the soldier for attempted rape.[32]

Additionally, in 2015, several new FARDC Rapid Response Units were established to operate in partnership with MONUSCO. These units have conducted several internal operations against armed groups in the East, and have reportedly performed far better than armed forces in the DRC typically do. These units may represent a new capability within the FARDC and, if they can be maintained and replicated, could mark a turning point for the force.[33]

However, with the positive come painful steps backward. In 2010, US Special Forces assigned to US Africa Command completed training of the FARDC's 391st Commando Battalion. Training and equipping the battalion cost US taxpayers US$15 million to complete. Initially seen as a success, the 391st was deployed to hunt down the rebel Lord's Resistance Army, but in 2012 the troops were diverted as part of an effort to confront the M23 rebel group, which had seized territory in the country's eastern region. As the tide turned the M23's favor, the 391st fled before M23 forces advancing near the city of Goma. According to a report issued by the United Nations Joint Human Rights Office, as they fled, members of the 391st engaged in a range of atrocities, including the mass rape of women and young girls, the arbitrary execution of at least two people, and widespread looting.[34]

In 2015 the DRC deployed 807 military personnel and 108 police to the UN Multidimensional Integrated Stabilization Mission in the Central African Republic (MINUSCA), the first time that the nation contributed significant forces to a UN peacekeeping operation.[35] Controversial from the beginning, the deployment was cut short in January 2016 when the Congolese forces were repatriated amidst allegations of child sexual exploitation and abuse—allegations sadly similar to those regularly made against the FARDC within its own borders.[36]

Also in 2015, the US Center for Civil-Military Relations (CCMR) delivered a series of seminars on elections security across the DRC. The ambitious project, sponsored by the Africa Bureau, US Department of State, was designed to bring diverse groups of 60–70 participants from the FARDC, PNC, National Independent Elections Commission, media outlets, political parties, and civil society organizations to discuss civil-military relations and best practices in elections security. The vision was to conduct the seminars in all eleven provincial capitals of the DRC, and have each seminar culminate with participants developing action plans for what their organizations could do to promote security around the upcoming local elections. Between September 2014 and June 2015, site surveys were conducted in all eleven provincial capitals, and five seminars were delivered, starting with the inaugural seminar in Kinshasa in February 2015.

The elections security project was well on its way to successful completion when, at the sixth seminar, in Mbuji-Mayi, an undercover member of the ANR approached the course instructors at the morning coffee break and demanded to see written authorization for the seminar delivery. The instructors pointed to the fact that there was broad support for the project from the Government of the DRC (GDRC), and that five seminars had already been delivered. Without written approval, the ANR representative refused to allow the seminar to continue. A week after the instructors departed, the GDRC contacted the US Embassy, apologized for the misunderstanding, and stated that the ANR field representative had "made a mistake." The government said that the seminar series was approved and should continue as planned. Two weeks later the seventh seminar began as scheduled, but the exact same situation occurred. At this point, everyone involved began to realize that this was not a mistake, and that given the very tense political situation in the country (with the president maneuvering to stay in office after the end of his second term) the GDRC no longer supported the seminar series. After consultations with the ambassador and State Department in Washington, it was agreed to suspend the project.[37]

## ASSESSMENT

In addition to the Governance and Capacity Assessment framework (tables 5–8) used to evaluate the state security forces in preceding sections of this chapter, the other assessment tools introduced in chapter 2 provide further ways to analyze the state security forces in the DRC—and to compare them with other security forces across the continent.

**National Brand.** The Government of the DRC uses its armed forces in several ways. One such use is as a "Defender," protecting the citizenry (albeit not very effectively) from external armed groups such as the Lord's Resistance Army. Another brand is "Fireman," deploying the armed forces on domestic missions to protect the citizenry from internal armed groups such as the Mai Mai militia (again not very effectively) or assisting the police when they lose control during periods of civil unrest. Given the poor governance and bad behavior of the FARDC, a third brand for the armed forces must be that of "Troublemaker."

**Most Significant Threats.** Significant internal, external, traditional, and human security threats face the nation and citizenry of the DRC. Oxfam International has identified at least ten significant internal armed groups operating in the east of the country.[38] Regular allegations of cross-border clashes between the armed forces of neighboring states such as Rwanda and Uganda against DRC-based militia groups such as the Democratic Forces for the Liberation of Rwanda and the Allied Democratic Forces provide examples of external threats affecting the DRC's sovereignty and territorial integrity. Food insecurity, limited access to healthcare, banditry, and gender-based violence are among the many threats to human security already detailed in this chapter. Bad governance, rampant corruption, and impunity exacerbate all of these threats further.

**Roles of the Security Forces.** As has hopefully been made clear in the preceding pages, there is little coordination or clarity of roles between the military, law enforcement and intelligence agencies in the DRC. Depending on the time, location and, most importantly, priority of leaders (especially at the national level), different security forces are used in various ways to address the multitude of security threats facing the nation. Alternatively, in many cases they are not used at all—or contribute directly to the insecurity of the public.

**Political System.** Based on the characteristics of the different political systems identified in table 4, the DRC hovers between Personal Rule and a Minimally Institutionalized State. Corruption is rampant, coordination is minimal, and roles and missions lack clarity.

**Trends for Security Sector Institutions.** The security forces of the DRC have never been an accountable, professional, or efficient force. They have been effective at supporting the ruling regime but have never effectively defended the citizenry from internal or external threats. Rather, they have preyed upon the people, taking whatever they could with impunity. Trapped in a cycle of exploitation and bad governance, the experience of the average citizen has changed very little in the last century. It has been estimated that the DRC has US$24 trillion of untapped mineral potential, making it one of the most resource-rich nations on earth.[39] Access to this wealth has proven too tempting to the country's ruling regimes, which for centuries have used the security forces to enrich themselves at the expense of the common citizenry. Unfortunately, this situation is unlikely to change any time soon. Until it does, it is hard to imagine how the citizens of the DRC will rise above their current level of abject misery while being terrorized by their government and surviving on a per capita average of less than one dollar a day.[40]

Much depends upon the actions that President Kabila will take in the near future. If he honors the Constitution and steps down at the end of his second term, there is limited hope for improvement. If, as looks likely, he tries to hang on to power, civil unrest and another deadly civil war seem inevitable. Paradoxically, brutal conflict may be necessary for new leaders to come in and truly reform the country. The current leaders are simply doing too well as things are to push for change.

The Congo is sometimes described as the heart of Africa, and like any vital organ its condition will have a fundamental impact on the broader body. With a population of 80 million people, an enormous amount of territory, and nine neighboring countries, it is the key to stability in the region. If the culture of corruption and impunity can be replaced with

accountability, good governance—and democratically elected civilian
control of the armed forces—the DRC could become the breadbasket of
Southern Africa that it rightfully should be. If things continue as they are,
the ruling elite will use the security forces to enrich themselves at the
expense of the citizenry, and risk throwing the entire region into chaos.

**AFTERWORD**

On December 19, 2016 President Kabila reached the end of his constitutional mandate, without holding elections or leaving office. Protestors
took to the streets, resulting in clashes with the police that left at least
40 dead and hundreds arrested. After tense negotiations mediated by
the Catholic Church, a deal was reached on December 30, which allows
Kabila to remain in power until elections can be held in 2017. According
to the deal, Kabila must appoint a prime minister from the country's main
opposition bloc to oversee the transition by March. Tensions remain
high amidst concern that the deal will not be honored, and that the DRC
will miss the opportunity to experience its first peaceful transition of
political power in the nation's history.

# NOTES

1. All opinions expressed in this chapter are my own and do not reflect official positions of either the Naval Postgraduate School or the United States government.

2. For an excellent, if horrifying, account of King Leopold's reign, see Adam Hochschild, *King Leopold's Ghost* (New York: First Mariner Books, 1999). For a literary account of King Leopold's Congo, see Joseph Conrad, *Heart of Darkness*, (London: Blackwood's Magazine, 1899).

3. For an interesting account of Mobutu's Congo, see Michela Wrong, *In the Footsteps of Mr. Kurtz: Living on the Brink in Mobutu's Congo* (New York: HarperCollins, 2001).

4. Michela Wrong, *In the Footsteps of Mr. Kurtz: Living on the Brink in Mobutu's Congo* (New York: HarperCollins, 2001), 263.

5. The territory currently known as the Democratic Republic of the Congo was known as the Kingdom of Congo in pre-colonial times, the Congo Free State under King Leopold's rule, the Belgian Congo under Belgian administration, the Republic of Congo with national independence, the Democratic Republic of the Congo, then the Republic of Zaire as part of Mobutu Sese Seko's authenticity campaign. Laurent Kabila renamed it the Democratic Republic of the Congo in 1997.

6. Séverine I Autesserre, "Dangerous Tales: Dominant Narratives on the Congo and their Unintended Consequences," *African Affairs* (Oxford: Oxford University Press, 2012), 202–222.

7. United Nations Security Council, "Report of the Secretary-General on the Implementation of the Peace, Security and Cooperation Framework for the Democratic Republic of the Congo and the Region," March 5, 2014.

8. "Global and Inclusive Agreement on Transition in the DR Congo: Inter-Congolese Dialogue - Political negotiations on the peace process and on transition in the DRC," http://reliefweb.int/report/democratic-republic-congo/global-and-inclusive-agreement-transition-dr-congo-inter-congolese.

9. Henri Boshoff, "Overview of Security Sector Reform Processes in the DRC," *African Security Review* 13, no. 4 (2004).

10. "Security Sector Reform in the Congo," *International Crisis Group*, Africa Report no. 104 (2006), 2.

11. "Treated Like Criminals: DRC's Race to Silence Dissent in the Run Up to Elections," *Amnesty International*, London, 2015.
12. The annual *Country Reports on Human Rights Practices*, produced by the Bureau of Democracy, Human Rights and Labor, US Department of State, chronicle the abuses regularly committed by state security forces in the DRC.
13. McGerty, Fenella. "Jane's Democratic Republic of Congo Defense Budget Overview," IHS Markit, January 28, 2016, https://janes.ihs.com/CentralAfrica/DisplayHistory/961082.
14. McGerty, 7.
15. Constitution of the Democratic Republic of the Congo, Article 83, adopted February 18, 2006; see http://www.parliament.am/library/sahmanadrutyunner/kongo.pdf.
16. Jane's Sentinel Security Assessment – Central Africa, Armed Forces: Democratic Republic of Congo," IHS Markit, July 22, 2015, 6-7, https://janes.ihs.com/CentralAfrica/DisplayHistory/961082. Jane's Sentinel Security Assessment is part of the Jane's Information Group, a British publishing company that specializes in military topics. They produce periodic assessments of nations and their military capabilities, such as this and the IHS Jane's reports cited throughout.
17. "2015 Government Defence Anti-Corruption Index," *Transparency International*, http://government.defenceindex.org/countries/democratic-republic-of-the-congo/.
18. Christoph Vogel, "Reshuffle in the Congolese Army," (September 28, 2014) https://christophvogel.net/2014/09/28/reshuffle-in-the-congolese-army-cui-bono/.
19. "No Will No Way: US-funded security sector reform in the Democratic Republic of Congo," *Oxfam America*, 2010.
20. Simone Gorrindo, "Congo's military takes on new challenge: caring for army widows," *The Christian Science Monitor* (April 16, 2015).
21. Letter dated October 16, 2015, from the Group of Experts extended pursuant to Security Council resolution 2198 (2015) addressed to the President of the Security Council at http://www.securitycouncilreport.org/atf/cf/%7B65BFCF9B-6D27-4E9C-8CD3-CF6E4FF96FF9%7D/s_2015_797.pdf.
22. "Crisis in the Democratic Republic of the Congo," International Coalition for the Responsibility to Protect, http://www.responsibilitytoprotect.org/index.php/crises/crisis-in-drc.

23. "Justice on Trial: Lessons from the Minova Rape Case in the Democratic Republic of the Congo," *Human Rights Watch*, October 2015.

24. "Serious human rights violations committed during DR Congo elections – UN report," UN News Centre (March 20, 2012), http://www.un.org/apps/news/story.asp?NewsID=41583#.V15B6NayPVo.

25. Jane's Sentinel Security Assessment – Central Africa, Armed Forces: Democratic Republic of Congo," IHS Markit, July 22, 2015, 6-7, https://janes.ihs.com/CentralAfrica/DisplayHistory/961082.

26. Zongwe, Dunia, François Butedi, and Phebe Mavungu Clément, "UPDATE: The Legal System of the Democratic Republic of the Congo (DRC): Overview and Research," *Hauser Global Law School Program*, GlobaLex, January/February 2015.

27. "New Law a Boon for Police Reform," *IRIN, Kinshasa* (December 16, 2010), http://www.irinnews.org/report/91391/drc-new-law-boon-police-reform.

28. Issa Sikiti da Silva, "The ANR: a threat to DR Congo's media freedom," *Doha Centre for Media Freedom* (February 20, 2013) http://www.dc4mf.org/en/content/anr-threat-dr-congos-media-freedom.

29. "Treated Like Criminals: DRC's race to silence dissent in the run up to elections," *Amnesty International* (2015).

30. Author interview, conducted in Kinshasa, DRC (April 26, 2016).

31. European Union External Action Common Security and Defense Policy overview of activities in the Democratic Republic of the Congo (updated July 2015), http://eeas.europa.eu/csdp/missions-and-operations/eusec-rd-congo/pdf/factsheet_eusec_rd_congo_en.pdf.

32. Author interview with DIILS staff, conducted in Garmisch, Germany (April 22, 2016).

33. Jane's Sentinel Security Assessment – Central Africa, Armed Forces: Democratic Republic of Congo," IHS Markit, July 22, 2015, 6-7, https://janes.ihs.com/CentralAfrica/DisplayHistory/961082.

34. John Vandiver, "US-trained Congolese battalion among units accused of rape," *Stars and Stripes* (May 10, 2013).

35. In 2008 the DRC contributed a very small contingent of troops and military observers to the AU-UN Mission in Darfur (UNAMID).

36. "New Allegations of Sexual Abuse Emerge Against MINUSCA Peacekeepers," UN Multidimensional Integrated Stabilization Mission in the Central African Republic (press release; February 4, 2016).

37. Author's personal experience.

38. Oxfam International, "202 Oxfam Briefing Paper: Secure Insecurity: The continuing abuse of civilians in eastern DRC as the state extends its control" (March 6, 2015), https://www.oxfam.org/sites/www.oxfam. org/files/file_attachments/bp202-secure-insecurity-drc-protection-0603 15-en.pdf.
39. Gerard Prunier, "Why the Congo Matters," *Atlantic Council* (issue brief; March 2016).
40. World Bank, World Development Indicators, http://data.worldbank. org/indicator/NY.GNP.PCAP.CD/countries/CD-ZF-XM?display=graph. (The DRC's gross national income per capita is based on purchasing power parity.)

CHAPTER 4

# THE CASE OF GUINEA-BISSAU

*Thomas Bruneau*

There is general agreement that the Third Wave of democratization began on April 25, 1974, in Lisbon, Portugal, with a military coup that overthrew the Salazar–Caetano authoritarian regime that had been installed since the late 1920s.[1] The Third Wave has continued, with fits and starts, until today, forty-two years later. In fact, the military coup of April 25, 1974, began in Guinea-Bissau in 1973 when the Soviet Union furnished the guerrilla movement, the African Party for the Independence of Guinea and Cape Verde (PAIGC) with surface-to-air missiles, thereby denying air superiority to the Portuguese, who had been fighting the PAIGC since 1963. Despite efforts by the junior officers (and finally the Portuguese military commander, General António de Spínola, who knew that Portugal had lost Guinea-Bissau, and should negotiate independence there while retaining the incomparably more valuable settler colonies of Angola and Mozambique) to convince Premier Marcelo Caetano, the regime was intransigent. Consequently, the junior officers formed the

Armed Forces Movement (MFA), and overthrew the regime on April 24, 1974. In the resulting turmoil Portugal underwent a revolution, losing not only Guinea-Bissau but also Angola, Mozambique, and East Timor.[2]

Unfortunately, Guinea-Bissau has not participated in the Third Wave of democratization, or in the reforms of civil-military relations that have been part of the democratization process in most parts of the world.[3] According to the "Report of the Secretary-General on developments in Guinea-Bissau and the activities of the United Nations Integrated Peace-building Office in Guinea-Bissau" (UNIOGBIS), United Nations Security Council January 19, 2015: "Since its independence in 1974, the country has never seen a Government complete its term in office. *Coups d'etat* took place in 1980, 1998–1999, 2003, and 2012, attempted coups took place in 1985 and 1993, and alleged attempts took place in 2009, 2011, and 2012. The political instability in the country has been accompanied by repeated gross violations of human rights, including politically motivated assassinations, abductions, cases of torture, arbitrary arrests, detentions of political opponents and civil society representatives, and restrictions on the freedom of expression and assembly."[4] The coup in 1998 resulted in a civil war that lasted almost a year. During this period of conflict, what professional armed forces that remained from the independence movement against the Portuguese were diluted by armed gangs.[5] The lack of professional armed forces—and training facilities to raise forces to a professional level—continues to the present day. The civil war also destroyed some of the infrastructure that existed at the time, including the closing of the United States embassy which had been shelled, resulting in the death of a guard.

According to one analyst, "indeed narco trafficking is not only the 'core business' of the Armed Forces in Guinea-Bissau, it is also, due to the financial weight of cocaine trafficking, the reason the military has assumed previously unimagined levels of importance."[6] To paraphrase the Grand Jury document for the United States District Court, Southern District of New York, United States of America v. Antonio Indjai, Defendant: In April

2010, Antonio Indjai, the defendant, helped lead a military coup which resulted in the detention of the Prime Minister. By June 2010, Indjai had become Chief of Staff of the Guinea-Bissau Armed Forces. On or around April 12, 2012, the military staged another coup. In the aftermath of the coup, the first public communiqué by the "Military Command" that took responsibility for the coup was issued by the Armed Forces General Staff, led by Antonio Indjai. He was a defendant and pleaded guilty on four counts. The first was to engage in a narco-terrorism conspiracy with the Revolutionary Armed Forces of Colombia (FARC). The second was to import cocaine from Colombia and to oversee its distribution—including in the United States. The third was to support the FARC, a terrorist organization, with arms, including SAM (surface-to-air) missiles. And the fourth was to acquire the SAM missiles ostensibly for the Guinea-Bissau Armed Forces that would be transferred to the FARC with the intention to shoot down US helicopters in Colombia.[7] Later, in 2013, the chief of the Guinea-Bissau Navy was caught in a sting operation, involving drug trafficking, and pleaded guilty at the US District Court in Manhattan.[8]

## SOME POSSIBLE CAUSES FOR THE CURRENT SITUATION

There is no single reason for the current unfortunate situation in Guinea-Bissau.[9] There are, instead, at least seven reasons that must be reviewed and analyzed with the goal to identify what might be changed so that the overall political situation, including the security forces, can be improved.

First, according to the single most thorough and authoritative study of Guinea-Bissau, Professor Joshua Forrest claims that the Portuguese, in fighting the insurgents, including the PAIGC, engaged in what he terms "state terror" to retain the colony.[10] Again, according to Forrest, having defeated the Portuguese and taken control over the independent country, the PAIGC replicated the "state terror" and continued to use it after independence in September 1974.[11] From the beginning, then, extreme violence became the common currency in politics, including, but not limited to, the armed forces and politics. Correia de Nóbrega also highlights the use of extreme violence in all that concerns the armed political party, the PAIGC, that led the country to independence.

Second, Guinea-Bissau, unlike Angola and Mozambique, was not a settler colony. In contrast to these two colonies, Guinea-Bissau lacked the size, climate, and natural resources that could sustain a sizeable Portuguese settler population. Consequently, there was minimal investment in infrastructure and in human capital. Guinea-Bissau became independent with virtually nothing. For example, when Guinea-Bissau became independent, only 2% of the population was literate.[12] In short, Guinea-Bissau began life as an independent country with minimal assets. Politics, including violent politics, was a matter of attempting to capture the very limited resources that were available.

Third, Guinea-Bissau is among the bottom ten countries in the world in terms of economic and social development. Its only legal export crop is cashew nuts, virtually all of which go to India for processing. According to the United Nations Development Program's Human Development Index (2015), Guinea-Bissau is 178 out of 187 countries.[13] The misery and poverty are obvious in every imaginable respect. While there is a port in Bissau, it is in total disrepair and even lacks cranes. There is an international airport at Bissau, but scheduled flights are few and far between. The country began its independent existence poor, and has remained poor.

Fourth, unlike other postcolonial countries, including Angola and Mozambique, Guinea-Bissau did not begin its independence with an acknowledged leader. The main leader of the independence movement, Amílcar Cabral, was assassinated, apparently by rivals within the PAIGC, in January 1973, before independence. Much of the "state terror" that Professor Forrest refers to, was caused by rival elements in the PAIGC fighting for power. There was no independence leader, such as an Agostino Neto (of Angola), let alone a figure of the stature of Jawaharlal Nehru, who could lead the newly independent country. Not only was Amílcar Cabral murdered, but other similar leaders from Cape Verde were also marginalized; and the two independent countries, Guinea-Bissau and Cape Verde later went their separate ways.

Fifth, while the Revolutionary Armed Forces of the People (FARP) of the PAIGC was, as noted earlier, riven by factions and all were prone to use violence to assert themselves, with the civil war of 1998–1999 what little element of military professionalism there was largely disappeared. Whereas in 1990 there were 2,500 personnel in the armed forces, today the estimated numbers are at least double. Further, they are extremely top-heavy.[14] The armed forces are not professional. Indeed, there is no military academy, and there are absolutely no other training facilities for the armed forces. Based my experience at a seminar in Bissau the week of August 16, 2015, a great many of the senior officers seem illiterate and are unable to read or speak in Portuguese. They can converse only in creole, which admittedly, is the country's *lingua franca*. Guinea-Bissau lacked, and still lacks, a professional armed force.

Sixth, in view of the poverty of the country and the political instability, salaries and pensions for the armed forces are extremely problematic. We will see next that this fact may offer leverage for potential reform in civil-military relations. Everything very quickly becomes a matter of the use of force to obtain resources. In the meantime, however, there is a temptation for the military to engage in drug trafficking, and as we saw earlier—and will see even more later in this chapter—this takes place at the highest levels of the armed forces. Even if they were not involved, the lack of resources, including boats, would make it impossible for the armed forces to control the archipelago of islands off Bissau.

Seventh, according to the UNIOGBIS Report: "At the root of the cycle of instability in Guinea-Bissau lies the fact that there has not been serious and genuine dialogue aimed at national reconciliation among the various stakeholders in the country."[15] The country's political and military history since independence in September 1974 demonstrates again and again the accuracy of this damning statement. The most recent analyses of Guinea-Bissau by virtually all observers highlight the lack of dialogue and resulting instability. In its report on February 12, 2016, UNIOGBIS, states on page 1 under "Major developments in Guinea-Bissau" that: "The political environment in Guinea-Bissau has continued to be marked by tensions and divisions within the ruling African Party of the Independence of Guinea and Cabo Verde (PAIGC) and among the sovereign organs of the State."[16] And, in its most recent report, of August 2, 2016, UNIOGBIS states: "Since my previous report, the political situation in Guinea-Bissau has deteriorated."[17]

The International Crisis Group, in their Crisis Watch Database of February 1, 2016, has a long paragraph detailing the factional struggle within the PAIGC, the fragility of political institutions, and the disruption and chaos in the political system.[18] And, in *Jeune Afrique*, its article on February 11, 2016, was entitled "Guinée-Bissau: face à l'impasse politique, la communauté internationale exaspérée"[19] The most recent UNIOGBIS Report (August 2, 2016) provides chapter and verse on the political stalemate and the many efforts by other countries and international organizations to resolve the stalemate.[20] In short, the domestic political actors, which clearly include the armed forces, are so far unwilling and maybe even *unable* to negotiate and find solutions which might lead to political stability, and in which the armed forces are not the central political actors.

On the basis of this political background, which of course extends back to even before independence in 1974, it is no surprise that the assessment of Guinea-Bissau is extremely negative in terms of our assessment framework. In fact, it would be negative in terms of any assessment framework, as indeed virtually all of the articles about the country by social scientists are extremely negative. While I normally give the highest priority in the analysis of politics to *domestic* factors, I found in the case of Portugal in the 1970s from coup, to revolution, and ultimately to democracy, there was a very important role for foreigners in politics, national defense and security, and the economy. Portugal did indeed lead the Third Wave, but events there were very heavily influenced by foreign states (especially Germany and the United States), NATO, the IMF, World Bank, and European Investment Bank.[21]

In the current situation of Guinea-Bissau, I believe that if there is to be any solution to the seriously unstable political and political-military situation, it will to some degree have to be externally influenced. There are a huge number of external actors involved in Guinea-Bissau. This should not be surprising considering the country's instability in a region where terrorism is making inroads, its role as a transit location for illegal drugs, the concern of Senegal with Guinea-Bissau which borders on the Casamance region with strong separatist tendencies, the concerns of European countries regarding the implications of both instability and drugs, the aspirations of Portugal and Brazil regarding a Lusophone country, and the unscrupulous behavior of some military leaders who were prepared to provide SAM missiles to the FARC for money that would be derived by selling cocaine.

While there is a great deal of overlap, as one would expect in a small town such as Bissau, I believe that the main themes, or issues, to be described and analyzed are three. First (clearly a power issue), are the roles of the US Drug Enforcement Administration (DEA) and United Nations Office on Drugs and Crime (UNODC) in attempting to impede the use of Guinea-Bissau as a transit location for illegal drugs, mainly cocaine. Second is the role of neighbors (Brazil, across the South Atlantic) and Nigeria (mainly though ECOWAS) in attempting to bring political stability to Guinea-Bissau. And third is the role of UNIOGBIS in attempting to coordinate the policies of the donor community for the progress and benefit of Guinea-Bissau.

## DRUGS

There is an abundant, and sensationalist, literature on Guinea-Bissau as a drug transit state. Monograph titles capture the general sense. One is *Advancing Stability and Reconciliation in Guinea-Bissau: Lessons from*

*Africa's First Narco-State.*[22] Another telling title is *Africa's Cocaine Hub: Guinea-Bissau a Drug Trafficker's Dream.*[23] Authors such as Eduardo Costa Dias go into great detail on the how, why, and implications of the transit of drugs through Guinea-Bissau.[24] The journal *Perspectives* of the UNODC published a lead article entitled "Guinea-Bissau: New hub for cocaine-trafficking."[25] And, most recently, the US Department of State, Bureau of International Narcotics and Law Enforcement Affairs, in their 2015 International Narcotics Control Strategy Report state the following:

> Guinea-Bissau is a transit hub for cocaine trafficking from South America to Europe. The country's lack of law enforcement capabilities, demonstrated susceptibility to corruption, porous borders, and convenient location provide an opportune environment for traffickers. The complicity of government officials at all levels in this criminal activity inhibits a complete assessment and resolution of the problem. Despite a newly elected government that is seeking to establish the rule of law, Guinea-Bissau's political system remains susceptible to and under the influence of narcotics traffickers.[26]

These facts are well known. What is most important is that something is being done about the involvement of the highest levels of government (including the armed forces) in the trafficking of illegal drugs. The US Drug Enforcement Administration has a regional office in Dakar, Senegal, which is responsible for Guinea-Bissau (for there is no United States embassy in Bissau). General Antonio Indjai, Chief of Staff of the Guinea-Bissau Armed Forces, was arrested in a West African country on April 4, 2013, and transferred to American custody, where he was subsequently indicted in New York for trafficking in cocaine owned by the FARC, with distribution planned for the United States, and plans to furnish the FARC with SAM missiles which would be used to shoot down American helicopters.[27] And, on April 2, 2013, in a sting operation, the DEA arrested the chief of the Guinea-Bissau Navy, José Américo Bubo Na Tchuto for trafficking in cocaine. He was also transferred to New York and indicted.[28] Both of these highest-level officers from the Guinea-Bissau armed forces served time in prisons in the United States. The arrests demonstrated that while these officers might enjoy impunity within Guinea-Bissau, the international community could reach out, arrest them, try them, and put them in prisons in the United States. In the words of one of my contacts in Bissau, the arrests demonstrated the vulnerability of the officers, and it really got their attention.[29]

In short, while impunity might exist within Guinea-Bissau, it is strictly limited globally. In this regard, that of power, Guinea-Bissau is under a United Nations sanctions regime in which eleven designated individuals are under travel bans. The United Nations document states the following: "...the impact of sanctions in Guinea-Bissau has transcended the travel ban restrictions imposed by resolution 2048 (2012)...sanctions had acted as a deterrent to the direct involvement of the security and defence forces in the political crisis the country had faced since August 2015."[30]

## SUPPORT BY REGIONAL POWERS

Even while discounting the exaggerated rhetoric, Brazil, the regional power in the South Atlantic, has been active in supporting democracy and democratic civil-military relations in Guinea-Bissau. This includes initiatives at the level of the United Nations and also within the country.[31] Probably most important for the purposes of this chapter are those concerning education and training for the police and the armed forces. For the Guinea-Bissau Armed Forces, the Brazilian Federal Police created the Centro de Treinamento de Forças de Segurança and the Brazilian military began a Centro de Formação de Oficiais. However, work on this center was halted with the military coup of 2012.[32]

With the support of Portugal, elements in the military have now migrated into two new police organizations, roughly based on the models in Portugal of the Guarda Nacional Republicana and the Polícia de Segurança Pública. In Guinea-Bissau these are the *Guarda Nacional* and the Polícia de Ordem Pública. These two major police forces have been recently created; they total 4,758 officers and men, but so far their tasks or functions have neither been delineated nor has professional training been provided. They are formally under the Ministry of the Interior, and not the Ministry of Defense.[33]

At the regional level, ECOWAS, and in particular Nigeria, have been very active. ECOWAS has been involved in attempting to build peace in Guinea-Bissau since at least 1998.[34] At an Extraordinary Summit of ECOWAS on September 12, 2015 the Authority of Heads of State and Government of ECOWAS extended the mandate of its Mission in Guinea-Bissau (ECOMIB) through June 2016. They also mandated the presidents of Senegal and Guinea, in their respective capacities as ECOWAS Chair and ECOWAS Mediator for Guinea-Bissau (with the assistance of the former president of Nigeria, Olusegun Obasanjo, in his capacity as Special Envoy of the President of Nigeria) to facilitate dialogue with all stakeholders to find a lasting solution to the political crisis. Former President Obasanjo returned to Bissau in October 2015 to pursue consultations with political stakeholders. ECOWAS, the UN, African Union, EU, and the *Comunidade dos Países de Língua Portuguesa* (CPLP) were heavily involved in negotiations between President Vaz and the government in February of 2016. ECOWAS—with the support of the EU, Nigerian troops—continues to maintain a presence in Guinea-Bissau.

## Support by the International Community

International donors include individual countries such as East Timor, France, Great Britain, Portugal, and the United States, as well as a myriad of international organizations including the EU, UNICEF, UNDP, CPLP, the World Bank, International Fund for Agricultural Development, the Peace-building Fund, the African Development Bank, and the West African Development Bank. In March 2015, at an international partners' round-table, pledges were made for approximately $1.3 Billion. In an effort to coordinate programs and policies, the United Nations established in Guinea-Bissau a UN Peace-building Support Office on March 3, 1999.

On January 1, 2010 it was replaced by the UN Integrated Peace-building Office in Guinea-Bissau, UNIOGBIS. Since that time, its mandate has been extended every year.[35] As Guinea-Bissau stumbles from crisis to crisis, the UNIOGBIS continues until today, but little of the pledged $1.3 billion has been released.[36]

In addition to informing the UN and other sponsors, the UNIOGBIS has as its main task the implementation of several key elements in terms of a mandate. In the most recent report of the Secretary-General, dated February 12, 2016, they review the status of these ten elements. A review of this report will provide substantial information on the status of developments. They are as follows:

a) Inclusive political dialogue and national reconciliation process. Some, but fairly modest, progress.

b) Strategic and technical advice and support for national authorities in implementing the national security sector reform and rule of law strategies. Again, some progress, but little progress on demobilization efforts and on pensioning off excess military personnel.

c) United Nations good offices. Several meetings and ongoing tensions among state institutions and the PAIGC.

d) Support for the Government of Guinea-Bissau in the mobilization, harmonization and coordination of international assistance. Several meetings to establish effective mechanisms for aid coordination.

e) Strengthening democratic institutions and enhancing the capacity of State organs to function effectively and constitutionally. Numerous seminars and meetings.

f) Strategic and technical advice and support for the establishment of effective and efficient law enforcement, criminal justice, and penitentiary systems. Again, numerous meetings and training sessions.

g) Promotion and protection of human rights and human rights monitoring and reporting activities. Some progress, but "[D]espite intense lobbying by UNIOGBIS, efforts to review the status of the country's National Human Rights Commission to make it compliant with the Paris Principles have been delayed."[37]

h) Strategic and technical advice and support for the Government of Guinea-Bissau to combat drug trafficking and transnational organized crime. Again, several meetings and training sessions.

i) Incorporating a gender perspective into peace-building, in line with UN Security Council resolutions 1325 (2000) and 1820 (2008). More meetings and training sessions.

j) Work with the Peace-building Commission in support of Guinea-Bissau's peace-building priorities. One meeting.

Finally, under "Observations," the result of progress on these mandates is summed up in the following terms: "The political crisis within the main political party, PAIGC, and among the political leadership in Guinea-Bissau, which has prevented the country from moving forward with its national reform agenda for more than six months, is concerning. The current stagnation undermines the bright outlook for the country following the successful partner's round table in March, during which international partners expressed unprecedented support for the country's strategic and operational plan for the period 2015-2020. The crisis has the potential to further damage the already fragile State institutions and the overall peace-building process."[38]

## ASSESSMENT

**National Brand.** Given the extremely low degree of readiness, the country's armed forces are incapable of defending its borders (although there is some deterrent effect from simply *having* armed forces). The conduct of international peacekeeping operations, which require specialized skills and a high level of professionalism, would seem to be far in the future. By virtue of the military's central role in trafficking drugs, Guinea-Bissau is certainly a Troublemaker country. If the armed forces were better organized and more professional, it might be possible for the government to use them for a variety of public purposes, including law enforcement.

**Most Significant Threats.** There are traditional threats at the borders with Guinea–Conakry and Senegal, both of which have intervened in Guinea-Bissau, admittedly at the request of President Vieira. There is currently concern with Jihadist movements from the West Africa region, and particularly Mali. Guinea-Bissau is extremely vulnerable to smuggling activities. The country's geography, characterized by remote islands and rivers, has turned Guinea-Bissau into a regional hub for illegal trafficking.

**Roles of the Security Forces.** There is no formal delineation of roles (and the resources that go with them) for security force institutions. The embryonic police institutions complicate rather than complement the activities of the armed forces. Indeed, the clear articulation of roles for all security force institutions should form the first phase of security sector reform.

**Political System.** Guinea-Bissau's political development is too nascent for strict labeling, but the country has yet to form institutions worthy of the name. It is not a Collapsed State in the same sense as Libya or Somalia, but it has a lot of work to do. Chronic political instability has deprived Guinea-Bissau of strong leadership for long enough periods to make a difference.

**Contribution of the Security Forces to Good Governance.** The security forces of Guinea-Bissau contribute nothing to good governance but quite a lot to bad governance. It is noteworthy, however, that during the political crisis in August 2015, and continuing until late 2016, the military have not intervened in politics. Without serious and major reform of its security forces (armed forces, law enforcement, and intelligence), the country will fail to achieve gains in human security and good governance overall.

## TRENDS FOR SECURITY SECTOR INSTITUTIONS

In a September 2016 seminar in Bissau, the CCMR faculty utilized the Level 2 Assessment Framework, introduced in Chapter 2, as a teaching tool with the 50+ participants. The mean ratings for governability and effectiveness were 5.0 and 4.7 respectively. Two police forces have just been founded, but their roles have yet to be delineated with each other, let alone from the military. While the police forces are ostensibly under the Ministry of Interior, they retain a military training profile and mentality.[39]

Guinea-Bissau is widely considered a failed state in that no president has ever completed his term of office, and political paralysis is more the rule than the exception. So far, however, and as noted above, in the ongoing political crisis, the most positive observation in the February 2016 UNIOGBIS Report—and which still holds—is as follows: "I note with satisfaction that the armed forces have remained in their barracks and have not interfered in the political affairs of the country."[40]

The armed forces and the PAIGC were forged in a conflict where there was little distinction between the party and the military. Today, with some rudimentary elements of professionalism, the military may become separate from the government. So far, there is little good governance in any aspect of Guinea-Bissau, including security. In short, all remains a work in progress in security and civil-military relations in Guinea-Bissau.

## NOTES

1. For the term *the third wave*, see Samuel Huntington, *The Third Wave: Democratization in the Late Twentieth Century* (Norman: University of Oklahoma Press), 1991.

2. On the origins of the coup, see Joshua Forrest, *Lineages of State Fragility: Rural Civil Society in Guinea-Bissau* (Athens: Ohio University Press, 2003), 243; and Avelino Rodrigues, Cesário Borga, and Mário Cardoso, *O Movimento dos Capitães e o 25 de Abril: 229 Dias Para Derrubar O Fascismo* (Lisbon: Morães Editores, 1974), 248–262. On August 20, 2015, I met in Bissau with Manuel dos Santos, who went to the Soviet Union in early 1973 to be trained to use the "Estrella" surface–to–air missiles, which ultimately denied air superiority to the Portuguese Armed Forces which used Fiat and DC 6 airplanes. Manuel dos Santos later supported the MPLA in Luanda by holding off the South Africans with these same SAMs.

3. The issue of democracy and civil–military relations is dealt with in *Who Guards the Guardians and How: Democratic Civil–Military Relations*, edited by Thomas Bruneau and Scott Tollefson (Austin: University of Texas Press, 2006).

4. United Nations Security Council, "Report of the Secretary-General on developments in Guinea-Bissau and the activities of the United Nations Integrated Peace-building Office in Guinea-Bissau," January 19, 2015, S/2015/37, 11.

5. In his excellent book, *A Luta Pelo Poder Na Guiné-Bissau*, Álvaro Correia de Nóbrega notes that during the civil war many criminals were freed who then joined the military junta. (*Universidade Técnica de Lisboa Instituto Superior de Ciências Sociais e Políticas*, 2003), 121.

6. Eduardo Costa Dias, "From the Unbearable 'Resilience' of Coupism to Ethicisation: A Short Journey for the Armed Forces of Guinea–Bissau," *Nordic Journal of African Studies* 22 (nos. 1 & 2; 2013),18.

7. United States District Court. Southern District of New York United States of America v. Antonio Indjai. S 6 12 Cr. 839. See https://www.justice.gov/sites/default/files/usao-sdny/legacy/2015/03/25/U.S.%20v.%20Antonio%20Indjai%20S6%20Indictment.pdf.

8. See http://www.reuters.com/article/us-bissau-drugs-guilty-idUSKBN0EE2FO20140603.

9. Correia de Nóbrega gives particular attention to "heterogeneity" of society, religion and the PAIGC, but in his excellent analysis he includes many more factors than heterogeneity.
10. Joshua Forrest, 2003, 183.
11. Ibid., 117. In support of Forrest's allegation see the chronology of some examples of state terror under the PAIGC, http://www.gbissau.com/?p=1048.
12. Author interview with Manuel dos Santos, Bissau August 20, 2015.
13. Human Development Index, 2015, http://hdr.undp.org/en/countries/profiles/GNB.
14. The estimate of 2,500 was given to me by Manuel dos Santos on August 20, 2015. He was Minister of Finance in 1990 and knew the numbers because he was responsible for paying their salaries.
15. Report of the Secretary-General on developments in Guinea-Bissau and the activities of the United Nations Integrated Peace-building Office in Guinea-Bissau," UNIOGBIS Report (January 19, 2015), 17.
16. "Report of the Secretary-General on developments in Guinea-Bissau and the activities of the United Nations Integrated Peace-building Office in Guinea-Bissau," UNIOGBIS United Nations Security Council (February 12, 2016), 1.
17. Report of the Secretary-General on developments in Guinea-Bissau and the activities of the United Nations Integrated Peace-building Office in Guinea-Bissau," UNIOGBIS United Nations Security Council (August 2, 2016), 1.
18. Crisis Watch Database – International Crisis Group, "Guinea-Bissau" (February 1, 2016), http://www.crisisgroup.org/en/publication-type/crisiswatch/crisiswatch-database.aspx.
19. See http://www.jeuneafrique.com.
20. UNIOGBIS (August 2, 2016), 1–5.
21. Some of this information is found in Thomas Bruneau and Harold Trinkunas, "Democratization as a Global Phenomenon and its Impact on Civil-Military Relations," *Democratization* 13, no. 5 (December 2006): 776–790.
22. David O'Regan and Peter Thompson, ACSS Special Report no. 2 (2013). Washington, D.C.: Africa Center for Strategic Studies.
23. *Spiegelonline International* (March 8, 2013). See http://www.spiegel.de/international/world/violence-plagues-african-hub-of-cocaine-trafficking-a-887306.html.
24. Eduardo Costa Dias, 2013; see especially p. 9.

25. *Perspectives* Issue 5 (May 2008), Vienna: U.N. Office on Drugs and Crime. https://www.unodc.org/documents/about-unodc/Magazines/ perspectives_5_WEB.pdf.

26. U.S. Department of State, INL, Country Report: Guinea-Bissau. See http:// www.state.gov/j/inl/rls/nrcrpt/2015/vol1/238975.htm.

27. DEA press release. See http://www.dea.gov/divisions/hq/2013/hq0418 13.shtml.

28. DEA press release. See http://www.dea.gov/divisions/hq/2013/hq040 413.shtml. See also https://www.justice.gov/usao-sdny/pr/colombian-narcotics-trafficker-sentenced-manhattan-federal-court-25-years-prison.

29. My meeting with international official in Bissau on August 18, 2015. For the most recent scholarly article on this topic see Mark Shaw, "Drug trafficking in Guinea-Bissau, 1998– 2014: the evolution of an elite protection network," *The Journal of Modern African Studies* 53:3 (2015): 339–364.

30. Report of the Secretary-General on the progress made with regard to stabilization and restoration of constitutional order in Guinea-Bissau. No place or date; see page 3.

31. For extensive details on the positive role of Brazil see Adriana Erthal Abdenur & Danilo Marcondes De Souza Neto, "Rising Powers and the Security-Development Nexus: Brazil's Engagement with Guinea-Bissau," *Journal of Peacebuilding & Development* 9:2 (2014): 1–16. For a more skeptical view see Pedro Seabra, "A harder edge: reframing Brazil's power relation with Africa," *Revista Brasileira de Política Internacional* 27:1 (2014): 77–97. For details from the Brazilian Embassy in Bissau website see http://bissau.itamaraty.gov.br/pt-projetos.xml

32. For an update on the Brazilian initiatives in security and defense I rely on information provided by a Brazilian officer at UNIOGBIS e-mail of November 25, 2015.

33. Information on the numbers from meeting with U.N. officials in Bissau on September 14, 2016, and discussion with all seminar participants on September 16, 2016.

34. John M. Kabia, *Humanitarian Intervention and Conflict Resolution in West Africa: From ECOMOG to ECOMIL Farnham* (Surrey: Ashgate, 2009).

35. For further information, see http://www.whatsinblue.org/2016/02/ mandate-renewal-of-uniogbis-and-guinea-bissau-political-crisis.php.

36. For an update on UNIOGBIS, see http://www.whatsinblue.org/2016/02/ mandate-renewal-of-uniogbis-and-guinea-bissau-political-crisis.php.

37. Report of the Secretary-General on developments in Guinea-Bissau and the activities of the United Nations Integrated Peace-building Office in

Guinea-Bissau," UNIOGBIS (United Nations Security Council: February 12, 2016), 13–18.

38. Ibid., 17–18.
39. The 2016 seminar (which followed a similar event in 2015) illuminated an increased awareness among civilians, military, and police that progress in the development of security forces is necessary and possible. That awareness, if combined with commitment and dedication, could well bring about major changes in security and civil-military relations in Guinea–Bissau.
40. UNIOGBIS Report (February 2016), 18.

CHAPTER 5

# THE CASE OF GUINEA

*Paul Clarke*

The Republic of Guinea (La République de Guinée) is very poor by any standard, with a poverty rate of 55 percent, and a per capita GDP of just US$536, but it is not without its advantages.[1] The country is rich in water resources and has untapped agricultural potential.[2] It has a significant mining industry with the world's largest bauxite reserve.[3] Until the Ebola crisis of 2014–2016 disrupted Guinean society on every level, the economic conditions had been improving under democratic rule. The budget deficit was greatly reduced, inflation was falling, and the economy grew at 4.8 percent in 2012.[4] The mismatch between Guinea's potential and its reality has largely been a function of failure of governance, specifically of the roles of defense and security forces and their relationship to the chief executive.

Guinea came under French control in 1891. Guinea was one of the first countries in French West Africa to gain independence and was noted for being the only country to reject membership in the French Community, turning instead to the Warsaw Pact countries for its inspiration and sponsorship. The new nation was led by Ahmed Sékou Touré, who ruled the country from its independence in 1958 until 1984. Touré was followed by Colonel Lansana Conté (via a coup against the interim leadership); Conté ruled until his death in 2008. So for the first fifty years of its independence, Guinea knew only two leaders, both of whom were autocratic and used institutions, such as they existed, for their own regime's survival.

When President Lansana Conté died in 2008, a junta, led by army captain Dadis Camara, took control. A year of great chaos and abuse by the military soon followed, culminating in the September 28, 2009, stadium massacre, in which 150 opposition members were killed and scores of women were raped. Dadis Camara was seriously injured in an attack by fellow military members in December 2009, which lead to the installation of General Sékouba Konaté as interim leader. He was persuaded to engage the international community in an initiative to help save the state from collapse. International stakeholders, particularly the UN, AU, and ECOWAS, recognized the potential for another failure of a Western African state and worked to develop a program to stabilize Guinea and return it to normalcy and stability under democratic rule. In January 2010 the regime and the government agreed to twelve principles, referred to as the Ouagadougou Accord, which promised a quick handover to a democratic government. The Accord affirmed General Konaté as the interim leader, who would later step down according to plan. At the same time, a Senegalese officer of high regard, General Lamine Cissé, was chosen to undertake an assessment of the potential for Security Sector Reform (SSR).[5]

In 2010 Alpha Condé won a contested election for president (he was reelected in 2015), and SSR has been formally underway since 2011. While opposition members denounce him for being ethnically biased—and he has received much opprobrium for the state's handling of the Ebola crisis

—in general, President Alpha Condé has continued to embrace the SSR agenda, cooperate effectively with regional and international powers, and modestly advance the cause of civilian control of the security and defense forces. SSR is ambitious, aiming to end military control of government; to establish civilian, democratic control of the state; and to build the many institutions that enable a democratic state. For this reason, much of the analysis of Guinea's security and defense forces will be seen through the lens of this SSR effort. But, first we turn to the history and nature of the defense and security institutions.

## The Armed Forces

> In addition to the state's excessive use of force, in recent years order and discipline within the forces seem to have broken down for several reasons. The military has traditionally been the strongest institution in Guinea and for decades the stability of the country has relied on it. However, a series of events may have led to the army's destabilisation. [President Lansana] Conté's strategy of pitting groups and individuals against each other has increased competition among members of the forces,"
>
> —Ana Larcher Carvalho[6]

The defense forces, particularly the army, had a central role in Guinea's early years because they could be used by the political leadership for many tasks within society. Ahmed Sékou Touré came to power during the Cold War, and he benefitted from aligning with the USSR. Guinea had almost no military at inception but, with Warsaw Pact aid, it was able to develop a somewhat competent military, including an army, an air force with MiG jet fighters, and even a small navy.[7] Touré and his military were active in the region during the 1960s and 1970s, sending troops to the Belgian Congo in 1960–1961 and also later to Sierra Leone, Benin, and Liberia.[8] He also created a presidential guard to ensure regime survival and formed ethnically based militias to strengthen his political and ideological control; over time, he found the military to be less of a source of strength and more of a rival to his power. He favored the Malinké ethnic group, who were a majority in the military at that time, while he also used the militias to monitor the army for loyalty, fearing a coup attempt.[9] Touré's rule ended in 1984, and Lansana Conté ruled until 2008. He too found the military to be a both an instrument for ensuring regime control and a source of competing power, a function of the security forces becoming politicized. Conté's misrule set the stage for the modern era; as noted by one observer, "The army that General Conté has bequeathed his country knows little of the role and methods that it would need to employ in a democratic state respectful of its citizens' most basic rights."[10]

Estimates of the size of the military services vary, in part because of the large and unplanned growth in recruitment during the regional civil wars in the 1990s. A United Nations report from March 2012, placed the size of the armed forces (army, navy, air force, and gendarmerie) at 22,432, with the Army itself comprising two-thirds of that total.[11] There are also specialized units, such as the President Guard Battalion and the Special Forces Battalion, that are part of the army structure. As is the case for many African militaries, the army has long dominated the establishment, and the air force and navy remain modest.[12] SSR has focused on a major remaking of the military. Among these initiatives was the retirement of some 4,000 military members (so-called ghost soldiers) and the movement of many troops and units from the capital region—a peninsula that sticks into the Gulf of Guinea, a particularly vulnerable location for the lion's share of the military's forces.

## LAW ENFORCEMENT

Law enforcement, public order, and internal security responsibilities are divided between elements of the Ministry of Security (the Police) and the Ministry of Defense (the Gendarmerie). Security forces for many years have been accused of a variety of abuses, including corrupt practices, arbitrary arrest and detention, and acting against perceived threats (such as journalists and political activists) to the dictatorships.[13] Many of these activities remain as the norm in these ministries. As the US State Department noted in its 2015 Human Rights Report, "Police remained ineffective, poorly paid, and inadequately equipped. There were multiple reports of security service units disregarding their orders and resorting to excessive force."[14]

## The National Police
### (Ministry of Security and Civil Protection)

The National Police is responsible for public order, protecting the people and their goods, and border control, among other law enforcement duties. Following the French model, the National Police have a judiciary function, a role that they share with the gendarmerie of the Ministry of Defense, with the police performing that function in towns and cities, and the gendarmerie in rural areas (although that latter distinction has historically been ignored by the gendarmerie). The police form a directorate general under the Ministry of Security and Civil Protection.[15]

The major divisions of the police are:
- Central Directorate of Public Security;
- Central Directorate of the Judicial Police;
- Central Directorate of Surveillance of the Territory and Official Trips;
- Central Directorate of the Police and Border;
- Central Directorate for Road Safety;
- Central Directorate of Response Units;
- Central Directorate of Foreign Control and the Fight Against Illegal Migration;
- Central Directorate of Technical and Scientific Police;
- Central Directorate of General Information;
- Office for the Promotion of Gender, Child Welfare and Morals;
- Office of Intelligence and Criminal Investigation;
- Office for the Prevention of Economic and Financial Crimes;
- Central Drug Office.[16]

Much of the police's work is in the capital of Conakry, where 1.8 million of Guinea's 11.8 million people live and which constitutes much of the country's urban area.[17] The police service has 13,000 members; of those, approximately 10,000 have not been trained. The ratio of police to inhabitants is 1:1400, which is considerably below the international norm.[18] The 2010–2015 presidential and legislative elections, where violence or the threat of violence was ever-present, reflected the inadequacy of the security forces in the cities, even with special measures in place. After independence, Touré prioritized the military and, later, the militias, leaving few resources for traditional security functions or institution building. The long period of military rule left the police marginalized and a bit player in the political hierarchy. The institution was under-resourced and used for political chores by the ruling elite, gaining a reputation for corruption and low standards.

The SSR program made the military their first priority because they were the catalyst for so many of the nation's woes, but SSR is inclusive of all security forces, and the police are also in need of reform. Under SSR a national training school has been created, and 4,000 new officers are to be added to the service. In addition, community policing concepts are being introduced, and budget execution is being recentralized to ensure resources are available at the community level. In other security areas, a forest ranger service has been created with a goal of creating a force of 2,000 rangers.[19] Finally, a temporary force has been formed to provide security during elections: the Special Force for the Securing of the Electoral Process (FOSSPEL). These are not special forces in the military sense but rather a unique, temporary authority cobbled together from existing security forces.[20]

### The Gendarmerie (Ministry of Defense)

The gendarmerie is part of the Ministry of Defense but charged with law enforcement functions. It is tasked with the military justice and police justice missions, meaning it is responsible for investigating and arresting defense and security personnel. The police and gendarmerie work together in some roles; for example, in specialized units to fight organized crime and drug trafficking.[21] In theory, the police are responsible for cities and towns and the gendarmerie are focused on rural areas. This has been very loosely applied in the past. According to the UN, of the 22,432 members in the armed forces in 2012, about 6,000 belong to the gendarmerie.[22] As noted earlier, the gendarmerie has been involved in abuses (as have other security and defense forces). During the SSR era though, it has been given a new and larger role in ensuring accountability for the behavior of military and security forces. This was done by creating a new High Command for the Gendarmerie within the Ministry of Defense, providing for independent budget control. Many of its troops (along with those of the Army) have been moved out of the capital in order to perform this role in rural areas.

## INTELLIGENCE SERVICES

There are intelligence units within the army, gendarmerie, the police and the presidency. Traditionally, the intelligence units have supported three functions: military operations, law enforcement, and political intelligence. Despite the many intelligence efforts, there is little attention paid to the strategic appraisal of emerging security threats, forecasting, or the use of intelligence in military operations.

### Military Intelligence

The military maintains an intelligence function and, at times, they have taken the role in performing an intelligence appraisal function for the emerging threat environment, as well as in support of operations. With few current state threats and very few operations since the Dadis Camara era, Guinea has not been in need of such a function in the traditional sense. The most obvious regional concerns would have been in the civil wars in Sierra Leone, Liberia, and Bissau, and more recently the potential from the spillover from events in Mali. Guinea is again participating in regional peacekeeping operations, but the intelligence in these operations is provided by UN sources.

## Law Enforcement Intelligence

Both the police and gendarmerie maintain intelligence units that focus on law enforcement investigation, as well as organized crime and other transnational threats, although both efforts are underfunded and the output very modest. As capacity grows in these institutions, there will be a call for increased ability to perform intelligence functions to respond to transnational threats, such as narcotics trafficking.

## Political Intelligence and the Militias

Guinea has a long history of using formal and informal organizations to collect intelligence on citizens—particularly military and socio-political activists—to ensure regime rule. For example, in the early 1960s, the ruling Democratic Party of Guinea (Parti Démocratique de Guinée, PDG) formed youth militias that served to promote revolutionary zeal and monitor compliance in the general population. Over time the organizations became more formalized and were reformed in 1974 as the National and Popular Militia, assuming some functions from the army and, to a lesser extent, the police.[23] Similarly, due to concerns about potential coup threats, the Touré regime created a presence to monitor activities within the ranks, using the ruling Democratic Party of Guinea to create Military Section Committees, tasked with monitoring political infractions by service members. The committees eventually influenced the military force structure through changes in the recruitment and officer promotion processes.[24] These internal intelligence services turned combat forces drew resources away from the armed forces, which aided in the long decline of the military.[25]

## The Armed Forces and Governance

Drawing from our model in chapter 2, for civilian authorities to assert control over the defense and security services, the new government, abetted by its international sponsors, sought to do so by *limiting the size, budgets*, and *power* of these institutions.

**Size.** The government has also focused on resizing the military and security forces. Within the military, the primary focus has been on downsizing the army, which had grown substantially after 2000 in response to the spillover effects of crises in Liberia and Sierra Leone. In all, 7,500 youths were recruited into the military and given arms and a minimum of training to form a sort of auxiliary during the era of regional civil wars.[26] The SSR process also sought to remove 4,000 "ghost soldiers" from the payroll. The police have not been subjected to similar reductions in size because they were excluded or marginalized during the dictatorships; rather, the focus here has been on professionalization and a modest expansion in size.

**Budgets.** As noted earlier, the security forces are to expand modestly under SSR. The army, as evidenced by the reduction in numbers, is destined to be smaller and more professional, although major acquisitions will likely come mostly from foreign donors. Without serious investment, the military particularly will be unable to develop basic capabilities, such as mobility. The air force is illustrative. Investment in new equipment and maintenance soon fell off after President Touré began to fear a military coup. The air force suffered a fatal crash in February 2013, an accident that took the lives of eleven senior service members, including the chief of the armed forces and other officers.[27] This crash and the general inability to conduct basic operations are representative of the fall from grace of the armed forces under both Presidents Touré and Lansana Conté.

**Power.** Reducing military power, particularly that of the army, has been a key goal of the SSR effort. Downsizing has been the most successful part of the process, with the removal of army assets from the capital and an end to the military's responsibility for directing nonsecurity sector parts of the government. Even though the interim president was a military member, the quick appointment of a civilian prime minister —and two subsequent presidential elections along with one legislative election—suggest that the trend is clearly in the direction of increased civilian control.

## DESIRED OUTCOMES

We also see in the framework from tables 5 to 8 a series of weighted criteria designed to identify how well societies/governments manage their defense and security forces. The framework includes measurements of legislative oversight and transparency, civilian oversight, trust, role in the national economy, resources and human security. These are applied to the Guinea context in the following section.

**Legislative oversight and Transparency.** The Constitution adopted in 2010 lays out the role of the National Assembly in national security.[28] However, with a long history of autocratic rule, there is little experience in effective oversight by the legislature over security and defense forces, particularly given the political activism of security forces and the more or less direct military rule under President Lansana Conté. The SSR efforts have attempted to encourage engagement on civil-military relations through a series of national dialogues on security and defense issues. The political campaigns have also allowed more direct discussion of these issues by elected officials, although the political environment remains fairly undeveloped. Public discussion of the SSR documents was also useful for transparency.[29] Assembly representatives have few resources or staff to question, and some politicians have yet to undertake the many facets of their duties. The long delay in legislative elections, which were pushed back from 2007 to 2013, meant that this already-weak political body was not able to perform any function at all for several years.

Despite the improvements in the basic functions of the military and its return to barracks, there is little reason to believe that transparency into its operations and institutional practices have significantly improved. Areas where outside partners apply the most pressure and resources—such as in military justice—are heading in the right direction, as witnessed by indictments of crimes by security forces.[30] As Transparency International noted in 2015, Guinea ranked 139 (a tie with Papua New Guinea) out of 167 nations surveyed in its Corruption Perception Index.[31]

**Civilian Oversight.** Civilian participation remains a work-in-progress in the security institutions, with the Ministry of Defense remaining the biggest challenge, given the lack of a healthy relationship in the recent past. President Alpha Condé has opted to retain the Defense portfolio for himself, administrating via a delegate-minister. This is not an unusual arrangement in the world, and it is understandable given the past challenges with the military. There is no permanent civilian staff in the Ministry of Defense, which presents a challenge for civilian rule.

**Trust.** As evidenced by polling from the European Union's Institute for Security Studies, the Guinean military is not trusted by the population it is designed to serve, placing well below the mean for Sub-Saharan Africa.[32] This no doubt represents the legacy of recent decay in the professionalism of the military, particularly in the lead-up to the September 2009 massacre. No data is available for earlier eras, but one can assume that the professionalism and superior resourcing during the early years left a better impression with the public. Considering how the government had been increasingly unable to provide basic services during the dictatorships (Guinea ranked 178 out of 187 in the 2011 Human Development Index), it is not surprising that trust is an issue, even five years into the SSR initiative.[33] And as noted previously the evidence of abuses—both criminal and political—by the police and gendarmerie is compelling.

**Role in the National Economy.** The military had a significant role to play in the postindependence economy, generous support for which was provided by the Soviet Union. Units were created to undertake

agricultural activity and to provide engineers to assist private farmers—
by building and maintaining bridges and roads, for example. Additionally,
a factory was built that produced garments for the military. As the
early zeal for such functions diminished and resources became scarcer
(particularly after the end of the Cold War) such projects were shut down.
As of the writing of this chapter, there is very little such activity, and
even the garment factory has closed. The Government of Guinea still has
intentions to use the military for the purpose of "national development,"
but this requires resources that are not available. Further illustrating
change, the military no longer controls certain commodities, such as
fuel and rice.[34]

**Resources.** Except for the brief period when the USSR sponsored the
military, there has not been much investment in security and defense
forces. Currently, the armed forces can expect limited funds from the
government. Budgets are tight, and the Ebola crisis has put the economy
in recession. Yet, international assistance has increased under SSR. For
the military (mostly the army), there has been assistance to undertake
two goals: 1) professionalization and modernization of the force, and 2)
re-creating a peacekeeping operations capability. These goals are aided
by partners—France and the United States, among others.

**Human Security.** Article 5 of the 2010 Constitution says, "The human
person and their dignity are sacred. The State has the duty to respect
them and to protect them."[35] The Human Rights Watch reports that
the 2015 elections were largely fair—although challenged with logistical
problems, a deepening ethnic divide, and some election violence (including
ten deaths attributed to security forces). The report notes a marginal
improvement in professionalism and accountability (for example, in a case
from September 2009, fourteen suspects have been charged—including
the former junta leader Dadis Camara and his vice president, Mamadouba
Toto Camara).[36] Investigations have also been opened by the judiciary
into some of the most recent and notable abuses by security forces,

including deaths reported in 2007 and the torture of political opposition members in 2010. Still, no trials had occurred by the end of 2015.[37]

Another measure of human security would be how the people respond to security forces when their services are most needed by society. The Ebola crisis was just such an occasion. The World Health Organization reported that, as of April 2016, there were 3,814 cases of Ebola detected in Guinea, of which 2,544 resulted in death.[38] Despite the need to marshal all possible resources, the government did not utilize the military much in this crisis—despite its ability to provide troops and some mobility— due to lack of public trust in the institution. Similarly, security forces and health workers were opposed (and even attacked at times) when working in the interior, in part because the government and its security forces had not previously established good relations within the forest region.

## ASSESSMENT

An overall assessment, drawing from the major themes in chapter 2, provides an understanding of the interaction of the security sector, the threat context, and the population that the defense and security forces are designed to protect.

**National Brand.** One could argue that the SSR is not just an effort to remake the Guinean political and security landscape but also an effort to change its brand internationally. The timing was right for this on several fronts—most noticeably the broad movement in the region toward more multilateral cooperation, particularly in the area of peacekeeping. Another catalyst was the growing concern about fallout from the collapse of Libya and the increasing terrorist threat in the Sahel, which Guinea borders. International organizations and States have aided in this rebranding of Guinea. For example, the United States has responded to the political progress by providing some limited aid, for example, giving US$5.6 million in assistance specifically to develop peacekeeping capabilities, which it then used for multinational operations in support of its troubled neighbor, Mali.[39] This followed a familiar pattern from a generation earlier when Guinea received regional and international credit for its support of the peacekeeping mission (ECOMOG) in Liberia.[40] Of course, this deployment was in the 1990s when the Conté regime was still vigorous, if not democratic, and had not descended into the depths that allowed Dadis Camara to emerge. Still, Guinea has made a decision to ally itself with the broad regional and international set of norms, and to allow the sort of inspection and intrusions on power from outside forces that will aid its recovery.

**Most Significant Threats.** President Alpha Condé's National Defense and Security Policy (November 2013) lists Guinea's top external security issues, reflecting both a general agreement about the limited level of external threat from states, as well as the growing sense that transnational threats such as terrorism and criminality (drug trafficking and piracy, for example) threaten the states in the region, calling for an integrated regional response.[41] According to one political scientist using a data-based model, Guinea was the country most likely to face a coup in 2014, suggesting a high level of internal instability.[42] Indeed, internal security issues are an important concern, particularly given the recent history of ethnic strife in the states that border Guinea. Human security was greatly decreased during the final years of President Conté and during Dadis Camara's short rule; security forces were the primacy source of that decrease.

**Roles of the Security Forces.** SSR begins with an examination of institutional roles within society by evaluating the laws governing the service. The process has several steps. The first step was the drafting of the 2010 Constitution, which was done before the SSR process was officially launched. It ensured that roles were reevaluated in the context of the recent abuses and decay of the security and defense institutions. Next, the five individual security sector committees were invested with the review of all regulations and texts that govern the individual services and the ministries. These texts were in turn reviewed by the civilian leadership with some outside advice on best practices. Lastly, the SSR process had a goal of coordinating the activities of the five committees in order to de-conflict differences and indoctrinate inter-ministerial cooperation, since the products of the SSR process itself include setting government-wide goals, priorities, and resource allocation.

SSR requires the services to justify and rationalize roles, working with the new civilian leadership and international advisors. In the Guinea context, the roles remained true to their original design, so these were not changed significantly, but the services were required to toe the line and begin to posture themselves to actually perform their prescribed roles. Thus, the gendarmerie has moved its forces to rural areas, as is their writ, while the army has moved more forces to the borders (and out of the capital city) in order to perform their role of territorial defense.

**Political System.** Chapter 1 introduced Grindle's typology of political systems. Guinea has experienced all five categories. Immediately before the recent turn toward SSR, the country was nearing a "collapsed state." In the very early days of the republic, the government, while not democratic, was somewhat representative, and the security forces were well resourced and competent, arguably, an "institutionalized competitive state," with the ability to influence events in the region. For much of its life, Guinea experienced a form of personal rule, which gave way to a "minimally institutionalized state" under both autocrats as they aged. Currently, it is on the path to becoming an "institutionalized noncompetitive state," hoping to build the institutions of democracy and good governance, and to engage the international community.

**Relationships between Security Forces and Society.** Guinea has been involved in a concerted effort to move away from military dictatorship and toward democratic practices. The country held democratic elections in 2010, 2013, and 2015. For the past five years, Guinea has been undergoing UN-sponsored Security Sector Reform (SSR) to align its security ministries with democratic practices. The core of the SSR process underway in

Guinea is a bottom-up review of the five main security sectors of the government (defense, police, justice, customs, and environment).

The era of dictatorships resulted in severe economic underdevelopment, dysfunctional government, and increased social divisions based on ethnicity. Five years after the transition, there is little reason to believe that the national reconciliation process has overcome the legacy of this history. However, the SSR process and, more generally, the overall political environment have introduced senior military officers to a systematic civil-military relations review process. Additionally, as the SSR looks across the five different security sectors in order to shape and define the government's role in each, it provides a foundation that can be used to develop a long-term habit of civil engagement with—and democratic control of—security and defense forces.

**Trends for Security Sector Institutions.** While one can point to the modest successes of the SSR process—and the clear improvements in human security—much remains unsettled in the political landscape. For example, ethnic divisions permeate the current political culture, and no truth and reconciliation commission has been established to deal with the lingering impact of human insecurity. Democracy will be no panacea (in 2013, three years after the fall of the dictatorship, 57 percent of Guineans were not satisfied with their democracy, and half continued to pay bribes for the most basic of services, such as water).[43]

## Conclusion

The history of Guinea's governance is an unfortunate one, with only two presidents between 1958 and 2008, both of whom were undemocratic and misused the power inherent in security institutions. Such misrule eventually diminished the institutions and brought the country to the brink of collapse. Alternatively, one could look to Guinea's governance experience as a source of stability for most of its existence, particularly given the tendency toward civil war in the region (both presidents actually died in office). There were some coups and coup attempts, but Guinea was noted for its stability. Why, then, the sudden near-collapse in 2009? The simple answer is that the stability of the earlier era masked a steady build-up and then beat-down of institutions, particularly focused on the military, which was charged with the sole task of regime preservation. And when the armed forces proved too competent at that task, they were feared as a source of regime change and so were beaten down again.

Guinea remains a bit of a mystery to the world that came to know it only recently due to the Ebola crisis. Yet, it is a success on several levels: the country did not collapse into civil war, it transitioned away from chaos, and it has embraced, however tentatively, the concept of democratic control of security forces. Lastly, Guinea represents a modest success by regional and international players, whose rapid respond to, and aid for, an at-risk country, provided it with the opportunity to pull back from the abyss.

## NOTES

1. United Nations Development Programme, "Guinea," http://www.microsofttranslator.com/bv.aspx?from=fr&to=en&a=http%3A%2F%2Fwww.gn.undp.org%2Fcontent%2Fguinea%2Ffr%2Fhome%2Fcountryinfo.
2. Food and Agriculture Organization of the United Nations, "Country Fact Sheet Guinea," http://www.fao.org/nr/water/aquastat/data/cf/readPdf.html?f=GIN-CF_eng.pdf.
3. United States Geological Survey, "Bauxite and Alumina," http://minerals.usgs.gov/minerals/pubs/commodity/bauxite/mcs-2009-bauxi.pdf.
4. United Nations Development Programme, "Guinea."
5. "In full: declaration made in Burkina Faso between Dadis Camara and Sekouba Konate," *News Times Africa*, http://www.newstimeafrica.com/archives/10414.
6. Ana Larcher Carvalho, "Republic of Guinea: an analysis of current drivers of change," Norwegian Peacebuilding Centre (March 2011).
7. Harold D. Nelson, *Area Handbook for Guinea*, Department of the Army Pamphlet 550-174 (1975): 331–339.
8. International Crisis Group, *Guinea: Reforming the Army,* Africa Report N°164 (September 23, 2010): 3.
9. Ibid., 5.
10. Gilles Yabi, "Le Pire Cadeau Empoisonné de Conté à Son Pays: Une armée à la fois dangereuse et incontournable," *AllAfrica.com* (January 7, 2009).
11. United Nations Peacebuilding Commission, "Visit Report of the Mission to Guinea 11 to 15 March 2012," http://www.un.org/en/peacebuilding/cscs/gui/pbc_visits/PBC-GUI%20Visit%20March%202012%20-%20Report%20%28EN%20version%29.pdf.
12. The military has some progressive concepts that survived the period of decline; for example, women were encouraged to join the military, forming about ten percent of the gendarmerie and a smaller percentage of the Army. See Aboubacar Diawara, "The security sector reform of the Republic of Guinea," Gbassikolo.com, http://www.gbassikolo.com/5032-la-reforme-du-secteur-de-securite-en-republique-de-guinee-par-aboubacar-diawara.html.
13. US Department of State, *2009 Human Rights Report: Guinea,* http://www.state.gov/j/drl/rls/hrrpt/2009/af/135957.html.

14. US Department of State, *Guinea 2015 Human Rights Report,* http://photos. state.gov/libraries/guinea/231771/PDFs/guinea2015humanrightsreport. pdf.

15. *Constitution of the Republic of Guinea,* Article 142 (adopted May 7, 2010), http://www.ilo.org/wcmsp5/groups/public/---ed_protect/---protrav/--- ilo_aids/documents/legaldocument/wcms_127006.pdf.

16. Interpol, "Guinea," http://www.interpol.int/Member-countries/Africa/ Guinea.

17. United Nations Development Programme, www.GN.UNDP.org.

18. United Nations Peacebuilding Commission, "Visit Report to the Mission to Guinea, 31 May to 2 June 2015," http://www.un.org/en/peacebuilding/ cscs/gui/pbc_visits/Visit%20Guinea%20June%202015-Report%20EN.

19. Aboubacar Diawara, "The security sector reform of the Republic of Guinea," Gbassikolo.com, http://www.gbassikolo.com/5032-la-reforme- du-secteur-de-securite-en-republique-de-guinee-par-aboubacar-diawara. html.

20. United Nations Peacebuilding Commission, "Visit Report of the Mission to Guinea 11 to 15 March 2012," http://www.un.org/en/peacebuilding/ cscs/gui/pbc_visits/PBC-GUI%20Visit%20March%202012%20-%20Report %20%28EN%20version%29.pdf.

21. US Department of State, *Guinea 2015 Human Rights Report,* http://photos. state.gov/libraries/guinea/231771/PDFs/guinea2015humanrightsreport. pdf.

22. United Nations Peacebuilding Commission, "Visit Report of the Mission to Guinea 11 to 15 March 2012," http://www.un.org/en/peacebuilding/ cscs/gui/pbc_visits/PBC-GUI%20Visit%20March%202012%20-%20Report %20%28EN%20version%29.pdf.

23. Harold D. Nelson, *Area Handbook for Guinea,* Department of the Army Pamphlet 550-174 (1975): 339–340.

24. International Crisis Group, *Guinea: Reforming the Army,* Africa Report N°164 (September 23, 2010): 4.

25. Ibid., 5.

26. United Nations Peacebuilding Commission, "Mission Report of the PBC Guinea Configuration's Chairperson's Visit to Conakry (17-19 February 2013)," http://www.un.org/en/peacebuilding/cscs/gui/pbc_visits/PBC- GUI-mission_report_Chairperson_17-19_02_2013_EN_.pdf.

27. Alphonso Toweh and Saliou Samb, "Guinean military chief killed in plane crash in Liberia," *Reuters,* http://www.reuters.com/article/us-liberia- guinea-crash-idUSBRE91A0NW20130211.

28. *Constitution of the Republic of Guinea*, Article 142.
29. Alpha Condé, *National Defense and Security Policy* (November 2013), http://www.pbfguinee.org/sites/default/files/report-documents/politique_nationale_de_defense_et_de_securite_2013.pdf.
30. US Department of State, *Guinea 2015 Human Rights Report.*
31. Transparency International, *2015 Corruption Perception Index*, http://www.transparency.org/cpi2015#results-table.
32. David Chuter and Florence Gaub, *Understanding African Armies* (Paris: European Union Institute for Security Studies, 2016).
33. Transparency International, *2015 Corruption Perception Index.*
34. Alexis Arieff, "Guinea's New Transitional Government: Emerging Issues for U.S. Policy," Congressional Research Service (April 23, 2010).
35. Condé, *National Defense and Security Policy.*
36. Human Rights Watch, "World Report 2015, Guinea," https://www.hrw.org/world-report/2016/country-chapters/guinea.
37. Ibid.
38. International Organization for Migration, "Guinea Ebola Response," Situation Report (April 11–20, 2016).
39. Alexis Arieff, "Guinea: In Brief," Congressional Research Service (October 16, 2014).
40. Mamadou Diouma Bah, "State Resilience in Guinea: Mitigating the 'Bad Neighbourhood Effect' of Civil War Next Door," *ARAS* 33, no.1 (June 2012).
41. Condé, *National Defense and Security Policy.*
42. Max Fisher, "A worrying map of the countries most likely to have a coup in 2014," *Washington Post online*, https://www.washingtonpost.com/news/worldviews/wp/2014/01/28/a-worrying-map-of-the-countries-most-likely-to-have-a-coup-in-2014/.
43. Afrobarometer 2013 Country Study, "Guinea," http://www.afrobarometer.org/countries/guinea-0.

# CHAPTER 6

# THE CASE OF MALI

*Florina Cristiana Matei*[1]

Between 1992, when free and fair elections occurred for the first time in Mali, and 2012, when the military staged a coup against the government, Mali was a constitutional democracy, with separation of powers among the executive, legislative, and judicial branches. Thus, for almost two decades, Mali was one of the very few "successes" of democratization[2] in Africa. While prior to the coup Mali achieved significant progress in bringing about political and economic reforms, it made less progress in developing robust, democratic civil-military relations (a tradeoff between democratic civilian control and effectiveness of the Security Sector).[3] Even though Mali created fairly effective political and economic institutions, as well as a healthy civil society, it failed to establish capable security institutions and competent civilian control mechanisms.[4] Against this background, in March 2012, Mali's short yet promising experience with democracy was abruptly interrupted by a military *coup d'état*, followed by a short military rule. Under these circumstances, Mali represents a paradoxical case—democratization without the institutionalization of civil-military relations. Coupled with the bleak security context in Mali and in the region, this had negative effects on the relationship between elected officials and the security forces. This chapter assesses the governance and capacity of security forces as well as civil-military relations in Mali.

## THE FIRST DEMOCRATIC TRANSITION

Mali is a landlocked country in West Africa, with a population of approximately 14.5 million inhabitants. It gained independence from France in 1960, and became a one-party socialist style dictatorship under President Modibo Kéïta until 1968, when a military coup led by Moussa Traoré removed Kéïta from power. Traoré remained president until April 1991, when Amadou Toumani Touré (dubbed ATT), an army officer, staged a coup that overthrew Traoré.[5] A transition government took over and set the stage for free and fair elections in 1992, which resulted in the election of Alpha Oumar Konaré as president. Another successful transfer of power occurred in 2002, when Amadou Toumani Touré was elected president. Thereafter, Mali was regarded as one of the few democracies in Africa, garnering universal praise in the international arena.[6]

In 2011 (and even in 2012), the widely respected Freedom House listed Mali as one of only five fully free democracies in Africa.[7] Not only did Freedom House list Mali as "free" in terms of freedom of political rights and civil liberties, but it also listed it as "free" in terms of freedom of the press, a status many second- and third-wave democracies in Europe and Latin America still have not attained.[8] In sum, as Sako notes, after the 2002 elections, "it was generally accepted, especially among the international community, that democracy was taking root in Mali and that the country was well on its way to a mature, self-sustaining and stable Western-style democracy."[9]

## THE SECOND TRANSITION

On March 22, 2012 a group of junior officers and enlisted soldiers, which formed the so-called "green berets" of the armed forces and were led by army captain Amadou Haya Sanogo, overthrew the elected Touré government, looted the presidential palace, seized members of the government, suspended the constitution, imposed a curfew, and closed the country's borders.[10] The coup was supported by the public in Bamako, Mali's capital.[11] These events were followed by instability and violence, and quickly led to the loss of Malian government control in the Northern half of the country (including the well-known tourist city of Timbuktu) to several insurgent groups. These groups had long been operating in the north of Mali but were able to consolidate their power after the fall of the dictatorship of Muammar Gadhafi in Libya.[12]

On April 12, coup leaders officially relinquished power, and Dioncounda Traoré became interim president, while Cheick Modibo Diarra became interim prime minister. The interim president and prime minister assured the population that their unrelenting focus would be regaining democracy and civilian rule in Mali, as well as winning the war with the Tuareg separatists and Islamic radical groups in the North.[13] Despite these promises, the interim government had yet to pave the way for democratic transition. It was challenged by continuous conflicting internal divisions within the country; continuous military intervention in politics,[14] corruption and mismanagement within state institutions, and harsh economic restrictions due to a national recession and revenue crisis.[15]

Aided by international forces, Mali recaptured important territories in the North of Mali—including Timbuktu, Gao, and Kidal—took prisoners, and killed several hundred rebels, among them important Al Qaeda leaders (while it is not quite evident how the French came up with the numbers of deceased Islamists).[16] Moreover, the Government has reached several peace agreements with the rebels since July 2014.[17] Notwithstanding these achievements, Mali has been far from secure. Not only has there been significant resistance from rebels in the north, which involved clashes with the foreign and Malian troops, but there has also been an increase in organized criminal activities and terrorist acts throughout Mali.[18] A dramatic recent example is the terrorist attacks on the Radisson Blu Hotel in Bamako in 2015.[19]

In Mali, as elsewhere, democratic consolidation proved to be a difficult process, made more difficult by weak state institutions and the lack of a strategic vision. With regard to the latter:

> Mali's new democratic leaders made a strategic miscalculation. They assumed that because multiparty democracy was rolling back dictatorial regimes across Africa, the main threats to the country would be internal (i.e. law and order), as opposed to external ones. Therefore, they strengthened internal security forces such as the police, gendarmerie, and National Guard instead of the army. It is now clear that threats to internal security and law and order can be compounded by external threats, such as those Mali faced from AQIM. This explosive conjunction of forces can only be countered when the country has a strong, well-trained, well-equipped army with a competent officer corps. [20]

Ultimately, poor management of the defense sector (lack of effective intelligence; the inability of the Malian Defense Ministry to supply the armed forces fighting in the North; and the Defense Minister's denial of various rank-and-file complaints) resulted in the "accidental coup" in March 2012, which threw out two decades of democratization (the case of Mali also reveals the limits of Western security assistance). In sum, the void of power at the national level, the decline of the Army, and the rapid loss of the North to AQIM and its allies called for a serious overhaul of Malian security institutions.

## SECURITY FORCES AFTER THE COUP

Currently, Mali's security sector consists of the armed forces (army and air force),[21] charged with national defense, and the "security forces" (police, gendarmerie), and intelligence agencies (which share responsibility for internal security). The civilian elites utilize the security forces more as "firemen" and "policemen," occasionally as "peacekeepers," and less as "warfighters" or "defenders."[22] While the security forces have a slightly distinct status from the armed forces, they function in a similar way.[23] The routine relationship between the army and the rest of Mali's security institutions remains vague, the army appears to be much more powerful than either the police or the gendarmerie. As Jane's experts note, "[a]lthough the 4,800-strong gendarmerie comes under the control of the MoD for operations, daily control is exercised by the Ministry of Internal Security and Civil Protection. The national guard is under the control of the MoD but not formally part of the armed forces".[24]

**Armed Forces**

The Malian Army, which consists of around 14,700 personnel, comprises two battalion-strength formations of special operations forces—tasked with counter-insurgency (COIN) and counterterrorism (CT) operations against AQIM—two commando companies, and a battalion of combat engineers.[25] The Malian Air Force is rather small (800 personnel) and appears to function autonomously from the army, except for its river patrol force, which belongs to the army. The air force is tasked with air defense and counter insurgency.[26] Reportedly, Mali's armed forces do not have any active reserve personnel.[27]

Both the army and the air force belong to the Ministry of Defense and Veteran Affairs, which is in charge of devising the defense policy. The president is the commander in chief of the armed forces, while the Minister of Defense and Veterans Affairs exercises operational control.[28] The Malian Armed Forces are tasked with safeguarding the country's territorial defense and integrity, but they also have civil protection roles.[29] Interestingly, they are not required to operate abroad unless they participate in United Nations Peacekeeping Operations. As such, the armed forces' doctrine focuses on self-defense and internal security.[30]

In late 2013 several Combined Arms Tactical Groups (GTIA) were created to improve ground/air interoperability. Their main role is to transmit information on enemy location. GTIAs have their own armor, artillery, engineering, logistics, special forces and other components, as well as Tactical Air Control Patrols (TACPs) from the air force.[31] Of these, "GTIA 7" is a special group, since it includes a company from the gendarmerie, two army companies, and other enablers.[32] What is more, there are plans to integrate the "red beret" elements into these task forces (the red berets will comprise a sub-unit, called the "Commando Detachment", within the GTIA).[33]

## National Police
The Ministry of Internal Security and Civil Protection (MSIPC) is charged with utilizing the "security forces" for safeguarding law and order, public order on the Malian territory, as well as natural disaster relief actions.[34] Mali's national police comprises approximately 7,000 personnel, and shares internal security roles with the gendarmerie, including public security, public order, and fighting against organized crime.[35]

The general directorate of the national police fulfills a variety of roles, including the protection of individuals and goods; maintaining public order, safety, security and peace; ensuring respect for laws and rules by police force personnel; ensuring the control of regulations pertaining to arms and ammunition; controlling the activity of private security services; overseeing the air and border police; ensuring the protection of state institutions and high level officials; participating in Peace Support Operations; and humanitarian and civil protection operations.[36]

The General Directorate comprises six subordinate directorates: the Directorate of Public Security, Directorate of Judicial Police, Directorate of Intelligence and Territorial Surveillance, Personnel and Finance Directorate, Border Police Directorate, and Directorate of Training. In addition, the General Directorate has regional and territorial offices. Of the six directorates, the Public Security Directorate fulfills several important roles, including developing the general doctrine for public security, as well as strategies for enforcing traffic laws and minor crime.[37] The Directorate of Intelligence and Territorial Surveillance is responsible for collecting and analyzing intelligence related to the Malian Police Force roles, missions, and activities.[38] The Judicial Police Directorate (DCPJ), which is made up of policemen, gendarmes, and customs officers, is charged with fighting organized crime (including trafficking and money laundering) and serious crimes.[39] The National Central Office (BCN) of the Judicial Police—tasked with fighting international crime—works with INTERPOL. The BCN also works with other Malian security institutions at the domestic level. [40]

## The Gendarmerie

Similar to the Guardia Civil in Spain or the Gendarmerie in France, Mali's gendarmerie is a paramilitary police force, consisting of some 1,800 personnel. Its mission is threefold: judicial and administrative police; military police, territorial defense police, protection of sensitive points on the Malian territory; and execution of missions related to judicial decisions and tribunals. In addition, it is charged with response against any type of attack against Malian territory and citizenry, including terrorist attacks.[41] The gendarmes report to the Ministry of Security, yet they are part of the Armed Forces, fulfilling specific military roles such as border-control missions.[42] Since 2012 the gendarmerie has been fighting against Jihadist groups operating in three northern regions of Mali.[43]

## Intelligence Agencies

Mali has two known intelligence agencies: The State Security General Directorate (DGSE) and the General Intelligence Directorate of the National Police (noted earlier). There is little reliable information, however, on the exact roles, capabilities, and effectiveness of these agencies. While media accounts reveal that DGSE is involved in counterterrorism operations along with the French intelligence agencies, no additional information exists. Likewise, there is no information on the budget or the number of personnel.[44] Reports indicate that the DGSE lacks both clandestine operational capabilities and analytical abilities and resources; they also stress that the agency does not have an antiterrorist unit, which is highly needed in the country.[45] The same applies to the General Intelligence Directorate. Reports indicate that the agency is "incapable of making a difference between information and intelligence."[46]

## DEMOCRATIC CONTROL OF SECURITY INSTITUTIONS

Democratic Civilian Control of the Malian security sector is rooted in the constitution of Mali. Formal control and oversight is exercised by the executive, legislative, and judicial branches of government. Just as importantly, informal oversight is exercised by the media and civil society.

Executive control and oversight involves shared responsibilities between the president (who is the supreme commander of the armed forces), the prime minister (who oversees the implementation of security and defense related policies), Mali's Supreme Defense Council (similar to the United States' National Security Council), and specific ministries. It oversees the direction and guidance for the main components of the security forces. Executive control also includes control of budgetary expenditures exercised by the Department of Public Accounts, the Department for the General Control of Public Service, the Department of Financial Control, and the Auditor General.[47] The Office of the Auditor General in particular is reportedly tasked with investigating corruption in defense contracts, and it operates independently from political power and the armed forces.[48]

Legislative control and oversight of the security sector in Mali is the prerogative of the Malian Parliament (National Assembly), which devises the main principles and organization of the defense and security sectors. Since the return to civilian rule in 2013, the Malian Parliament has taken several initiatives related to security and defense—these include voting on proposed negotiations with rebel groups in the North, as well as creating a Committee of Truth, Justice and Reconciliation to investigate allegations of abuses.[49] The Defense and Security Committee (DSC), functioning in the National Assembly, examines the defense budget and debates Malian Armed Forces potential missions.[50] On paper, if any irregularities are noted with regard to the budget, the National Assembly is lawfully entitled to establish an ad hoc inquiry committee.[51] It should be noted, however, that there is no intelligence oversight committee in the Malian Parliament.[52]

There is little reliable information on the judicial review of the security sector activities. Some reports on the armed forces reveal that the Supreme Court has units, which specialize in budgeting, that check the armed forces' accounts and approve the annual auditing bill.[53]

Mali's formal control and oversight of the security sector is complemented by the "informal"[54] scrutiny of civil society, in particular the media. Many scandals involving corruption, nepotism, blackmail, and human rights issues have been exposed by the media. It is unclear, however, if the media in Mali has been able to prompt responsive government (i.e., forcing the hand of the government institutions to take measures against transgression and wrongdoing by the security sector). At a minimum, however, evidence that the media is acting as a watchdog is a good indicator of the country's possible return to democracy; as mentioned earlier, before the coup the media in Mali was considered fully free by Freedom House.

## ANALYSIS OF CIVIL-MILITARY RELATIONS IN MALI

A glance at Mali's post-coup civil-military relations reveals a few modest accomplishments and several serious challenges in terms of democratic civilian control and effectiveness of the security sector. After the coup in 2012 and the elections in 2013, the Malian security forces—in particular the armed forces—have adapted well to the reinstated civilian rule and appear to no longer be a threat to the civilian government. In addition, Mali's civilian elites have created or reinstated formal oversight mechanisms of the security sector, at the executive, legislative, and judicial levels. Nevertheless, it appears that while these formal oversight mechanisms exist on paper, they have been far from effective, challenging not only the efficacy of civilian control/oversight of the security institutions, but also the effectiveness of the security forces.

In this context, while the Malian elected and appointed executive and legislative officials have been interested in reforming the security sector, they have yet to develop a strategic vision for defense and security that would provide clear guidance for the security sector with regard to their roles and missions in defense and security matters. Although in December 2014, the Supreme Defense Council adopted a draft National Defense and Security Policy (as well as a draft law on the military) stipulating significant reforms, Mali still lacks a formal defense policy.[55] This lack of strategic vision is a result of their limited expertise in defense and security matters. The rapidly changing security environment in Mali (and hence the need for adapting the roles and missions of security forces) also poses a challenge. Further, corruption and cronyism across Malian state institutions fuel personal, economic, and political competition, placing defense and security low on the policymakers' agenda.

With regard to the legislative branch, despite the parliament's modest progress in debating security and defense issues, as well as in approving various defense related issues, concerns over its effectiveness have occasionally been raised. Specifically, there are concerns on the unequal balance of power between the executive and legislative branches. For example, while the parliamentarians can debate the military budget, the executive branch can disregard or reject their recommendations. At the same time, the Ministry of Defense can hide expenditures from the parliament on grounds of national security. Additionally, nepotism is rampant (e.g., the president's relative was appointed as head of parliament).[56] Finally, the judicial review of security and defense activities in

Mali is far from effective because of internal corruption and the lack of interest in these areas.[57]

Inadequate civilian control, lack of expertise, and absence of vision have additional negative implications for the effectiveness of the security sector. According to Christopher Holshek, "Mali Defense and Security Forces (MDSF) are poorly led, equipped, and trained as well as fragmented and incapable of preventing soldiers from committing atrocities against civilians, as evidenced in widespread reports of post-coup human rights abuses and MDSF retaliation in northern Mali, where it has had a history of repressive military administration. Then there is corruption."[58] In addition, there is involvement on the part of security sector personnel in organized crime activities. That may be because the existing code of conduct for all Malian military and civilian personnel avoids any mention of corrupt activities. Ethnic divisions within the security sector have not disappeared, threatening institutional stability, and even Mali's security. Political affiliation is often key in military promotions, military personnel do not always receive their full salaries on time, and high-level officials are involved in unlawful activities and businesses.[59] All of this "has implications for military effectiveness and morale, and poses security risks as disenfranchised personnel look for other opportunities to supplement their income, or simply do not show up at all."[60]

Ultimately, corruption—one of the most deleterious effects of civilian elites' lack of strategic vision and expertise in defense and security issues —"is undermining public trust in the government and the armed forces, as well as posing a major threat to the success of operations."[61] Indeed, not only have the Malian troops reportedly encountered difficulties in fighting the rebels in the north effectively, but they also have allegedly been abusive against the local populations. The military lacks a robust human resources management system with careers and promotions based on merit, impartiality, and justice, as well as a culture of military education and training.[62] The effectiveness of the security forces has been challenged by a perpetuation of old mentalities and practices.[63]

Mali's intelligence agencies have been far from effective. They appear to be plagued by cronyism and nepotism as opposed to having professional career paths for their officers; and they have allegedly been involved with organized criminal groups.[64] As a result, their activities seem to have focused more on spreading rumors and disinformation than on providing policymakers with intelligence related to national security. Furthermore, despite the creation of the GTIAs, the effectiveness of these forces has also been negatively affected by a lack of discipline, cohesion, and trust —and by limited capabilities.[65] For these reasons, militias have stepped up in Northern Mali and undertaken security roles to compensate for the lack of effectiveness of the Malian Armed Forces and Police.[66]

Under these circumstances, Mali has yet to develop security forces that are effective and under democratic civilian control. Western countries have invested considerable resources and time in helping Mali's security sector, prior to and after the coup, yet their efforts have yet to beget professional and effective security forces, more knowledgeable civilian elites, or robust oversight of the security sector.

As a 2015 article noted,

> Security sector reforms, for now, focus on improving the army's capacity to defend the country by building tactical skills. Current security sector reform packages aim at bringing quick fixes and short-term results to face the emergency, but proper in-depth reforms will need to be considered: improving civilian control of the military, increasing professionalization, and rethinking recruitment are three challenges that must be tackled for a real and robust reform of the security sector.[67]

Hopefully, over time there will be significant transformations in Mali's civil-military relations. The president has proposed an overhauling of the army, including anticorruption safeguards, better career paths for military officers, as well as increased salaries for civilians.[68] In 2016 the Malian and US governments carried out the initiative to send several military officers and civilians to the United States Naval Postgraduate School so that they could pursue master's degrees; these efforts to boost their expertise and knowledge in defense and security matters are commendable.

## Assessment

**National Brand.** This chapter examined Mali's security forces and civil-military relations after the military coup in 2012. It found that the government utilizes the security forces more as "firemen" and "policemen," occasionally as "peacekeepers," and less as "warfighters" or "defenders."[69]

**Most Significant Threats.** Mali faces several significant internal security threats from armed insurgent groups fighting for autonomy in the north of the country. These threats are exacerbated by regional external threats, specifically from jihadist militants such as Al-Qaeda in the Islamic Maghreb. These threats are further intensified by the bad governance and endemic corruption that plague the country.

**Roles of the Security Forces.** The security forces have to take the lead in addressing both both internal and external security threats that Mali faces. However, while there is some interagency coordination among the security institutions—and internal roles are coordinated between the armed forces, law enforcement agencies, and intelligence services—there is no official defense or security strategy to guide and direct the security sector. Security sector personnel have yet to obtain the education, training, and equipment necessary to perform necessary bureaucratic tasks and expected operational missions. Adding to this problem is the fact that there is no merit-based promotion system in place within the security forces. In addition, militias operate in Mali, especially in the troubled North. There is no continuous legislative oversight of the security forces, and the formal oversight mechanisms lack expertise and authority. Until this situation is remedied, it will be difficult for the security forces to fulfill their role of providing effective defense for the nation.

**Political System.** Despite considerable security assistance to Mali by the West, before and after the 2012 coup, Mali currently finds itself a

Minimally Institutionalized State—a rather weak government which has frail state institutions—with marginally effective and largely corrupt security forces.

**Contribution of the Security Forces to Good Governance.** The state of the civilian government remains fragile, even after the elections of 2013. The armed forces do not pose a direct threat to the democratic state but, as the 2012 coup has demonstrated, they could easily emerge as a threat in the future. The Constitution allows for adequate civilian oversight of the military, but the government does not exercise it.

**Trends for Security Sector Institutions.** Mali's future remains uncertain. Internal and external threats remain strong while the security sector remains weak. Mali's civilian elites need to continue to focus on defense and security institution-building in order to boost progress in Mali's political stabilization and that of its security sector. Toward this end, foreign presence and assistance remain cardinal. In addition to providing foreign financial aid, the West needs to continue to help strengthen Mali's efforts to achieve effective rule of law and democratic civilian control of security institutions, as well as build linkages between security forces, elected civilians, and Malian society at large.

## NOTES

1. All opinions expressed in this chapter are my own and do not reflect official positions of either the Naval Postgraduate School or the United States government.

2. Here, Linz and Stepan's definition of electoral democracy is considered and their warning of the "electoral fallacy" is taken into account. See Juan J. Linz and Alfred Stepan, *Problems of Democratic Transition and Consolidation. Southern Europe, South America, and Post-Communist Europe*, (Baltimore: Johns Hopkins University Press, 1996), 7–15.

3. I utilize the framework of civil-military relations (proposed by Bruneau and Matei), which consists of democratic civilian control and effectiveness of the armed forces, police, and intelligence agencies. For a comprehensive review of the framework, see Thomas C. Bruneau, and Florina Cristiana (Cris) Matei, "Towards a New Conceptualization of Democratization and Civil-Military Relations," *Democratization*, vol. 5, no. 5, 2008, 909–929; Thomas C. Bruneau and Florina Cristiana Matei, *The Routledge Handbook of Civil-Military Relations* (London: Routledge, 2012).

4. All of these occurred, even despite significant aid provided by the West to Mali before and after the coup.

5. Touré almost immediately returned power to civilians and organized democratic elections, and the opposition leader Alpha Oumar Konaré, won and became president. See Alexis Arieff and Kelly Johnson, "Crisis in Mali," Congressional Research Service (CRS) Report, R42664 (August 16, 2012): 1–16.

6. Especially since 2002 when Konaré stepped down at the end of two constitutionally permitted terms, and Touré was elected president. Alexis Arieff and Kelly Johnson, "Crisis in Mali," Congressional Research Service (CRS) Report, R42664 (August 16, 2012): 1–16.

7. See http://media.crikey.com.au/wp-content/uploads/2011/01/14-01-2011-mapoffreedom2011.png; http://www.freedomhouse.org/reports.

8. For example, Italy, Chile, and Brazil are partially free in terms of freedom of the press. See http://www.freedomhouse.org/reports. It should be noted, however, that scholars of democratic transition and consolidation such as Larry Diamond, Mark Plattner, and Zeric Kay Smith point out some flaws in Mali's democracy. See Larry Jay Diamond and Mark M. Plattner, "Francophone Africa in Flux," *Journal of Democracy*, vol. 12, no.

3 (July 2001), 35–36; and Zeric Kay Smith "Mali's Decade of Democracy," *Journal of Democracy*, vol. 12, no. 3 (July 2001), 73–79.

9. Soumana Sako, "Crisis in Mali: Lessons from an ongoing democratic transition," *Legatum Institute (LI;* February 2014), 1–15.

10. Adam Nossiter, "Soldiers Overthrow Mali Government in Setback for Democracy in Africa," *The New York Times* (March 22, 2012).

11. Juan Carlos Castilla Barea, "The Malian armed forces reform and the Future of EUTM," *ieee.es*, (October 7, 2013).

12. Thomas C. Bruneau and Florina Cristiana Matei, "The military coup in Mali, 22 March 2012. Reflections on the demise of democracy and the importance of civil-military relations" *Journal of Defense Resources Management* 5, issue 1 (2014), 8.

13. "Mali's new leader threatens 'total war' against Tuareg rebels," *The Telegraph* (April 13, 2012); and "Mali names Microsoft Africa chief as interim PM," *Reuters* (April 17, 2011).

14. On April 30, for example, the "red berets" attempted to stage a counter coup and reverse the situation, but to no avail.

15. See Alexis Arieff, "Crisis in Mali," Congressional Research Service (CRS) Report, R42664, (January 14, 2013): 1–18; and David J. Francis, "The Norwegian Peacebuilding Resource Centre (NOREF) Report" (April 2013): 1–16.

16. Media reports, however, indicate it is unclear how the French came up with the numbers of deceased Islamists. See Defense Institution Reform Initiative (DIRI) Mali Country Paper, prepared by CCMR (March 1, 2013).

17. Jane's Sentinel Security Assessment – North Africa, Executive Summary: Mali," IHS Markit, September 16, 2015, https://janes.ihs.com/NorthAfrica/DisplayHistory/963102. "Jane's Sentinel Security Assessment – North Africa, Political Leadership: Mali," IHS Markit, January 27, 2016, https://janes.ihs.com/Janes/Display/1303745. "Jane's Sentinel Security Assessment – North Africa, Security: Mali," IHS Markit, August 6, 2015, https://janes.ihs.com/NorthAfrica/DisplayHistory/963103. "Jane's Sentinel Security Assessment – North Africa, Armed Forces: Mali," IHS Markit, October 6, 2015, https://janes.ihs.com/WestAfrica/DisplayHistory/966707.

18. Ibid.

19. For background on the attacks, see Lauren Ploch Blanchard, Emily Renard, Alexis Arieff "The November 2015 Terrorist Siege in Mali," CRS INSIGHT (November 23, 2015) (IN10401), https://fas.org/sgp/crs/row/IN10401.pdf.

20. Soumana Sako, "Crisis in Mali: Lessons from an ongoing democratic transition," *Legatum Institute* (*LI*; February 2014), 1–15.
21. As a landlocked state, Mali has no formal navy or coast guard. There is no separate navy and historically the primary role of the relatively small air force has been to furnish air support for the land forces.
22. Per chapter 2.
23. Jane's Sentinel Security Assessment – North Africa, Executive Summary: Mali," September 16, 2015 "Jane's Sentinel Security Assessment – North Africa, Political Leadership: Mali," January 27, 2016. "Jane's Sentinel Security Assessment – North Africa, Security: Mali," August 6, 2015. "Jane's Sentinel Security Assessment – North Africa, Armed Forces: Mali," October 6, 2015.
24. Ibid.
25. Ibid.
26. Ibid.
27. Ibid.
28. Ibid.
29. Fati Mata Dicko-Zouboye et Kadidia Sangaré-Coulibaly, "Genre Et Sécurité Au Mali État Des Lieux Et Nouvelles Perspectives" DCAF et PGPSP (2011): 1–44.
30. Jane's Sentinel Security Assessment – North Africa, Executive Summary: Mali," September 16, 2015 "Jane's Sentinel Security Assessment – North Africa, Political Leadership: Mali," January 27, 2016. "Jane's Sentinel Security Assessment – North Africa, Security: Mali," August 6, 2015. "Jane's Sentinel Security Assessment – North Africa, Armed Forces: Mali," October 6, 2015. As of August 2014 it had sixteen experts, sixty-five police, and one troop member (in Darfur) on mission to various UN missions.
31. Jane's Sentinel Security Assessment – North Africa, Executive Summary: Mali," September 16, 2015 "Jane's Sentinel Security Assessment – North Africa, Political Leadership: Mali," January 27, 2016. "Jane's Sentinel Security Assessment – North Africa, Security: Mali," August 6, 2015. "Jane's Sentinel Security Assessment – North Africa, Armed Forces: Mali," October 6, 2015.
32. http://www.eutmmali.eu/wp-content/uploads/2015/12/English-version1.pdf
33. Juan Carlos Castilla Barea, "The Malian armed forces reform and the Future of EUTM," ieee.es, October 7, 2013.

34. Fati Mata Dicko-Zouboye et Kadidia Sangaré-Coulibaly, "Genre Et Sécurité Au Mali État Des Lieux Et Nouvelles Perspectives" DCAF et PGPSP (2011): 1–44.
35. http://www.interpol.int/Member-countries/Africa/Mali
36. http://police.gov.ml/index.php/directions-et-services/service-de-sante-et-des-affaires-sociales/
37. http://police.gov.ml/index.php/directions-et-services/service-de-sante-et-des-affaires-sociales/
38. http://police.gov.ml/index.php/directions-et-services/service-de-sante-et-des-affaires-sociales/
39. Fati Mata Dicko-Zouboye et Kadidia Sangaré-Coulibaly, "Genre Et Sécurité Au Mali État Des Lieux Et Nouvelles Perspectives" DCAF et PGPSP (2011): 1–44, http://government.defenceindex.org/generate-report.php?country_id=5613.
40. http://www.interpol.int/Member-countries/Africa/Mali; http://maliactu.net/mali-direction-generale-de-la-police-nationale-du-mali-un-nouveau-plan-de-communication-pour-recreer-la-confiance-entre-policiers-et-citoyens/.
41. http://www.maliweb.net/armee/gendarmerie-nationale-mali-force-humaine-service-peuple-1495172.html
42. http://www.eutmmali.eu/wp-content/uploads/2015/12/English-version1.pdf; http://government.defenceindex.org/generate-report.php?country_id=5613.
43. http://www.force-publique.net/index.php?page=3&ch=9&ti=146&idd=1440666447. However, militias also operate in the north. Marc-André Boisvert, "Failing at Violence: The Longer-lasting Impact of Pro-government Militias in Northern Mali since 2012," *African Security* 8, issue 4 (2015): 272–298.
44. http://government.defenceindex.org/generate-report.php?country_id=5613.
45. http://maliactu.net/le-mali-un-pays-sans-services-de-renseignements/.
46. Ibid.
47. http://government.defenceindex.org/generate-report.php?country_id=5613
48. Ibid.
49. Ibid.
50. Ibid.
51. Ibid.
52. Ibid.

53. Ibid.

54. For a complete account on the role of the media in a new democracy, see Florina Cristiana Matei, "The Media's Role in Intelligence Democratization," *International Journal of Intelligence and CounterIntelligence* 27:1 (2014): 73–108.

55. http://government.defenceindex.org/generate-report.php?country_id=5613

56. http://government.defenceindex.org/generate-report.php?country_id=5613; Tehmina Abbas, Eva Anderson, Katherine Dixon, Hilary Hurd, Gavin Raymond, "Regional Results Africa. Government Defence Anti-Corruption Index," Transparency International, 2015, 1–28; http://malijet.com/actualite-politique-au-mali/93651-karim-ke%C3%AFta,-pr%C3%A9sident-de-la-commission-d%C3%A9fense,-s%C3%A9curit%C3%A9-et-pro.html; http://maliactu.info/politique/defense-et-securite-fermete-et-assurances; http://www.mali24.info/mentions-legales?id=1256.

57. http://government.defenceindex.org/generate-report.php?country_id=5613

58. Christopher Holshek, "Mali and the Primacy of Civil Authority," *The WorldPost* (May 28, 2013).

59. Tehmina Abbas, Eva Anderson, Katherine Dixon, Hilary Hurd, and Gavin Raymond, "Regional Results Africa. Government Defence Anti-Corruption Index," Transparency International (2015): 1–28, http://government.defenceindex.org/generate-report.php?country_id=5613.

60. "Jane's Sentinel Security Assessment - North Africa, Executive Summary," ihs.com, September 16, 2015; Jane's Sentinel Security Assessment - North Africa, Political Leadership," ihs.com, January 27, 2016; "Jane's Sentinel Security Assessment - North Africa, Security," ihs.com August 6, 2015; "Jane's Sentinel Security Assessment - North Africa, Armed Forces," ihs.com October 6, 2015.

61. Tehmina Abbas, Eva Anderson, Katherine Dixon, Hilary Hurd, Gavin Raymond, "Regional Results Africa. Government Defence Anti-Corruption Index," Transparency International (2015): 1–28.

62. Juan Carlos Castilla Barea, "The Malian armed forces reform and the Future of EUTM," ieee.es, October 7, 2013.

63. http://www.maliweb.net/insecurite/col-major-salif-traore-ministre-de-la-securite-interieure-et-de-la-protection-civile-nous-sommes-la-pour-securiser-la-population-1262752.html

64. http://maliactu.net/le-mali-un-pays-sans-services-de-renseignements/; http://government.defenceindex.org/generate-report.php?country_id= 5613

65. "Jane's Sentinel Security Assessment - North Africa, Executive Summary," ihs.com, September 16, 2015; Jane's Sentinel Security Assessment - North Africa, Political Leadership," ihs.com, January 27, 2016; "Jane's Sentinel Security Assessment - North Africa, Security," ihs.com August 6, 2015; "Jane's Sentinel Security Assessment - North Africa, Armed Forces," ihs.com October 6, 2015.

66. Marc-André Boisvert, "Failing at Violence: The Longer-lasting Impact of Pro-government Militias in Northern Mali since 2012," *African Security* 8:4 (December 2015): 272–298, http://dx.doi.org/10.1080/19392206.2015 .1100505.

67. Marc-André Boisvert, "Failing at Violence: The Longer-lasting Impact of Pro-government Militias in Northern Mali since 2012," *African Security* 8:4 (December 2015): 272–298, http://dx.doi.org/10.1080/19392206.2015 .1100505.

68. http://government.defenceindex.org/generate-report.php?country_id= 5613; Jane's

69. Per the framework proposed in chapter 2.

CHAPTER 7

# THE CASE OF TOGO

*Madoua Teko-Folly*

Togo is a small, French-speaking country in West Africa with approximately 7.5 million inhabitants. Measuring 56,785 sq. km (21,925 sq. miles),
it is roughly the size of West Virginia, with a narrow southern coastline.
The country enjoys territorial integrity, which is easily enforced by a
government that wants security for the nation, its citizens, and, most
importantly, the continued existence of the ruling regime. Indeed, if
there is a sector of the Togolese government that controls more than any
other, it is certainly the security sector—for both external and internal
purposes.[1] Since the late 1960s, a well-organized security sector has been
put in place at immense human and financial expense. In fact, on an
African continent where public policy sectors (especially health, economy,
education, employment, housing, and research) are stunted, the Togolese
security apparatus, in contrast, appears colossal with the efficiency and
organization through which it intimidates the Togolese people.

What would normally be the case in Western countries—that is, a government carries out its duty and moral obligation to protect the nation, its citizens, and their property as part of the social contract that binds a state and its citizens—is reversed in Togo, where the state seeks to protect itself from its own citizens. In this respect, the regime views peaceful populations as an internal enemy requiring constant monitoring and control by the armed forces and intelligence services.

To put all this in perspective and to better understand this state of affairs, it is important to revisit Togo's unusual political history and background. Following the country's independence on April 27, 1960, from a French-administered trusteeship, Togo experienced exceptionally troubled beginnings with a series of coups and assassinations. The turbulence began in January 1963 when a group led by General Gnassingbé Eyadéma overthrew the nascent, democratically elected government of Togo, the first military coup in post-independence Africa, which resulted in the assassination of President Sylvanus Olympio. In January 1967, Eyadéma led a second coup, this time against Nicolas Grunitzky, the second president of Togo, gaining power that he would not relinquish until his death on February 5, 2005.

Throughout his tight four-decade rule, with the security forces firmly under his control, President Eyadéma wielded much personal power which he used to oppress the population, disregarding the constitution and placing himself above state institutions and the people he governed. Immediately following his death, the Togolese armed forces (Forces armées togolaises; FAT) engineered his replacement by thrusting his son, Faure Gnassingbé, into power. After national protests and international outcries, Gnassingbé stepped down only to reclaim power a few months later in an election symbolized by systematic and continual violence waged by the state security forces and pro-regime militias on the Togolese population.

Since then, there have been two other presidential elections in 2010 and 2015 (and legislative elections in between in 2013), which, according to the Bureau of Public Affairs at the US Department of State, "were substantially better than the first election [in 2005], and in fact represented only the third time that the country had had anything that remotely resembled elections in a multiparty process".[2] While the international community viewed these elections as credible, they were decried as flawed and rigged by civil society organizations, voter groups, and the Togolese people in its entirety.

Evaluating the governance and capacity of the security sector in Togo is a complex process, which is undertaken in a series of analyses in the following pages using the criteria laid out in tables 5–8 of this book. Chapter 2 provides a simple but effective tool to evaluate the state of national security forces, civil-military relations, and overall good governance.

## THE ARMED FORCES

From the outset of post-colonial authoritarian rule, the Togolese security sector was expressly designed to maintain regime security. This concept has not changed much today. The security structure remains dominated by the Togolese Armed Forces (FAT), which operate independently from civilian authority and control, oppress, and repress civilian populations, often times assuming expanded internal law enforcement duties at the expense of police forces.

Under General Eyadéma, the FAT grew from a paltry force of 300 soldiers in the 1960s to more than 13,000 today. It is important to note that the FAT is a deeply tribal and ethnic institution lacking in diversity. This rather unusual ethnic configuration is the direct result of several decades of recruiting along ethnic lines. In fact, worried about his personal security, General Eyadéma made it a habit to systematically build the military around his own ethnic group, the Kabye from the north. Of a total of 13,000 men, at least 10,000 reportedly come from the north and the remaining 3,000 from the center and southern regions of the country.

Once exclusively reserved for the Kabye under Eyadéma's rule, the FAT officer corps remains dominated by northern personnel—out of a total of about 300 FAT officers, only 50 come from the south. Ethnic homogeneity has been debated numerous times at the Military Function High Council (Haut conseil de la fonction militaire), resulting in the military stating that the seeming ethnic imbalance is simply the representative percentage per ethnic groups and per district at the time of military recruitments.

With a force of at least 12,212 men, the FAT eclipses by far both the air force and navy, with forces of 636 and 226 men, respectively. From the outset of the Togolese military force, the armed forces has been favored by Eyadéma. The Togolese Air Force (Armée de l'air togolaise) was established in 1964 and its operations are largely concentrated at the Lomé Transport Base at the International Airport where its transport aircrafts are stationed, and the Niamtougou International Airport where the combat units are located. The Togolese Navy (Marine togolaise) was initially established in 1976 to solely secure the fifty-five kilometers of coast and the seaport in Lomé. Today, it carries out patrol missions throughout the maritime domain to deter high seas piracy, drug trafficking, and terrorist attacks.

Attempts have been made to keep the armed forces out of internal security affairs. The Global Political Agreement (APG)—signed in Burkina in 2006 between the Togolese government and political actors to solve the ongoing political crisis—clearly states a distinction between the mission of the FAT to defend national integrity, and that of the gendarmerie and the police to carry out law enforcement and public security missions.[3] The FAT, which is managed by the defense minister, lack the republican characteristics that are so prevalent in Western democracies. At the 1991 national conference in Lomé, the Commission on Defense and Security pointed out that the FAT was created for the exclusive protection of a single individual and rooted in political and ethnic favoritism.[4]

Under the Eyadéma regime, the Togolese military lacked proper military procedures and an effective schedule for career advancement and officer promotion. This lack of process, combined with the deep-rooted practice of ethnicity-based recruiting, makes it difficult to refer to the FAT as a truly republican army, bound by a strict framework outlining its legitimate functions and prerogatives.

In total disregard for existing texts, laws, and decrees, the military sought civilian jobs to augment their salaries and its officers were often appointed to top political positions, regardless of whether they possessed the required skills and experience. This led to the further expansion of military power into the Togolese civil service and government, and thus, to the military's role as an inevitable political actor. The 2005 example of the military catapulting Faure Gnassingbé into power following his father's death demonstrates the great influence the armed forces exert in politics.

A small degree of reform arrived two years after Eyadéma's death, when a General Status decree (2007) outlined specific roles for each military service, ultimately benefiting the armed forces as a whole with clarification of what each service would do and trainings designed to support missions that support the specific roles assigned to each service. The decree forbade the FAT from directly or indirectly taking part in any parallel and lucrative economic activities (as was the case in the past) and allowed only retired military personnel to work for private security companies. While progress should be considered incremental at best, there are notable changes, such as benefits, gender diversity, as well as advancement and training opportunities that do represent real progress.

## LAW ENFORCEMENT

Law enforcement in Togo is primarily a responsibility shared by the national police and national gendarmerie. The Global Political Agreement (APG) of 2006 clearly makes the distinction between the FAT's mission to defend the nation's territorial integrity and law enforcement and the public security responsibilities shared by both the gendarmerie and the police.[5] Despite this stated distinction, law enforcement remains dominated by the army, with the September 23, 1986, terrorist attack on President Eyadéma's regime being a major reason. Similar to the armed forces, the ethnic configuration of police force and the gendarmerie is very homogeneous, which, following several presidential decrees, has only recently seen incremental reform.

### The National Gendarmerie

The decree No. 95-064/PR of October 13, 1995, sought to reorganize the Togolese national gendarmerie, which is the nation's paramilitary police force and a branch of the FAT. The national gendarmerie is composed of 2,710 gendarmes who carry out administrative police duties and conduct criminal investigations, protect the people and their property in rural areas, control roads and communications, and provide relief assistance in emergency situations.[6] The national gendarmerie is made up of five central bodies primarily located in Lomé:

1. The Directorate General (Direction générale)
2. The Legions of the National Gendarmerie (Légions de la Gendarmerie nationale)
3. The Republican Guard (Garde républicaine)
4. The Unit of Trained Divisions (Groupement des formations spécialisées)
5. The National Academy of the Gendarmerie (École nationale de gendarmerie).

The national gendarmerie has regional bodies as well. Similar to the French Republican Guard, the Togolese Republican Guard provides security for the head of state and government officials. While the national gendarmerie is placed under the authority of the Ministry of Defense, the very nature of its functions also places it under the leadership of the ministries of interior and justice, as well as the Attorney General's office.

## The National Police

Decree No. 92-090 of April 1992 called for the reorganization of the 4,400-strong national police force which operated under the leadership of the Ministry of Security and Civilian Protection. Its principal duties are to enforce laws; protect people and their property; deter crime, and prevent the risks of disturbances to public order.[7] The national police operate under the authority of a managing director (directeur général) who is in charge of the Directorate General of National Police (Direction générale de la Police nationale; DGPN) and tasked to holistically coordinate and control police services. The DGPN is made up of five directorates:

1. The Directorate of Common Affairs (Direction des affaires communes; DAC), which is in charge of personnel and national police asset management;

2. The Central Directorate of Public Security (Direction centrale de la sécurité publique; DCSP), which manages police stations and posts throughout the country;

3. The Central Directorate for General Intelligence (Direction centrale des renseignements généraux; DCRG), which provides intelligence to the government and performs safety and security missions along the country's borders;

4. The Central Directorate for the Territory's Surveillance (Direction centrale de la surveillance du territoire; DCST), which combats foreign interference and meddling, and defends the country's economic, cultural and financial interests; and

5. The Central Directorate of the Judicial Police (Direction centrale de la police judiciaire; DCPG), which exists under the oversight of the Judicial Authority and is in charge of investigating criminal law violations, gathering evidence and looking for law violators and crime perpetrators.

Between 2005 and 2007, the recruitment policy initiated within the new reform framework saw a wave of female recruits, and a "statut particulier" (special status) for the police was approved by the National Assembly on July 10, 2015, so that the police could utilize a more modern framework better suited to contemporary security challenges.[8] "The police mission," according to the Ministry of Security and Civilian Protection, "has significantly changed over the past 15 years, especially with the increase in transnational organized crime, cyber criminality, etc. There is a recognized need to open the police to a more diverse pool of skills in order to meet the population's increasing security needs."

## INTELLIGENCE SERVICES

Set up in the wake of the 1960 Togolese independence, and mirroring both the French model of special intelligence services and the overwhelming military fixation on regime security, the Togolese intelligence services, from their modest origins, have embraced an internal approach to intelligence which focuses more on the surveillance of members from political opposition groups, detection of so-called unpatriotic activities, political troublemakers, activists, and potential coup plotters.[9] The intelligence services exist within both the gendarmerie and the central police authority.

Within the gendarmerie, the intelligence services are made up of:

1. Anti-crime Brigade (Brigade anti-criminalité; BAC);
2. Research and Response Brigade (Brigade de recherche et d'investigation; BRI);
3. Processing and Research Center (Centre de traitement et de recherche; CTR); and
4. Intelligence and Investigation Service (Service de renseignement et d'investigation; SRI).

These services are staffed by agents who function like political police and neighborhood spies.

Within the police, the intelligence services are made up of the Central Directorate for the Territory's Surveillance (*Direction centrale de la surveillance du territoire*; DCST) and the Central Directorate for General Intelligence (*Direction centrale des renseignements généraux*; DCRG).

These services combat foreign interference and meddling; defend the country's economic, cultural, and financial interests; and provide intelligence to the government while performing safety and security missions along the country's borders.

In theory, the government has the available tools within the national gendarmerie and the national police's respective intelligence services to carry out intelligence missions. However, several instances of alleged law and legal process infringements prompted their reorganization following decree No. 92-090 of April 8, 1992, for the police, and decree No. 95-064/PR of October 13, 1995, for the gendarmerie.[10] Within the organizational structure of the intelligence services, a new and more robust department placed directly under the head of state was created in 2006 to collect and use intelligence within the framework of internal and external state security, as a way to reinforce the other services and confront new security threats appearing on the horizon.

To replace the Processing and Research Center (Centre de traitement et de recherche; CTR) which, at the time, was functioning as a central intelligence agency, the National Intelligence Agency (Agence nationale de renseignement; ANR) was created by presidential decree No. 2006-001/PR of January 26, 2006, and placed under the direct authority of the president, but also under the supervision of a directeur général, pursuant to the decree's first article. The fourth article outlines the staffing of the ANR by both military and civilian personnel. Thus, members from the military and gendarmerie were working together with civilian police and ordinary citizens from all walks of life.[11] These included information technicians; data analysts; legal, communications, and finance experts; cab and motorcycle taxi drivers; students; young men and women speaking several local dialects and foreign languages; and sex workers, among others.

While there are no official figures, there are reportedly 1,000 such agents working throughout the country, but mostly in the capital, working at the international airport, the port, bus stations, state administrations, hotels, banks, police stations, prisons, and border checkpoints. They discreetly monitor phone conversations, e-mails, bank accounts, travelers, bystanders, and the activity of political opposition group members. With operating and material budgets estimated to reach millions of US dollars, the agency is well informed on high-level officials and ordinary citizens' movements, and on all that is happening in the subregion.

The intelligence services operate with both formal and informal structures. In the formal structure, the head of state oversees all security- and intelligence-related matters and is assisted by the ministries of defense, security, and civilian protection as well as territorial administration, decentralization, and local government bodies. At the intermediate and local levels, appointed prefects, mayors, village chiefs, and traditional leaders provide close-quarter surveillance and control over the areas they administer and, occasionally, even on one another.

Private militias and security companies conduct much of the informal intelligence collection, while an invisible system of surveillance involving thousands of individuals shares information with the regime. Thus, a very tight security net is cast over the country, both vertically and horizontally.[12]

## Other Forces

In addition to the armed forces and law enforcement, there are other forces which complement security forces, including the corps of firefighters, customs, prefecture guards, forest rangers, and prison guards.

## MILITIAS AND PARAMILITARY GROUPS

Although evidence of their existence is scarce, there are a number of militias in Togo operating under the auspices of student associations primarily at campuses of the University of Kara and the University of Lomé. Usually emerging during election seasons, these militia members, especially the High Council of Student Association Movements (HACAME), appear to enjoy close ties to the armed forces which allegedly train and equip them with weapons.[13] They were initially established to disturb and break up any dissident movements and strikes on the University of Lomé campus and to intimidate the student population. In the 1990s, they were involved in fierce combat with the Ekpemog, the now-defunct opposition's militia.

During the 2005 presidential elections, President Eyadéma's children and close associates reportedly formed militias that were trucked in from the north and heavily involved in the postelectoral violence which resulted in 500 deaths and the displacement of more than 50,000 people. The troubling aspect about all these militias operating with impunity in the country is their increased militarization. What started as pro-regime student associations and unions in the 1970s shifted in the early 1990s to armed support for President Eyadéma's regime and, in the late 2000s, to Faure Gnassingbé's political survival. To this day, such organizations continue to deny and counter any efforts to seek democracy and good governance, end corruption, and establish the rule of law.

## PRIVATE SECURITY COMPANIES

Private security companies abound in Togo and are well established in Lomé. There are about a dozen of these companies; they are mainly foreign-owned and began operations in the 1990s when Togolese were increasingly making demands for democracy, security and their safety. Today, they and their local associates participate in this very profitable private security market, where demand for their services is high among well-to-do individuals, local and foreign companies, and regional and international organizations. For their staffing, these companies rely on militiamen and a readily available pool of retired military personnel eager to supplement their pensions.[14]

While totally separate from the armed forces, private security companies enjoy close ties with them and some of the militias. A few of them with high-level connections have privileged access to the executive and key high ranking individuals within the FAT. In the 1990s, the French-owned Security Advisory Services (SAS-Togo), founded by a former French gendarme, trained and equipped the national gendarmerie's antiriot forces. Private security companies not only train Togo's antiriot forces but are also sometimes involved in riot control; for example, during the violent 2005 elections, witnesses reported seeing another private security company, Optimal Protection Services, lending a helping hand to the FAT to control protestors.[15]

## SECURITY THREATS

Security efforts have intensified over the past several decades due to a litany of both real and perceived threats. Most notably was the September 23, 1986, coup attempt on General Eyadéma's life, which resulted in the creation of a 750-strong Rapid Intervention Force (Force d'intervention rapide; FIR) to respond to internal and external threats. "Each coup attempt provided the state with an opportunity to further tighten the screws. The government took excessive advantage of the September 11, 2001 attacks in the United States, and the anti-terrorist policy of President George W. Bush, to serve its own ends."[16]

In 2014, the FIR was reorganized into two Rapid Intervention Battalions (Bataillons d'intervention rapide; BIR), staffed with 550 troops each, one for the south region located in the Maritime Region (in Lomé) and the other for the north region located in the Central Region (in Sokodé). This well-equipped and well-trained force is tasked to respond to both maritime and land-based threats. As the armed forces' chief of staff, General Abalo

Félix Kadhanga put it, "this new unit is equipped with modern means and will be able to effectively perform the missions assigned to defense and security forces. It is the embodiment of the reorganization process initiated by the head of state, and thus takes into account a new kind of security challenge, chiefly the emergence of terrorism, rebellions, transnational organized crime, and all types of trafficking."[17]

With the globalization of terrorism and today's various crises in Northern Africa and sub-Saharan Africa, the Togolese government is, more than ever, aware of its own vulnerability. The regime now views its threats as both "internal" (from its own population and the opposition) and external, coming from chronic regional instability and shifting global security dynamics.

To demonstrate its preparedness for a Jihadist terrorist threat, the regime organized a large-scale military exercise at the Hôtel Radisson Blu in Lomé. The operation, code named "Bouclier étanche" (Waterproof Shield), mobilized a specialized unit from the national gendarmerie, in the presence of the head of state and other government officials, to deter and prevent terrorist acts. The police and the military were also mobilized and remained on high alert, ready to intervene in support of the antiterrorist unit.

According to the first military region commander, "this exercise will help the different commands to evaluate the operational level of our forces in crisis management in urban environments." For several months now, and in anticipation of terrorist attacks in the country, the Togolese authorities reinforced security measures in Lomé and the rest of the country. Military patrols and controls were doubled to provide for contingencies.[18]

While it may seem that given their numerous training exercises and significant resources, the Togolese armed forces and security forces are prepared and ready for such attacks, it is imperative to note that former French colonies in Africa (Côte d'Ivoire, Central African Republic, Mali, and Burkina Faso, to name but a few) have had to rely on French military intervention periodically over the last several decades to defend themselves. Yet, the French are likely less capable of defending their "sovereign" national territories than they propose.

## DEMOCRATIC CONTROL OF SECURITY FORCES

Generally speaking, civilian oversight of the military or security forces is unheard of in Togo. Even though both the 1992 constitution and its 2002 amended version clearly call for the democratic control of security forces, in practice, civilians are routinely denied control over military and security matters. Public and civilian control of defense and security forces is de facto nonexistent because regulatory institutions (such as the Togolese National Assembly), the legal system, and administrative institutions all function poorly. Furthermore, constitutional decrees are generally not applied.

The national assembly, which would normally oversee the national security forces, lacks a control mechanism to do so. Comprising eighty-one members (of whom only thirty-one are from the opposition), the assembly is routinely criticized for its inability to initiate legislative reform or hold security forces accountable in any manner. As a whole, it is poorly organized, inefficient, and understaffed. Its personnel (members and staff) are ill-equipped and poorly—if at all—qualified.[19]

This seemingly important institution appears to have no working legal framework, nor the necessary resources to function. A divide clearly exists between these members, their parliamentary groups, their political parties, and their constituencies, who all too often are ignored or neglected. Several assembly members can hardly engage in political debate due to the great difficulty they have expressing themselves in French, the country's official language.

It is no secret that a civilian, whether he is a judge, a lawyer, or even a member of parliament does not wield the same power as a man in uniform, especially a ranking officer. As clearly stated by the Togolese

Human Rights League, "men in uniform are clearly above the law and the justice system." Despite the presence of a Defense Commission at the National Assembly headed by a former general, its members seem to exert no influence whatsoever on the armed forces, let alone other actors involved in the security sector.[20]

## HUMAN SECURITY

Article 49 of the 2002 constitution[21] states that the mission of the security and police forces is to protect the free enjoyment of rights and freedoms and guarantee the security for citizens and their property. However, given the perpetual state of insecurity facing civilian populations, whether in the capital or beyond, the vast majority of Togolese find themselves under constant threats for their lives, property, and well-being, and they face unceasing infringements on their civil liberties and basic rights from both security forces and common criminals.

Distrust of the police services is widespread in Togo. According to a survey conducted by Afrobarometer, a pan-African research network, when faced with crime, violence, or robbery, the Togolese people no longer have the desire or patience to wait for the police to protect them. Their answer to the increasing insecurity is simply lynching the criminal. Indeed, 79% of respondents argued that, because police stations are too far away, patrols in certain neighborhoods are rare, and officers routinely ask for bribes to do their job, they rarely involve the police in matters of crime. Civil-police relations are at their lowest because distrust for the police is common and is further undermined by extortion and racketeering practices, leaving the population to fend for themselves.[22] According to Boubacar N'Diaye, "African police forces must carry their own 'cultural revolution' if they are eager to re-establish trust with the people."[23]

## PEACE MISSIONS

The FAT regularly participate in peacekeeping missions mandated by the United Nations, African Union, and ECOWAS. These missions are notably in Côte d'Ivoire, the Central African Republic, Chad, Darfur, and Burundi. Most recently, the FAT participated with a contingent of well over 1,000 serving in the United Nations Multidimensional Integrated Stabilization Mission in Mali (MINUSMA). The FAT also take part in several regional military exercises and train with the French military through the African Capabilities Reinforcement in Peacekeeping (RECAMP) program and also count on US foreign assistance for "efforts made toward a professional military that respects civilian leadership and institutes reforms."[24]

The Togolese armed forces are working hard to shed their image of political meddling at home and abroad in the subregion, as well as of perpetrating atrocities against civilian populations by increasingly involving themselves in peacekeeping missions and providing relief assistance to local populations affected by floods and other small-scale natural disasters.

## TEXTS AND DECREES

Following the 2005 presidential elections, to show good faith and make good on his promises, President Faure Gnassingbé took several actions on the defense and security forces, including immediately replacing twenty corps and specialized unit commanders within the armed forces. Later in 2008, he enacted a number of decrees, including:

- Decree No 2008-006, confirming the attributions of the army chief of staff and director general of the national gendarmerie;
- Decree No 2008-007, calling for the reorganization of the army;
- Decree No 2008-009, calling for the reorganization of the navy;
- Decree No 2008-011, establishing a higher military council;

- Decree No 2008-014, requesting the reorganization of the air force; and

- Decree No 2008-012, defining the functioning of investigative councils involving the military.

Interestingly, while these decrees appear to touch upon practical and specific matters within the armed forces themselves and are hailed as progress, they ultimately fall well short of addressing substantive issues, such as civil-military relations or the relationships between defense and security forces themselves.

## ASSESSMENT

**National Brand.** Based on the table 1 of chapter 2, Togo, due to its unique history and very peculiar past, has for a long time been a "policeman" when taking into account the way the country used its armed forces to repress civilian populations, and all too often entrusted them with internal law enforcement duties. However, in recent years it has abandoned the "policeman" role to progressively become a "peacekeeper," increasing training and deployment of its armed forces for international peacekeeping missions.

**Most Significant Threats.** Considering the points discussed in table 2, Togo faces some traditional and human threats. While the country has not (yet) been directly targeted by terrorist groups such as Al-Qaeda in the Islamic Maghreb (AQIM), Ansar Dine, the Movement for the Unity and Jihad in West Africa (MUJAO), and other groups operating in the Sahel, these groups (when considered alongside Boko Haram's incessant attacks in Nigeria, Niger, Chad, and Cameroon) represent significant threats in the form of Jihadist terrorism facing the country. International organized crime (money laundering, drug trafficking, and cyber-attacks) represents another. In addition to these external traditional threats, Togo also faces some external human threats like illegal fishing. Togo is also vulnerable to internal human threats which plague many African countries—bad government, cronyism, nepotism, and corruption at various levels.

**Roles of the Security Forces.** The Togolese security forces follow the rules of thumb laid out in table 3. Though in the not-so-distant past, the armed forces held a law-enforcement role, today they continue to protect the country's territorial integrity and help maintain peace in postconflict regions. Both the police and the gendarmerie share law enforcement and public security roles by providing security to citizens, conducting criminal investigations, and protecting critical infrastructure. While the intelligence services are notorious for focusing their energy and resources on monitoring citizens, they also provide the government with vital intelligence.

**Political System.** Because the armed forces still dominate the security sector, they receive a significant portion of the defense budget and were until recently collectively an inescapable political entity. This coupled with the fact that the head of state appears to enjoy absolute power and the supreme protection of the armed forces, based on the rubric set out in table 4, Togo falls somewhere between status as an "institutionalized noncompetitive state" and "personal rule". On the one hand, its security forces are diverse and well established; they have coordination mechanisms and share power and influence. Decisions are made top-down by the same ruling political party which has ruled without real consensus for nearly half a century. The state is headed by a powerful individual, assisted by family and friends. On the other hand, the security forces preserve the territorial integrity of the country, maintain total order, and are fixated on ensuring regime survival and do not hesitate to quash political dissents or protests.

**Trends for Security Sector Institutions.** In spite of shortcomings and under international pressure, President Faure Gnassingbé has taken the difficult steps of reorganizing the defense and security forces, and in 2007 he signed a bill restating the status of the military as a republican and apolitical entity, reiterating the words of the 2002 constitution. Since then, many institutions with democratic control and a civilian management mandate have been put in place, while numerous seminars, trainings and workshops have been held to promote good civil-military relations, and the demilitarization of state institutions. Despite these incremental reforms, the legacy of decades of authoritarian rule has stunted the rule of law, which to this day struggles to materialize and take hold. Until that happens, Togo will continue to rely on security institutions and a militarized state security apparatus that operates with minimal control of democratic institutions and the Togolese people.

## NOTES

1. "Togo: Les Forces Armées Togolaises et le Dispositif Sécuritaire de Contrôle (1&2)," *letogolais.com* (October 7, 2008), http://www.letogolais.com/article.html?nid=2370.
2. "Background Briefing en Route Liberia," *U.S. Department of State* (January 12, 2012), http://www.state.gov/r/pa/prs/ps/2012/01/180798.htm.
3. "Dialogue Inter-Togolais: Accord Politique Global," *United Nations Peacemaker* (August 20, 2006), http://www.peacemaker.un.org.
4. Toulabor, Comi M. "Togo," in *Security Sector Governance in Francophone West Africa: Realities and Opportunities,* edited by Alan Bryden, and Boubacar N'Diaye (Geneva: Geneva Centre for the Democratic Control of Armed Forces [DCAF], 2011): 229–253.
5. "Le Projet d'Accord Politique Global (Texte Intégral)," *Ici Lomé* (May 6, 2016), http://www.icilome.com/nouvelles/news.asp?id=1&idnews=6968.
6. "Gendarmerie," *Forces Armées Togolaises,* http://www.forcesarmees.tg.
7. "Togo," *Interpol,* http://www.interpol.int/Member-countries/Africa/Togo.
8. "La Police Togolaise Aura un Statut Particulier pour S'adapter à Son Temps," *aLome.com* (December 25, 2014) http://news.alome.com/h/35365.html.
9. "Togo: Les Forces Armées Togolaises et le Dispositif Sécuritaire de Contrôle (Parts 1 & 2)," *letogolais.com* (October 7, 2008), http://www.letogolais.com/article.html?nid=2370.
10. Toulabor, "Togo," 229–253.
11. Ferdi-Nando, "L'ANR ou l'Agence de Renseignement Vraiment à la Togolaise," *Elomvitschinfo* (September 18, 2012), https://elovitschinfo.wordpress.com/2012/09/18/lanr-ou-lagence-de-renseignement-vraiment-la-togolaise/.
12. Toulabor, "Togo," 303–321.
13. "Togo: Les Forces Armées Togolaises et le Dispositif Sécuritaire de Contrôle (1&2)," *letogolais.com* (October 7, 2008), http://www.letogolais.com/article.html?nid=2370.
14. Toulabor, "Togo," 229–253.
15. "Togo: Les Forces Armées Togolaises et le Dispositif Sécuritaire de Contrôle (1&2)," *letogolais.com* (October 7, 2008), http://www.letogolais.com/article.html?nid=2370.
16. Toulabor, "Togo," 303–321.

17. "La Nécessaire Adaptation de l'Armée Togolaise," *République Togolaise* (October 15, 2014), http://www.republicoftogo.com/Toutes-les-rubriques/ Politique/La-necessaire-adaptation-de-l-armee-togolaise.

18. "Togo: Simulation d'Attaques Terroristes à l'Hôtel Radisson Blu « 2 février »," *Jeune Afrique* (last modified February 18, 2016), http:// www.jeuneafrique.com/303422/politique/togo-simulation-dattaques-terroristes-forces-armees-a-lhotel-radisson-blu-2-fevrier/.

19. Toulabor, "Togo," 229–253.

20. Toulabor, "Togo," 303–321.

21. "Constitution Togolaise de 1992," *Ici Lomé,* http://www.icilome.com/ togo/const.asp?site=2.

22. "Enquête Afrobaromètre: Le Togo, Figure de la méfiance envers la police," *Radio France Internationale* (last modified November 16, 2015), http:// www.rfi.fr/afrique/20151115-africains-pas-confiance-police-togo-benin-afrobarometre.

23. "Enquête Afrobaromètre: Le Togo, Figure de la méfiance envers la police," *Radio France Internationale*, last modified November 16, 2015, http:// www.rfi.fr/afrique/20151115-africains-pas-confiance-police-togo-benin-afrobarometre.

24. "U.S. Relations with Togo," *U.S. Department of State* (May 6, 2015), http:// www.state.gov/r/pa/ei/bgn/5430.htm.

CHAPTER 8

# THE CASE OF NIGERIA

*Thomas Mockaitis*

Occupying an area of 923,768 square kilometers (574,003 miles) and twice the size of California, the West African country of Nigeria stretches from the Gulf of Guinea in the South to the edge of the volatile Sahel region in the North. It borders Benin in the west, Cameroon in the east, and Chad in the northeast. Nigeria has a population of 181,562,056, which is divided into more than 250 ethnic groups, making it the most populous country on the continent and one of the most diverse. As in other Sahel countries, Christians comprising 50% of the population live in the south and Muslims comprising 40% live in the north. Like most developing nations, Nigeria has a serious youth bulge with more than 60% of its population under the age of 25.[1] With an estimated GDP of $1.1 trillion in 2015, Nigeria has the largest economy in Africa. Most of its wealth derives from large oil reserves in the Niger Delta. Unfortunately, this wealth has not improved the lives of most Nigerians. More than sixty per cent of the population lives in poverty, while government resources have been lost through waste, corruption and mismanagement. Relatively little of the revenue from its oil reserves has been spent on infrastructure and social services.

Since achieving independence from Britain in 1960, Nigeria has had a turbulent history, marred by ethnic and regional conflict and a series of military coups. In 1967 three eastern provinces seceded, forming the Republic of Biafra and sparking a three-year civil war that killed over a million civilians, many of them by starvation.[2] Nigerian military officers seized power in 1966, 1975, 1983, 1985, and 1993. Military rule ended in 1999, and a modicum of stability has characterized national politics ever since. Elections are held on a regular basis, and while there have been accusations of impropriety, these elections have resulted in orderly and peaceful transfers of power. However, intermittent ethnic conflict has continued, and sectarian violence has become endemic.

## ARMED FORCES

On paper, Nigeria has an impressive military establishment. The strength of the armed forces is 130,000 active duty and 32,000 reserve personnel. The army has 148 tanks, 1,420 armored fighting vehicles, 25 self-propelled and 339 towed artillery pieces, and 30 multiple rocket launchers. The air force has 105 aircraft, including ten fighters, twenty-two attack aircraft, and nine attack helicopters. The navy has seventy-five ships, including two frigates and forty-eight coastal defense vessels.[3]

Despite its impressive list of hardware, the Nigerian military has been described as a hollow force. Poor training, aging equipment, lack of maintenance, and failure to invest in newer weapons system hampers effectiveness. Of the $5.8 billion allocated for defense in 2015 (one quarter of the entire national budget), only 10% went to capital spending.[4] Corruption further cuts into the money intended for equipment. For example, a former national security advisor and a former defense minister were recently charged with stealing $2 billion and $1.5 billion respectively of funds intended for arms purchases.[5] The government has limited defense spending to deter the coups that have plagued the country in the past, but this move has hampered the military's ability to combat the threat posed by the Islamist group Boko Haram.[6]

One whistle blower, an air force corporal, described the impact of corruption on operational effectiveness:

> Nigerian military is too ill-equipped to combat the ravaging insurgency in the North. Forget about what the Defense spokesman is saying from Abuja. Here [in the conflict zone], it's visible to the blind and audible to the deaf. In my unit here in Yola, despite the global technological progress, we are still using the *Fabrique Nationale* rifles that were used in the Biafran War! Meanwhile, the insurgents are carrying advanced weapons. They have light machine guns, new AK-47 rifles, general-purpose machine guns, to mention a few.[7]

Corruption also extends to theft of soldiers' pay and allowances. In 2014, soldiers fighting Boko Haram deserted when they came under attack, insisting that they were angry over a fifty percent pay cut they believed resulted from graft.[8] Inadequate pay and poor supply result in low morale and high desertion rates.

## POLICE

The Nigerian Police have undergone a significant expansion since the end of military rule. Police strength increased from 140,000 in 1999 to 371,800 in 2008, where it has remained.[9] Each of Nigeria's thirty-six states and the capital has a state command under a commissioner of police. Each state command belongs to one of twelve zones (consisting of 2–3 state commands) under an Assistant Inspector General of Police, who in turn reports to the Inspector General in Abuja. In addition to this regional distribution of forces, the police force also has specialized functional units.[10]

Increasing the number of police while reducing the size of the military was a healthy development in a country racked by coups, but the expanded force has not been given the resources to do its job effectively. Each zone complains of constraints under which its forces operate. These constraints include shortages of funds, manpower, vehicles, weapons, and office equipment.[11] Such shortages have the same negative effect on performance and morale as they do for the armed forces.

An endemic culture of corruption further diminishes the effectiveness of the Nigerian Police Force. Recruits pay a bribe for admission to the police academy and for promotions during their career. This practice encourages officers to recoup their losses by taking bribes from the public. The police extort money from suspects and shake down ordinary motorists at checkpoints. These illegal activities are rampant throughout the force, from the Inspector General to the lowest-ranking policeman. A former Inspector General was believed to have stashed away $350 million in foreign bank accounts.[12]

Where corruption is openly tolerated and even encouraged, human rights abuses are sure to follow. Amnesty International reported that in 2015–2016 "Torture and other ill-treatment by police and military remained pervasive. Extrajudicial executions, extortion, and arbitrary and prolonged detention were rife."[13] These practices seriously erode public trust in the police. Citizens are reluctant to report ordinary crime and even less likely to cooperate in fighting serious internal threats like Boko Haram.

## INTELLIGENCE SERVICES

Like most modern states, Nigeria has an array of civilian and military intelligence agencies to gather information necessary to protect its state and society. During the years of military rule, the intelligence establishment developed a reputation for supporting repression by focusing not on threats to the states but on threats to whatever junta was in power. A 1986 decree disbanded the distrusted National Security Organization and replaced it with three new intelligence agencies: the National Intelligence Agency, the Defense Intelligence Agency, and the State Security Services. All three agencies report to the Coordinator of National Security in the Office of the President. The Nigerians appear to have based their intelligence system on the American model.[14]

The National Intelligence Agency (NIA) is charged with foreign, non-military intelligence gathering and counterespionage within Nigeria. The State Security Service (SSS) gathers intelligence to combat crime and counter internal threats. The SSS works closely with the Federal Investigation and Intelligence Bureau, the body charged with liaising between law enforcement and the intelligence community.[15] The Defense Intelligence Agency (DIA) gathers military intelligence to protect the territorial integrity of Nigeria. According to its own mission statement, "The DIA is to produce comprehensive, contextual and timely intelligence support to defense planners and decision makers in order to effectively enhance national security."[16] The DIA is subdivided into defense sections, and it also facilitates cooperation with foreign militaries.[17] Each of the armed services also has its own intelligence service. The DIA is the only one of the three intelligence agencies not authorized to operate within Nigeria.

## CIVILIAN OVERSIGHT OF THE MILITARY

Given the repeated intervention of the Nigerian military in politics, the framers of the 1999 constitution took great care to include provisions for its civilian oversight. The president appoints the Chief of the Defence Staff and the Chief of Staff of each of the armed services. The president also serves as commander in chief, determining when and how the military may be employed in defense of the nation or for internal security operations. In specific situations, he may also delegate the operational control of its forces to a member of the military.[18] The National Assembly has the power to set the defense budget and regulate the powers of the commander and chief and "the appointment, promotion and disciplinary control of members of the armed forces of the Federation."[19] Both the Nigerian Senate and House of Representatives have Defense Committees charged with overseeing the military. To be properly implemented, the Nigerian Constitution requires civilian oversight of the military.

Legal clauses alone do not, however, guarantee civilian control. Unless political leaders demonstrate the will to exercise control, constitutional guarantees will have little meaning. Since the end of military rule in 1999, the record of oversight has been mixed. On the positive side, the military has not interfered directly in politics. Not only have there been no coups, but the country has also weathered two political crises without military intervention. A threatened coup was nipped in the bud in 2005, and an effort by President Obasanjo to stand for a third term in defiance of the constitution was thwarted by civilian opposition.[20] Furthermore, education and training of military personnel has emphasized proper civil-military relations in a democracy.[21] On the negative side, the legislature has not exercised meaningful oversight of the armed forces. From 1999 to 2006, neither the House nor the Senate Defense Committee proposed a single bill, auditing of defense spending rarely occurs, and procurement information (deemed confidential) is left out of what audits do occur.[22] This lack of transparency contributes to graft and corruption.

On balance it seems that although the civilian government has the ability to regulate the armed forces, it has been reluctant to do so to the full extent necessary for complete transparency. This reluctance may stem from history and the security situation in the country. Given the past propensity of the military to intervene in politics, elected officials may be reluctant to push the oversight envelope too far for fear of provoking a coup. The expanded role of the military in internal security may also make politicians reluctant to antagonize the armed forces upon which the country depends for its survival. Ironically, this reluctance encourages corruption, which in turn erodes morale, and thus makes the armed forces less effective. Finally, the corruption of politicians and civilian bureaucrats probably discourages them from pointing the finger at corrupt officers for fear of drawing attention to their own malfeasance. This pervasive culture of corruption remains a serious threat to democracy as the military has previously used poor governance as an excuse to stage coups.[23]

## SECURITY THREATS

While ordinary people have a clear vision of what security means, analysts require more precise definitions. Narrowly defined, national security entails protecting the state from direct threats to its sovereignty. These threats may come from foreign states or internal insurgent or terrorist groups. The United Nations Development Program (UNDP) has, however, argued for a more comprehensive definition of *human security*. "The concept of security must thus change urgently in two basic ways," the foundational 1994 UNDP report proclaims:

> - From an exclusive stress on territorial security to a much greater stress on people's security.
>
> - From security through armaments to security through sustainable human development.[24]

Threats to human security may be economic and environmental as well as political. Put another way, people need adequate food, shelter, health care, and protection from crime and violence.[25]

Nigeria currently faces no direct threats to its sovereignty from foreign states. Indeed, the absence of regional or local threats has allowed Nigeria to be a significant troop contributor to peacekeeping missions, such as those in Sierra Leone and Liberia during the 1990s. The deteriorating internal security situation has, however, made it difficult to continue participating in peace operations.

Absence of foreign enemies does not, however, mean that Nigeria enjoys either traditional national security or human security. The country faces a wide array of internal threats that challenge both the sovereignty of its state and the security of its people. These threats include insurgencies in the north and south, intercommunal violence, and pervasive crime.

## Niger Delta Militancy

The vast oil-rich Niger Delta has been a hotbed of conflict over the past several decades. This conflict has involved a toxic blend of ethnic strife, eco-terrorism, and criminality. Ecological degradation and poverty lie at the heart of the strife. Indigenous groups resent encroachment on and destruction of their ancestral lands. Ordinary people resent failure of the government to invest oil revenue in improving the local quality of life. Inhabitants of the delta bear all of the costs of oil extraction while reaping few of its benefits. This resentment manifests itself in organized and spontaneous resistance as well as criminality.

The Niger Delta covers 27,000 square miles and is home to 27 million people from forty ethnic groups. The region consists of nine states with 185 local governments.[26] A collection of local and international oil companies runs the extraction industry, including Shell, Exxon Mobil, and TotalFinaELF. Residents have deduced correctly that collusion between the oil companies and the federal government led to the brutal suppression of unrest by the Nigerian military on behalf of the extraction industry.[27] Politicians in Abuja line their pockets with oil revenue while people in the Delta live in abject poverty.

In late 2005, discontent exploded into a full-blown insurgency. The Movement for the Emancipation of the Niger Delta (MEND) evolved out of protest groups and small militia-style organizations active in the 1990s. It subsumed other groups such as the Niger Delta Volunteer Force and the Niger Delta Vigilante Group. From the outset, MEND adopted a different strategy than its predecessors, preferring to disrupt oil production rather than engage in violent confrontation with the security forces. MEND Commander Ebikabowei "Boyloaf" Victor-Ben explained the logic of the new approach:

> I believe the economy is the power. Like you may have known, I don't believe in fighting human beings, I believe in crumbling the economy. On my way crumbling [*sic*] the economy, if any military man comes across me and tries to stop me, I mean those people will kiss their graves. My bullet, nozzle is always targeted at the flow stations, pipelines etc, I don't believe in fighting human beings. Before we formed the MEND, our people were fighting, but it was a war between the Ijaw and Itsekiri, that was not the Niger Delta struggle.[28]

True to its word, MEND conducted a series of attacks against oil facilities. It also kidnapped oil workers for ransom. To fund its operations MEND relied on "oil bunkering," syphoning oil from pipelines and selling it on the black market.

To avoid the fate of earlier movements, MEND adopted a highly decentralized organization. It eschewed a hierarchical command structure in favor of a highly decentralized cell system. This approach has prevented the government employing the decapitation strategy that had proven effective against previous, leader-based resistance organizations.[29] MEND has thus unified diverse groups and harnessed widespread discontent to launch a very effective campaign of economic disruption. Because of its impact on world oil trade, this campaign has drawn favorable international attention to the plight of people in the Delta.[30]

Faced with an extensive insurgency based upon legitimate grievances held by a large, diverse segment of the Nigerian population, the government made no real attempt to win the people over. With the help of the oil companies, it flooded the Delta with troops and used excessive force to crush the insurgents. The strategy killed many innocent civilians but it did not defeat the insurgency. MEND retaliated by stepping up attacks on oil facilities and pipelines. By 2009, insurgents and criminals were stealing 200,000 barrels of oil a day.[31] This theft not only seriously disrupted production and, therefore, government revenues; it also provided MEND funds to buy weapons.

The government realized that repression alone would not work. In September 2008, President Umaru Yar'Adua created the Technical Committee on the Niger Delta to study the region and make recommendations on how to end the conflict. In November the Committee issued a comprehensive report with recommendations grouped into three broad categories: 1) Governance and the Rule of Law, 2) Regional Development, and 3) Human Development. Most of its recommendations under categories 2 and 3 reduced to a simple imperative: spend more of the profit from oil on improving living conditions for the people of the Delta.[32]

The president implemented one major recommendation almost immediately. On June 25, 2009, he inaugurated an amnesty and reintegration program, which included educational and vocational training for former insurgents. By May 2011, 30,000 had signed up for the program; and by March 15, 2015, there were 451 graduates from various schools. Another 3,482 were still in training while 11,200 were awaiting training and receiving temporary stipends.[33] These numbers suggest both good faith on the part of the government and significant buy-in by the insurgents. The program has led to improved security and, as a result, an increase in petroleum production. Output has increased from 700,000 barrels per day in mid-2009 to 2.2–2.4 million barrels per day since 2011.[34]

Despite these impressive results, the issue of the Niger Delta has hardly been resolved. Beyond the amnesty and reintegration program, the government has done little. A recent study concludes that "the government has failed to carry out other recommendations that addressed the insurgency's root causes, including infrastructure, environmental pollution, local demands for a bigger share of oil revenues, widespread poverty and youth unemployment."[35] The report also notes that the ceasefire in the delta owed much to Good-luck Jonathan, the first president of Nigeria from the region. His defeat in the March 2015 elections has introduced a new element of uncertainty to the security situation.[36]

Fortunately, the oil companies have been proactive in mitigating at least some of the causes of unrest. For example, Shell Oil has realized the

importance of community engagement to its industry. The company has
invested in sustainable projects to reduce pollution, improve public health,
advance education, and encourage economic development.[37] As desirable
as such corporate efforts are, they nevertheless cannot compensate for
the failure of the national government to meet the needs of its own
people. The Niger Delta must thus be considered an active security issue.
The potential for renewed violent conflict remains a serious concern.

### Boko Haram

Over the past seven years, the greatest threat to Nigerian security has
come from the Islamist extremist group Jama'atu Ahlis Sunna Lidda'awati
wal-Jihad, "people committed to the propagation of the Prophet's teach-
ings and jihad." Founded in 2002, the group is better known by its
popular name "Boko Haram," loosely translated as "Western education is
sin."[38] The popular name reflects a split in the broader Nigerian Islamic
movement over whether or not to participate in secular education and
other government programs. Like other Islamist extremist groups, Boko
Haram wishes to impose strict Sharia law on all Muslims in Nigeria.
However, like the Taliban in Afghanistan, the group is defined more by
what it opposes than by what it supports. One of its leaders proclaimed
in a 2014 video:

> I am going to kill all the imams and other Islamic clerics in Nigeria
> because they are not Muslims since they follow democracy and
> constitution. It is Allah that instructed us, until we soak the
> ground of Nigeria with Christian blood, and so-called Muslims
> contradicting Islam. We will kill and wonder what to do with their
> smelling corpses. This is a war against Christians and democracy
> and their constitution.[39]

The conflict with Boko Haram has its origin in the complex demographics of the country and the wider region. Nigeria lies in the Sahel, a
broad band of territory dividing the desert from the equatorial zone. This
geographic demarcation corresponds roughly to the boundary between
Africa's Islamic and Christian populations. In the case of Nigeria, the

north-south division also demarcates a gross inequity in quality of life. In the Muslim north 72% of the population lives in poverty as compared to 27% in the south and 35% in the Niger Delta.[40] A pervasive feeling that the government in Abuja neither meets their needs nor safeguards their interest has encouraged many to support the extremists. Corruption and heavy handedness exacerbate this problem. In June 2009, for example, the security forces shot seventeen motorcyclists (though none fatally) for failing to wear helmets as required by law.[41]

In 2009 Boko Haram launched a violent campaign against the Nigerian government. It has attacked police stations and made extensive use of suicide bombers, many of them children. As often happens in such conflicts, many of the dead have been innocent civilians. By the fall of 2015, Boko Haram had killed at least 17,000 people.[42] Besides the military and police, the group targets Christian communities and Muslims who do not comply with its dictates. Many of its victims have been women and children. In addition to murder, the group also employs kidnapping as a terrorist tactic. The 2014 abduction of 276 girls from a school, presumably for forced marriage and sexual slavery, outraged world opinion and highlighted the brutality of the group. Boko Haram also burns down schools.

Those whom they do not kill, Boko Haram often make homeless. According to the Internal Displacement Monitoring Centre, Nigeria has an estimated 2,152,000 internally displaced persons (IDPs) as of December 31, 2015. Eighty five percent of these IDPs have fled because of Boko Haram, 12.6% have been displaced by intercommunal violence, and the rest by natural disasters.[43]

Despite its local roots, Boko Haram has an international dimension. It is affiliated with al-Qaeda and has ties to that umbrella organization's other affiliates in the region: al-Qaeda in the Islamic Maghreb, al-Shabab in Somalia, and the Movement for Unity and Jihad in West Africa based in Mali. These links have caused Boko Haram's rhetoric to become more international, emphasizing hatred of the West, not merely the Nigerian government.[44] In March 2015, the group swore allegiance to the Islamic State, but it remains unclear what if any material support ISIS provides the Nigerian terrorist group.

The Nigerian government has responded to Boko Haram in much the same manner it had responded to MEND. It has overrelied on military force while doing little to address the root causes of unrest. Even under the best of circumstances, military measures alone seldom suffice to defeat determined insurgents. The circumstances in Nigeria are far from the best. Demoralized, riddled with corruption, lacking sufficient equipment, and poorly trained for counterinsurgency, the Nigerian military has performed poorly against Boko Haram. An influx of foreign aid—especially from the United States—has helped but cannot alone compensate for these deficits.

Not only has the military performed poorly; its activities may have exacerbated the situation. Considerable evidence suggests that the security forces engage in widespread human rights abuses. These abuses include detention without trial, torture, and extrajudicial killings. During 2013, the security forces detained 1,400 people in the northeast; only 50 have been tried.[45] The army also allies informally with local vigilante groups, some of whom employ child soldiers.[46] Without a comprehensive counterinsurgency strategy that attacks the causes of discontent as well as the insurgents themselves, Nigerian security forces can do little but contain Boko Haram.

### Crime and Ethnic Strife
In addition to these major threats, a host of lower level, chronic security challenges plague Nigeria. Pervasive ethnic tensions often flare up into open violence. From 2010 to 2015, ethnic violence in just five states in central and northern Nigeria killed approximately 4,000 people and displaced 120,000 others.[47] Much of this violence involves grazing rights and competition for political power; the federal government has generally failed to prosecute the perpetrators.[48]

Crime rates are high throughout the country. Criminal activity includes robbery, murder, cattle rustling, and kidnapping for ransom. Nigeria ranks third among African nations and sixth in the entire world for its crime rate.[49] Abject poverty accounts for much of this activity as desperate people struggle to survive. The police are stretched very thin and lack the transport and other equipment to provide security. Poor infrastructure, especially lack of roads, further compromises their effectiveness. Ordinary crime does not, of course, pose an existential threat to the state, but it erodes confidence in government and ties up resources badly needed to combat more serious threats.

## Assessment

While Nigeria is a unique state with its own institutions, culture, strengths and problems, it is also an African nation that must for the purposes of this study be examined in the context of the continent. The assessment rubric developed in chapter 2 provides a framework for situating Nigeria within that larger context. Such an assessment suggests how the challenges that Nigeria faces compare with those of other African states, how it might benefit from the experience of its neighbors, and how its experience can help them in return.

**National Brand.** Twenty years ago Nigeria would have been classified as a "peacekeeper," a relatively stable nation whose armed forces contributed substantial contingents to peacekeeping missions in Africa and farther abroad. Ethnic violence, Niger Delta insurgency, and the rise of Boko Haram have forced the state into the "policeman" category. Its security forces have been increasing called upon to engage in internal security operations. Against heavily armed insurgents and terrorists, the armed forces have been pushed to the fore with the police relegated to a subordinate role, at least in the north and in the Niger Delta.

**Most Significant Threats.** The insurgent/terrorist group Boko Haram poses the greatest threat to Nigerian security. Violence in the Niger Delta has subsided but could flare up at any time. Crime and ethnic violence are endemic. Bad governance and endemic corruption exacerbate all security threats.

**Roles of the Security Forces.** Nigeria currently faces no external threat to its territorial integrity, so the armed forces need devote little energy and few resources to protecting borders. Internal threats require the armed forces and intelligence agencies to concentrate on internal security and law enforcement operations. The police, who should be playing a greater role, if not taking the lead in these roles, lack the resources and equipment to do so.

**Political System.** Based upon the typology outlined in chapter 2, Nigeria is an "institutionalized competitive state." It has a strong government and distinct armed forces, intelligence services, and police. These institutions, however, do not function synergistically. They are hierarchical and often corrupt. The armed forces receive the lion's share of the security sector budget, but defense funds are appropriated by ministers and senior officers. While the civilian government is no longer threatened by the armed forces, it does not exercise adequate oversight of them.

**Contribution of the Security Forces to Good Governance.** The armed forces no longer threaten the democratic state as they did until the turn of the twenty-first century. Although the constitution allows for adequate civilian oversight of the military, the government does not exercise this.

**Trends for Security Sector Institutions.** There have been a few encouraging trends in the development of the Nigerian Security Sector, but real reform has not occurred. Pervasive corruption syphons off weapons procurement funds and even soldiers' pay. The police in particular suffer from lack of resources, low pay, and poor morale.

## NOTES

1. Details on geography and demographics from "Nigeria," *The World Fact Book* (2016), https://www.cia.gov/library/publications/the-world-factbook/geos/ni.html.
2. Barnaby Philips, "Biafra: Thirty Years On," *BBC* online (January 13, 2000), http://news.bbc.co.uk/2/hi/africa/596712.stm.
3. Figures are 2016 estimates from *Global Firepower*, "Nigeria," http://www.globalfirepower.com/country-military-strength-detail.asp?country_id=nigeria.
4. "Nigeria," *Global Security*, http://www.globalsecurity.org/military/world/nigeria/army.htm.
5. Conor Gaffey, "Nigerian Army Orders Officers to Declare Assets in Corruption Clampdown," *Newsweek* (January 21, 2016), http://www.newsweek.com/nigerian-army-chief-orders-officers-declare-assets-418165.
6. "Nigeria," *Global Security*.
7. "Corporal of Airforce on Corruption in Nigerian Military," *Nigeria News Today* and *Breaking News* (updated 2014), https://www.naij.com/284295-corruption-nigerian-military.html.
8. Ibrahim Abdul'Aziz and Dulue Mbachu, "Nigerian Troops Say Corruption Saps Will to Fight Islamists," *Bloomberg* online (July 16, 2014), http://www.bloomberg.com/news/articles/2014-07-15/nigerian-troops-say-corruption-saps-will-to-confront-islamists.
9. Nigeria Police Watch, http://www.nigeriapolicewatch.com/resources/about-the-nigeria-police/.
10. See Nigeria Police Watch for details on force structure.
11. See http://www.npf.gov.ng/index.php. For details on area of operation, manpower, crime statistics, and constraints in each zones, click on "Zones."
12. Alhaji Ahmadu Ibrahim, "Police Corruption and the State: Prevalence and Consequences," *Global Journal of Arts Humanities and Social Sciences* 3, no. 3 (March 2015): 25. For details on corruption , see pages19–29.
13. "Nigeria 2015/16," *Amnesty International* report, https://www.amnesty.org/en/countries/africa/nigeria/report-nigeria/.

14. Jimi Peters, "Nigeria's Intelligence System: An Analysis," *Africa Spectrum* 22, no. 2 (1987), 188. For discussion of intelligence reforms, see pages 181–191.
15. "Nigeria, Intelligence and Security," 2004, http://www.encyclopedia.com/doc/1G2-3403300532.html.
16. DIA Mission Statement, http://www.dia.gov.ng/more?page=Pages&title=History%20of%20DIA&menu=About%20Us&view=Single&itemType=Pages&location=history_of_dia&itemid=1.
17. Ibid.
18. Constitution of Nigeria (1999), Section 218, 1-3, http://www.wipo.int/wipolex/en/text.jsp?file_id=179202.
19. Ibid., Section 218, 4.
20. Adegboyega Isaac Ajayi, "Subordinating the Military to Civilian Control in Nigeria since 1999: Enabling Factors, Strategies," *European Journal of Social Sciences*, vol. 25, no. 1 (2013): 1289.
21. Ibid., 1291.
22. Patrick I. Ukase, "Subordinating the Military to Civilian/Legislative Control in Nigeria's Fourth Republic: Issues, Challenges and the Way Forward," *SCSR Journal of Social Sciences and Humanities* I, issue 1 (March 2013): 17.
23. Ajayi, "Subordinating the Military to Civilian Control in Nigeria," 1293.
24. UNDP, *Human Development Report 1994* (New York: Oxford University Press, 1994), 24.
25. Ibid.
26. Demographic and geographic data on the Niger Delta from Paul S. Orogun, "Resource Control, Revenue Allocation and Petroleum Politics in Nigeria: the Niger Delta Question," *GeoJournal* 75, no. 5 (2010): 462.
27. Ibid.
28. Elias Courson, *Movement for the Emancipation of the Niger Delta (MEND)* (Uppsala, Sweden: Nordiska Afrikainstitute, 2009), 18, http://nai.diva-portal.org/smash/get/diva2:280470/FULLTEXT01.
29. Ibid., 19.
30. Ibid., 19.
31. Orogun, "Resource Control," 467.
32. *Report of the Technical Committee on the Niger Delta* 1 (November 2008): 57–58.
33. *Curbing Violence in Nigeria (III): Revisiting the Niger Delta* (International Crisis Group, September 29, 2015), 2.
34. Ibid., 2.

35. Ibid., i.
36. Ibid.
37. "Royal Dutch Shell PLC Sustainable Development and Community Relations," October 2012, http://www.shell.com/investors/investor-presentations/2012-investor-presentations/sri-shell-operations-nigeria-10102012/_jcr_content/par/textimage.stream/1447704841054/9251e4513395420099d6f6dacd68af022c4e5986b7a2bc0341186577043f37ed/community-developmentsrishelloperationsnigeria.pdf.
38. "Boko Haram," Council on Foreign Relations Backgrounder, http://www.cfr.org/nigeria/boko-haram/p25739.
39. John Campbell, *U.S. Policy to Counter Nigeria's Boko Haram* (Washington, DC: Council on Foreign Relations, 2014), 12.
40. "Boko Haram," Council on Foreign Relations Backgrounder.
41. Roman Loimeier, "Boko Haram: the Development of a Militant Religious Movement in Nigeria," *Africa Spectrum* 47, no. 2/3 (2012), 51.
42. "Boko Haram Death Toll Escalates," *E-news Africa* (October 1, 2015), https://www.enca.com/africa/boko-haram-death-toll-escalates.
43. "Nigeria IDP Figures Analysis," *International Displacement Centre* (2015), http://www.internal-displacement.org/sub-saharan-africa/nigeria/figures-analysis.
44. Campbell, *U.S. Policy to Counter Nigeria's Boko Haram*, 11.
45. Human Rights Watch, *World Report 2015: Nigeria*, https://www.hrw.org/world-report/2015/country-chapters/nigeria.
46. Ibid.
47. Ibid.
48. Ibid.
49. Crime Index by Country, 2016, http://www.numbeo.com/crime/rankings_by_country.jsp.

CHAPTER 9

# THE CASE OF KENYA

*Lawrence Cline*

Due to the British colonial history, much of the Kenyan security structure is based on the British model. Since independence, the Kenyan government of course has adapted its security services to face new regional and internal security threats. In many ways, the current structure has been shaped by four specific major security events. The first was the 1998 terrorist bombing against the US Embassy in Nairobi that resulted in 213 killed. The second was the internal violence surrounding the 2007 presidential elections. More recently, the Kenyan military deployment into Somalia in 2011—and the subsequent series of terrorist attacks inside Kenya in response—have further shaped the Kenyan perception of the regional security threat. Finally, the terrorist siege of the Westgate Mall in Nairobi in 2013 sparked efforts to improve Kenyan security. All these specific events, together with a number of other attacks and regional security problems, have impacted the Kenyan security system.

## ARMED FORCES

The Kenyan Constitution of 2010 specifies the control of the military as being under the National Security Council. The National Security Council comprises the president, deputy president, the cabinet secretary responsible for defense, the cabinet secretary responsible for foreign affairs, the cabinet secretary responsible for internal security, the attorney general, the chief of Kenya Defence Forces (KDF), the director general of the National Intelligence Service, and the inspector general of the National Police Service.

The parliament has a standing National Security and Foreign Relations Committee that meets regularly. There is parliamentary oversight of the KDF, and the military formally responds to parliamentary inquiries. The Kenya Defense Forces regularly post responses to inquiries by individual members of parliament. Kenyan press reporting suggests that there is very open public and political debate about many aspects of the KDF and its use.

Three roles are specified in the Constitution for the Kenya Defence Forces (KDF):

> a) are responsible for the defence and protection of the sovereignty and territorial integrity of the Republic;
>
> b) shall assist and cooperate with other authorities in situations of emergency or disaster, and report to the National Assembly whenever deployed in such circumstances; and
>
> c) may be deployed to restore peace in any part of Kenya affected by unrest or instability only with the approval of the National Assembly.

Beyond the constitutional provisions, the KDF is managed through the Kenya Defence Forces Act No. 25 of 2012. This provides further details of how and when the KDF will be employed for external and internal operations.

Although the employment of the KDF for external operations may be fairly straightforward in terms of statutory authority, some notes should be made about its use in internal missions. The KDF Act of 2012 provides the following structure:

> [T]he Defence Council may deploy the Defence Forces in any part of Kenya affected by unrest or instability to restore peace... Whenever the Defence Forces are deployed to restore peace in any part of Kenya..., the Chief of the Defence Forces shall be responsible for the administration, control and overall superintendence of the operation...The Defence Forces may be deployed in a joint operation and in support of the National Police Service in situations of emergency or disaster. (2) The Defence Forces may, with the approval of the National Assembly, be deployed to restore peace in any part of Kenya. (3) Whenever the Defence Forces are deployed pursuant to subsection (2), the Inspector-General of the National Police Service shall be responsible for the administration, command, control and overall superintendence of the operation... [There will be] joint operation plan and guidelines issued by the Chief of the Defence Forces and the Inspector-General of National Police Service regarding— (A) co-operation between the Defence Forces and the National Police Service; and (B) co-ordination of command over and control of members of the Defence Forces and the National Police Service during the operation.[1]

These details are noted because they appear to offer a reasonable legal structure for coordination in internal operations. At the same time, however, the statutes do not adequately address the normal expected command and control system in interagency operations. At the more practical bureaucratic level, the National Security Council provides a mechanism for controlling the KDF at strategic level, but coordination with law enforcement agencies at tactical level may be problematic.

The Westgate Mall attack of 2013 displayed all the hallmarks of poor coordination as responsibilities for response shifted from the police to the military.[2] More specifically, according to the official Kenyan government public report, "The RECCE [reconnaissance] Company from the General

Service Unit (GSU) had contained the terrorists in one corner of the Mall. There was, however, poor coordination during the changeover between the Kenya Defence Forces and the Police."[3] Based on the problems with coordinating an effective response, the KDF announced the formation of a new command, the Nairobi Metropolitan Command for improved counterterrorism and natural disaster operations. Nevertheless, the details released thus far do not appear to indicate a significantly increased day-to-day coordination between the KDF and police services for internal security.[4]

According to a 2014 survey sponsored by the (Kenyan) *Daily Nation*, only 30 percent of Kenyans have confidence in the KDF, which suggests significant issues in gaining popular support. In fairness, however, the military is considerably more trusted than are the police at 11 percent confidence and the intelligence services at 10 percent.[5] In large measure, the lack of trust in the security services can be ascribed to a series of "successful" terrorist attacks, but the trend appears to be longer term. As discussed later, the police in particular have created an environment not conducive to public confidence. The relationship between the KDF's long-term intervention in Somalia and Kenyan public support for the military may be complex. On the one hand, Kenyan press and opinion makers demonstrated the "rally around the flag" pattern in supporting the troops and the KDF leadership. Over time, however, the long deployment and subsequent increase in al-Shabaab cross-border attacks appear to have soured many Kenyans on the operation. Likewise, at least some of the official public reporting emerging from the KDF regarding its operations in Somalia has not been particularly forthcoming.[6]

There is no formal role of the KDF in the Kenyan economy through operating legal businesses. There have, however, been allegations of the KDF becoming involved in illegal trade during its occupation of Somalia. The issue of charcoal sales and export in Somalia under KDF auspices remain very contentious, with arguments ranging from views that it is a tactical necessity, that it is an effort to maintain some semblance of economic activity, and that such activity is a thinly-disguised attempt at smuggling.[7] Likewise, there have been allegations of illegal sugar smuggling coming into Kenya from Somalia.[8] Again, there are considerable uncertainties regarding the details of this illegal trade—particularly whether the KDF is actually involved, or the extent of its involvement—but given the extent of corruption within various Kenyan governmental agencies, many Kenyans are very likely to view KDF involvement as being quite likely.

In addition to the various legally organized security forces in Kenya, a number of various paramilitary, vigilante, and militia groups (in many cases, the characterization of an individual group is subject to considerable debate) continue to operate in the country. The most significant in terms of its impact on internal security in recent years was the Mungiki, a local militia organized to protect the Kikuyu, the major ethnic group, especially in slum areas. In many ways, the Mungiki viewed themselves as something akin to a neighborhood watch group, albeit more willing to use violence to protect local interests. The actual strength of the Mungiki is vague, but leaders claim up to two million members and supporters.[9] As is typical, this level of membership almost certainly is exaggerated, but the Mungiki likely numbered at its peak several hundred thousand. The group became heavily involved in extortion of local inhabitants and businesses for funding.

Following the election violence surrounding the 2007 election, the group began attacking members of other tribes, particularly the Luo. According to one Mungiki, the goals of the violence were rather direct: "Mainly our strategy is to be brutal and to send a message. Sometimes it means beheading or dismembering. But the goal is to instill fear and send a message that unless they don't change what they are doing something bigger will happen to them."[10] Although exact figures are hard to confirm, somewhere around 1,000 persons were killed in the violence surrounding the elections, with the majority of the casualties likely caused by the Mungiki.

The net result of the Mungiki-inspired violence was a wave of communal killing, seriously exacerbated by very heavy-handed responses by the Kenyan security services.[11] The Kenyan government's concern over the group led to the creation of a special anti-Mungiki police squad composed of multiple police and intelligence agencies. Following a very violent police crackdown, in which large numbers of Mungiki members and supporters were killed, some level of stability was restored, but members of the group reportedly continue similar activities, albeit more quietly.[12] Although the Mungiki have had the most direct impact within Kenya, a number of other militias remain, and they constitute potential competing internal power centers and threats.[13]

## LAW ENFORCEMENT

The Kenyan police system is rather complex. There are two major police services. The first is the Kenya Police Service, which has about 18,000 officers. It is further subdivided into a number of agencies. One of the most significant agencies for internal security is the General Service Unit, with about 5,000 members. This institution provides security for key personnel and infrastructure, along with counterterrorism operations. Other police agencies include, but are not limited to, the Kenya Airports Police Unit, Marine Police Unit, Railway Police Unit, Tourist Police Unit, Anti-Stock Theft Unit.[14] The Directorate of Criminal Investigations is established as a separate agency for more complex investigations.

The second police service—operated as a separate system—is the Kenya Administration Police. The service, historically based on the colonial tribal police, consists of about 47,000 members. Its control system involves reporting to local district commissioners, who in turn report to the office of the president. The mandate of the Administration Police entails many missions similar to those of the regular police service.[15] Importantly, it also has a primary role in border security and border patrols. Beyond the normal police activities, it has three specialized units: Rapid Deployment Unit, Rural Border Patrol Unit, and Security of Government Buildings

Unit. There is no available evidence that particular ethnic groups are over- or under-represented in the police forces.[16]

Two other agencies are very important in law enforcement. The first is the Kenya Wildlife Service, a paramilitary force responsible for wildlife conservation and general protection. Over time, its units have become increasingly well-armed and prepared for increasing violence by poachers. The second service is the Kenya Forest Service. Its principal roles are forest protection, enforcing revenues, and evictions of illegal squatters on national lands.

The roles for the police services are laid out in The National Police Service Act, 2011 (and amended in 2014). There has been significant formal oversight of the police, with a particular stress on oversight following the 2007 violence. The Independent Policing Oversight Authority (IPOA), established by an Act of Parliament in 2011, is the main organization for providing independent review of the police forces. Its responsibilities include "to investigate deaths and serious injuries caused by police action"; "to investigate police misconduct"; "to monitor, review and audit investigations and actions by Internal Affairs Unit of the police"; "to conduct inspections of police premises"; "to monitor and investigate policing operations and deployment"; and "to review the functioning of the internal disciplinary process."[17]

Although the IPOA has provided a structure for external oversight of the police, some questions have been raised as to its actual effectiveness. According to a Kenyan press report, as of February 2014, "Since its inception in June 2012, the authority has received 1,090 complaints. Of these, only 27 cases are currently under investigation."[18] More recently, according to the US State Department: "During the year [2014] the IPOA investigated 200 incidents, of which 69 involved death at the hands of police. Only one IPOA investigation led to a prosecution, which was underway at year's end."[19]

The other body that reports directly to parliament is the National Police Service Commission (NPSC) The NPSC consists of six civilians, including two retired police officers, and two deputies of the police inspector general. The NPSC is responsible for recruiting, transferring, vetting, promoting, and removing police officers in the National Police Service. Perhaps the most important function of the NPSC is the vetting (and revetting) of police officers, which has become a major priority of the Kenyan government. This process, however, has faced numerous challenges:

> While Cabinet Secretary for the Interior Joseph Ole Lenku announced that all 77,500 domestic police officers would be vetted by June, the NPSC itself reported that it intended to complete the vetting exercise in 2015. Vetting required an assessment of each officer's fitness to serve based on a review of documentation, including financial records, certificates of good conduct, and a questionnaire, as well as consideration of public input regarding allegations of abuse or misconduct. Between December 2013 and June 2014, only 198 senior police officers had been vetted. Of these, 17 officers were removed, 10 officers opted for early retirement rather than undergo the vetting process, and one officer was reinstated after challenging his removal. The vetting process was subject to numerous court challenges by individuals who failed their vetting.[20]

More recently, there have been further developments in terms of the results of the vetting process. In October 2015, sixty-three senior police officers were removed for cause. At the same time, however, the vetting officials reportedly began receiving death threats, "including a severed head being sent to their office with a note warning them to tread carefully."[21]

The reason that the vetting system is so important is that the Kenyan police have demonstrated what might be termed endemic corruption. According to Transparency International, the Kenyan public believes the police to be the most corrupt institution in the country.[22] According to a Kenyan government report:

The study findings indicate that one third (30%) of respondents had experienced police malpractice including: assault/brutality, falsification of evidence, bribery, and threat of imprisonment within 12 months prior to the study. The incidence of police malpractice is higher in rural areas at 61% than in urban areas at 39%. In terms of gender, 62% of men compared to 38% of women were exposed to police malpractice in the last 12 months. The incidences of police violations is [sic] higher among younger people aged less than 35 years (64%) than those aged above 35 years (34%). Only 30% of those who experienced incidences of police malpractice reported the crime to the relevant authorities. More respondents in the rural areas (68%) reported cases of police misconduct than their counterparts in the urban areas (32%). More males (62%) than females (38%) reported cases of police malpractice.[23]

The lack of public confidence in the police as noted in the levels of crime reporting was reflected in a further study by a nongovernmental organization cited by the US State Department: "According to a September study by the NGO Usalama Reform Forum, less than 40 percent of crime victims made a report to the police due to lack of confidence in the police and the criminal justice system, lack of support for witnesses and victims, and fear of retribution. Usalama estimated that only 20 percent of crimes were reported."[24]

Various private security companies play a key role in providing security for corporations, small businesses, and, in some cases, local communities. A bill was introduced in 2014 to establish the Private Security Regulatory Authority. Purposes of this body revolve around supervising and regulating the large number of security companies in Kenya. The authority will be governed by a board chaired by someone appointed by the president and will include representatives from internal security, finance, labor, and the National Police Service, together with representatives from associations for private security firms, employee organizations, and "registered residents associations." A key provision of this bill is to regulate the licensing and relicensing of private security companies and individual guards.

Although this bill provides further guidance for the legal status of private security companies, it remains a bit vague and general on the exact relationship between these private companies and governmental security services. The only two provisions regarding this issue are:

> 45.(I)-Whenever called upon by a National Security Organ, the Inspector General of the National Police Service or the Cabinet Secretary, a private security service provider shall cooperate in the maintenance of law and order or in any other manner as may be provided for in the instrument of request.

> (2) The Cabinet Secretary in consultation with the Inspector-General and the Authority shall make regulations generally to provide for any matter relating to the cooperation, scope, mechanism and command in the case of cooperation with the private security service provider.[25]

As of the date of this writing, a formal process for coordinating police services and private security companies does not appear to have been fully implemented.

One further aspect of the Kenyan legal system should be mentioned. This is the actual effectiveness of preparation for trial and the trials themselves. Overall, 64% of the felony cases reviewed never met the minimum evidentiary threshold to charge a person with an offense.[26] Although commonly not receiving the same level of attention as the police services themselves, the judiciary in all countries is at least as critical for the overall law enforcement system. Kenya has had a number of issues with the judiciary. A Kenyan government study noted:

> Administration of justice in Kenya has been associated with political servitude, low standards of professionalism, widespread corruption and delinquent jurisprudence, financial insecurity, elitist legal system, and expensive adjudication and enforcement

hence undermining realization of just outcomes. Institutions serving the chain of justice have been viewed as not independent enough to expeditiously administer justice for all without discrimination.[27]

In fairness, however, the Kenyan government has recognized the issues with the judiciary and, in cooperation with various international organizations and nongovernmental organizations, has made considerable efforts over the last few years to improve the system. Even one nongovernmental organization that is otherwise very critical of the government has noted these efforts:

> The Judiciary has also seen a raft of reforms, key among them the vetting of judges and magistrates that began in 2011. Additional judges have been appointed to ease the backlog of cases that for a long time bred fertile ground for corruption. The Judiciary also invested resources in improving physical infrastructure and embraced information, communication and technology (ICT) to expedite services, and increase transparency. But with all these developments, and a seemingly more accessible and transformative leadership, the Judiciary remains bribery prone, with its aggregate score increasing in 2014. The suspension of some key Judiciary administrative staff over procurement irregularities in 2013 and 2014 further lends credence to claims of bribery and corruption at large in the sector.[28]

Finally, outside the "pure" legal system itself, corruption by customs and immigration officials reportedly has led to the ability of terrorists and other threats to internal security to enter and operate in Kenya: "There is nationwide systemic failure on the part of the Immigration Services Department, Department of Refugee Affairs; and Registration of Persons Department attributed to corruption at the border control points and registration centres, mainly in Nairobi, Coast and North Eastern areas."[29] Among other problems, persons in the country illegally reportedly have been able to acquire Kenyan identification documents or to be released early when caught in "suspicious criminal activities."[30]

## Intelligence Service

As with virtually every nation, open-source information on the intelligence services in Kenya is (justifiably) rather scarce. The primary intelligence organ for the country is the National Intelligence Service (NIS), which is responsible for both external and domestic intelligence collection and analysis and which reports directly to the president. The NIS is formally established in the Constitution, but the only constitutional provisions are that the NIS "(a) is responsible for security intelligence and counter intelligence to enhance national security in accordance with this Constitution; and (b) performs any other functions prescribed by national legislation."[31]

Further statutory authority for the NIS is through The National Intelligence Service Act, 2012 (and amended in 2014). This law lays out the range of NIS responsibilities.[32] It also specifies that the NIS will not carry out police or paramilitary functions. The NIS director general is appointed jointly by the president and the national assembly. The NIS must submit a report annually to the national assembly regarding its activities, and there is an appointed oversight board. A degree of judicial oversight is provided by requiring warrants for some NIS collection activities.[33] Along with the NIS, the Kenya Defence Forces also receive intelligence support from the Military Intelligence Corps. Details on this formation are minimal, but it appears to focus on tactical-level intelligence.

One other key player in internal security national intelligence is the National Counter Terrorism Centre (NCTC). This was established by the December 2014 Security Laws Amendment Bill. It includes representatives from "(a) the Director appointed by the National Security Council; (b) the National Intelligence Service; (c) the Kenya Defence Forces; (d) the Attorney General; (e) Directorate of Immigration and Registration; (f) the National Police Service; and (g) such other national agencies as may be determined by the National Security Council," all seconded to the center for three years.[34] The most critical roles of this center are to focus analysis specifically on the terrorist threat and to coordinate intelligence efforts for counterterrorism.

The NIS operates the National Intelligence Academy, but it is unclear if it provides training to all intelligence-related agencies in Kenya. There appear to be issues with cooperation among intelligence services, and between intelligence services and operational agencies.[35] In the case of the Westgate Mall attack in particular, "There was general information on the impending terror attack on all the malls and other strategic Western interests especially in Nairobi. The information was made available to the relevant Security officers in Nairobi County."[36] The extent to which such sharing and interoperability problems can be resolved likely will be the most critical aspects of the Kenyan intelligence system in the future.

## ASSESSMENT

**National Brand.** Kenya is primarily a "defender" state. With its involvement in Somalia, it also has somewhat increased its identity as a "peacekeeper" state, but Kenyan military missions in Somalia have included a number of offensive operations, perhaps increasing a mindset of "warfighter."

**Most Significant Threats.** Using the framework in table 2, Kenya faces significant threats in all four quadrants. It is experiencing traditional internal and external threats and human external and internal threats. The most immediate threat comes out of Somalia. This includes al Shabaab in Somalia itself as well as its cross-border operations. The Kenyan government is justifiably concerned as to threats emerging from the Somali refugee population, most notably from the massive Dadaab refugee camp. It also faces traditional internal threats based on political violence and tribalism. Based on recent election history, the violence engendered by ethnic group militias that support different political parties (largely based on ethnicity) could be a recurring fixture of future political campaigns.

Likewise, both external and internal human security remain problematic. Migration into Kenya—particularly of course from Somalia—have strained resources and presented a number of international complications for the Kenyan government. Kenya has faced increasing desertification, in large measure based on poor land management practices. One very traditional problem for Kenya, particularly along the border areas, has been cattle rustling. This has become even more significant as tribal rustling groups have acquired military-grade weaponry, sharply increasing the human toll among the victims. Similarly, responding to wildlife poaching has evolved into something akin to military operations, with both government wildlife rangers and their poacher opponents engaging in bloody firefights. Internally, governance remains rather problematic, largely due to widespread corruption, particularly among the security services.

**Roles of the Security Forces.** The Kenyan Armed Forces previously focused on traditional military roles, with the police and other security services the principal tools for maintaining internal order. With the rise of terrorist attacks, these distinct roles have become somewhat blurred, but the government has maintained distinctions in the operational roles of the military and the police. Instruments for coordination and cooperation almost certainly remain a work in progress.

**Political System.** Using the categories in table 4, Kenya falls somewhere between "institutionalized noncompetitive state" and "institutionalized competitive state." The security services remain under firm government control, but a true political system has not yet been firmly established.

**Contribution of the Security Forces to Good Governance.** Relations between security forces and civil society are very poor. The army seems to be somewhat better respected than the police forces, but this is faint praise. The police and the internal security forces are widely distrusted, and this seems unlikely to change any time soon.

**Trends for Security Sector Institutions.** Overall, the major systemic weakness in the Kenyan security system appears to be interagency coordination and cooperation; this of course applies to many (if not the overwhelming majority of) other countries. Kenya has incorporated some measures such as the National Counter Terrorism Centre that should help improve the interagency process, but this remains very much a work in progress. In particular, police-military cooperation has displayed major gaps. Likewise, although obviously less publicly discussed, there appear to be gaps between the Kenyan national intelligence system and operational units. Given such known failures as the Westgate Mall attack and a number of smaller terrorist attacks—even with governmental statements that at least some intelligence warnings were provided—either appropriate intelligence information is not being provided to operational units or these units are not incorporating intelligence products.

Probably even more important, the extent of corruption among some Kenyan security services, most notably the police, has created long-term problems for Kenyan internal security. This issue certainly has been recognized by the Kenyan government, and together with some outside support, officials have focused on this weakness. Unfortunately, current reporting suggests that there is still a considerable distance to go. Such corruption not only directly reduces the effectiveness of those agencies with a high number of corrupt officials, but it almost certainly lowers the willingness of the public to cooperate. Until significant progress is made in sharply reducing the level of corruption among security forces, Kenya will face major gaps in public security.

# NOTES

1. National Council for Law Reporting with the authority of the Attorney-General, *Kenya Defence Forces Act* No. 25 of 2012, Published by the National Council for Law Reporting with the Authority of the Attorney-General (Nairobi, Kenya: 2012), 29–30.
2. Edmund Blair, "Analysis: Kenya's intelligence work hurt by corruption, rivalries," *Reuters* (October 4, 2013), http://www.reuters.com/article/us-kenya-attack-security-analysis-idUSBRE9930G620131004.
3. Kenya National Assembly Eleventh Parliament—First Session—2013, *Report of the Joint Committee on Administration and National Security; and Defence and Foreign Relations on the Inquiry into the Westgate Terrorist Attack, and Other Terror Attacks in Mandera In North-Eastern and Kilifi in the Coastal Region*, Nairobi, December 2013, 7. [Hereafter referred to as the *Westgate Report*]
4. For example, in a response to a parliamentary inquiry, the KDF stated that the new command would (among other things) "co-ordinate KDF's efforts in Counterterrorism operations..." and " strengthen relationships between KDF and other agencies and authorities involved in emergency and disaster management operations," but it did not provide any specifics as to how such improved coordination was planned. The response also stated that the Nairobi Metropolitan Command would be modeled after the already-existing Eastern and Western Commands of KDF. Cabinet Secretary for Defence, "Statement in Response to the Question by Member of Parliament for Wajir West Constituency on the Establishment the Nairobi Metropolitan Command of the Kenya Defence Forces" (June 18, 2014).
5. Nic Cheeseman, "What Kenyans think of their new institutions," *Daily Nation* (April 12, 2014), http://www.nation.co.ke/oped/Opinion/What-Kenyans-think-of-their-new-institutions-/-/440808/2277346/-/7pp5j7z/-/index.html. Perhaps more significant for the government overall, about 41 percent of Kenyans have "a lot of trust" in the president. This can be compared to findings that "a majority of Kenyans (54 percent) think that foreign NGOs help Kenya 'somewhat' or 'a lot'." The figures are also fairly high for the IMF (35 percent), the European Union (29 percent), and the ICC (24 percent). Even the UK (33 percent) and USA (43 percent), which have received considerable public criticism from the government

in recent times, enjoy more favorable ratings than important Kenyan institutions such as the police and even the new county governments.

6. For a recent example, see Tomi Oladipo, "What happened when al-Shabab attacked a Kenyan base in Somalia?" *BBC Online* (January 21, 2016), http://www.bbc.com/news/world-africa-35364593.

7. For a detailed examination of the questions surrounding the charcoal trade, see United Nations, *Letter dated 12 July 2013 from the Chair of the Security Council Committee pursuant to resolutions 751 (1992) and 1907 (2009) concerning Somalia and Eritrea addressed to the President of the Security Council* (New York: 12 July 2013), 421–428.

8. Journalists for Justice, a project of the International Commission of Jurists, Kenya Chapter, Nairobi, Kenya, *Black and White: Kenya's Criminal Racket in Somalia* (Nairobi: 2015), 1–28. This report argues that the KDF has been involved in both sugar and charcoal smuggling in Somalia.

9. Nancy MacDonald, "A Banned Sect's Reign of Terror," *Maclean's*, 120/23 (June 18, 2007).

10. Statement by "Peter," whose real name was withheld. Quoted in Scott Baldauf, "Kenya's Critical Moment," *Christian Science Monitor* (January 29, 2008): 12.

11. For one report on the police response, see Kenya National Commission on Human Rights, *'The Cry of Blood': Extra-Judicial Killings and Disappearances* (Nairobi: August 2008), 3–76.

12. CCI Team, "The Reincarnation of Mungiki," *The Standard* (August 18, 2010); Radio France Internationale, "Kenya: Over 100 Mungiki Sect Members Held for Extortion" (July 6, 2010).

13. For good thumbnail sketches of some of these groups, see Mahathir (no other name), "Rag-Tag" militia groups that control Kenya" (April 23, 2008) http://muthumbi.blogspot.com/2008/04/rag-tug-militia-groups-that-control.html. Some of these militias include Kalenjin Warriors, Sabaot Land Defence Force, Taliban (no relation to the Afghanistan group), Chinkororo, Baghdad Boyz, and Kamjesh. Although this site is somewhat dated, with various groups changing names and becoming more or less important over time, the basic details remain accurate.

14. For official descriptions of the roles and responsibilities of each of the various units, see "Kenya Police Service," http://www.kenyapolice.go.ke

15. For details of the specific missions, see "Administration Police," http://www.administrationpolice.go.ke/2015-02-16-09-14-42/mandate.html.

16. Although now very dated, a police official testified before the parliament that there was a deliberate decision to spread recruitment among all

ethnic groups. The National Assembly, House of Representatives, *Official Report: Fourth Session Friday 1st July 1966 to Friday, 29th July 1966*, Nairobi, 2117-2118. No contradictory evidence has been found to refute this stated policy.

17. For further details, see "Independent Policing Oversight Authority," http://www.ipoa.go.ke/about-us/ipoa-mandate.

18. Joe Kiarie, "Is the Independent Policing Oversight Authority (IPOA) the new toothless bulldog in town?" *Standard Media* (February 22, 2014), http://www.standardmedia.co.ke/article/2000105207/is-the-independent-policing-oversight-authority-ipoa-the-new-toothless-bulldog-in-town.

19. *US State Department, Country Reports on Human Rights Practices for 2014*, http://www.state.gov/j/drl/rls/hrrpt/humanrightsreport/#wrapper.

20. Ibid.

21. Tom Odula, "63 police officers fired over corruption in Kenya reforms," *AP Radio News* (October 15, 2015) http://bigstory.ap.org/article/12453 aba8bbf40f0b28b9bf09f9c71db/63-police-officers-fired-over-corruption-kenya-reforms.

22. *Corruption by Country / Territory: Kenya, 2014*, Transparency International, https://www.transparency.org/country/#KEN_PublicOpinion. For further statistical evidence, see Transparency International—Kenya, *The East African Bribery Index—2014*, Nairobi: 2014, 15–25.

23. Independent Policing Oversight Authority, Baseline Survey on Policing Standards and Gaps in Kenya, 2013, 6.

24. US State Department, Country Reports on Human Rights Practices for 2014, http://www.state.gov/j/drl/rls/hrrpt/humanrightsreport/#wrapper.

25. *Kenya Gazette Supplement No. 18 (Bills No. 3)*, 'The Private Security Regulation Bill, 2014 Nairobi, March 3, 2014, 64.

26. *National Council on the Administration of Justice Strategic Plan, 2012-2016*, Nairobi, 8.

27. Ibid.

28. Transparency International—Kenya, *The East African Bribery Index—2014*, Nairobi: 2014, 16.

29. *Westgate Report*, 7.

30. Ibid., 15.

31. Kenya Constitution, Article 242.

32. *Kenya Gazette Supplement* No. 143 (Acts No. 28), Nairobi (October 5, 2012): 1555–1558.

33. For details, see *Kenya Gazette Supplement* No. 143 (Acts No. 28), 1587-1591.
34. *Kenya Gazette Supplement* No.167 (Acts No.19), Nairobi (December 22, 2014): 351.
35. For example, see *The Star* (Nairobi), "Kenya's Intelligence Service Is Worried About Who Their New Chief Will Be" (August 19, 2014), http://www.matthewaid.com/post/95188546861/kenyas-intelligence-service-is-worried-about-who.
36. *Westgate Report*, 7.

CHAPTER 10

# THE CASE OF ETHIOPIA

*Bruce Sweeney*[1]

The Ethiopians, uniquely among African nations, have no colonial history. Although Ethiopia was defeated by the Italians and briefly occupied from 1935–1941 (the British then exercised control until 1944 as the liberators of Ethiopia)[2], this was a very brief period during World War II, and as such, left little colonial structure in place. Thus, Emperor Haile Selassie developed his own security structure from ancient traditions and adapted it after World War II.

Sadly for Ethiopia, there have been three post–World War II administrations, and the first two came to a violent end. The first, which lasted from 1944 to 1975 was Haile Selassie's empire. The emperor was overthrown and killed by the Derg military junta regime (along with many other Ethiopians) in 1975. The Derg was a leftist, communist-style group led by Mengistu Haile Mariam, heavily supported by the Soviet Union, and they were, in turn, overthrown by the Ethiopian Peoples

Revolutionary Democratic Front (EPRDF) in 1991. Significantly, each change of regime was also accompanied by a major drought and difficult famine. The current regime, the EPRDF, has now been in power twenty-five years and has necessarily adapted its security services to face current conditions internally, as well as externally in East Africa.

## OVERALL APPROACH TO SECURITY FORCES

The current government's approach to security has been shaped by the previous two regimes and rapidly became evident as the EPRDF set up their new government. The former rebels had closely observed the Emperor and the Derg, and noted that the Emperor had been dependent on the United States for security equipment, training, funding and advice. The Derg, in contrast, had depended on the Soviet Union for all of these things. Thus, the EPRDF determined that they would be independent and not rely on any one country for security assistance, advice, or funding. The EPRDF had won their long fight for liberation from the Derg without significant assistance from any other country, and they saw no point in changing that approach after being successful and taking over. This does not mean that Ethiopia does not accept funding or security assistance; it merely means that it will do so only when such assistance suits Ethiopia, with its own national interest in mind. In practice, this means that Ethiopia, the Ethiopian National Defense Forces (ENDF), and other Ethiopian institutions, will work with other nations from time to time, but not consistently. This independence means that Ethiopia has no reliable "partners" in security, frustrating governments that try to use aid, advice, and military training and equipment to further their own national interests.

In addition to the overall EPRDF government approach, the Ethiopian security structure and how the security forces are used has also been shaped by three major events since the EPRDF took charge. Those events are: the Ethiopia/Eritrea War of 1998, the Ethiopian election of 2005, and the evolving threat from the Islamic Courts in Somalia that began in 2006 and has evolved over time into Al Shabaab in Somalia. The war with Eritrea was the first significant use of the ENDF since the fight for independence concluded in 1991, and was essentially a border disagreement that took place around the town of Badme. As is true in many conflicts, after two years and approximately 100,000 deaths[3], a ceasefire was agreed to without much overall change to the borders and no comfortable peace. The "Badme War" has been most significant to the Ethiopians because it has resulted in making and keeping Eritrea as their number one military threat, enemy, and concern. For Ethiopians, the Eritrean threat is constant and visceral. The war also affected the structure and disposition of the Ethiopian army. Approximately one-third to half of the army is always on alert and arrayed along the Eritrean border to ensure that Ethiopia will not caught by surprise, and it is always prepared to counterattack any sign of Eritrean aggression or activity.[4]

The Ethiopian election of 2005 began with pre-election activities deemed free and fair. Unconfirmed preliminary election results began to circulate on election night that the opposition parties scored significant gains, especially in Addis Ababa. After unofficial reports circulated in May that opposition parties would control the majority of seats, preliminary results released over the remainder of May and through June showed the ruling EPRDF controlling the majority of seats. Opposition parties claimed fraud and organized protests, including taxi strikes and student demonstrations at the University of Addis Ababa. On June 3, the Carter Center released a statement on its postelection observation, noting observers' reports of improperly secured ballot boxes, as well as intimidation and harassment of opposition agents. It called on all sides to pursue legal channels to investigate complaints and resolve disputes.

Tensions spread across Addis Ababa in the following days and by June 8, more than forty people were reported killed by the security forces' crackdown on postelection protestors. The US Embassy, the Carter Center, and other organizations expressed alarm about the deaths and violence, calling on the government to curb the extreme measures of the security forces and urging all sides to pursue peaceful means to resolve disputes. Things calmed down while 179 disputed constituencies were reviewed and thirty-one were revoted in August. On September 5, final results were announced with the opposition winning 32% of the vote and the ruling EPRDF getting 60%. Further demonstrations and riots started after the results were announced. According to an independent commission, appointed to investigate postelection violence, the government response resulted in the deaths of 193 people at the hands of the security forces between June and November, along with the arrest of opposition leaders and supporters.[5]

Fundamentally, the EPRDF government demonstrated that stability was more important than a fair election outcome, and the government directed the army—and especially, the various police forces—to quell the protests, arrest opposition leaders, and restore stability. The role of enforcing stability has remained significant for the security forces ever since—in evidence during the election of 2010; the appointment of the deputy prime minister, Haile Miriam Desalegne, to the job of prime minister in 2012, following the death of Prime Minister Meles Zenawi Asres; and in the recent 2015 election, which was tightly run and resulted in continued domination of the EPRDF in parliament. Stability and continuity are paramount for the government, and the security forces will be used to ensure it.

Somalia's Islamic Courts and its successor fundamentalist group, Al Shabaab, have shaped the ENDF by their threat to Ethiopia and Ethiopian interests in Somalia. Somalia and Ethiopia have a long history of war that goes back hundreds of years; the last major interstate war between them ended only in 1978 with an Ethiopian win and a mutually agreed-upon border.[6] Although historic animosities resonate in both countries, Ethiopia respected the current border from 1978 through 2006. Ethiopia still recognizes the border, but it has violated the agreement in order to address threats to its territory and interests. As the Union of Islamic Courts (UIC) grew strong and marched through central Somalia, the

Ethiopian government sent an official message to the UIC not to advance on Baidoa in July 2006. This ultimatum was issued for two reasons: to protect the Transitional National Government of Somalia (TNG), based in Baidoa; and to protect the Ethiopian border (Ethiopia did not want the UIC operating on Ethiopian soil). When the UIC *did* march into Baidoa, the Ethiopian army crossed the border with tanks, artillery and infantry.[7] Ethiopian troops stayed in that part of Somalia through early January 2009. This particular intervention shows how the armed forces are prepared to operate outside of Ethiopia whenever the Ethiopian government feels it is in their national interest to do so. Ethiopian troops returned to Somalia in 2011 to fight al-Shabaab for similar reasons in 2006. It is noteworthy that Ethiopia did not join the African Union Mission to Somalia (AMISOM) until December 2013, shouldering this mission independently for two years—a clear example of how the national interest determines the actions of the Ethiopian government and its security services, with little regard to outside opinion or perspective.[8]

## ARMED FORCES

The Ethiopian Constitution of 1995 actually has little to say regarding the specifics of the national armed forces—only that they will be composed of all the nationalities and peoples of Ethiopia, that the Minister of Defense will be a civilian, that the forces are to protect the sovereignty of Ethiopia, and that they must be free of any political organization.[9] The armed forces are structured under the minister of defense and organized as the Ethiopian National Defense Force (ENDF), divided into the Ethiopian air force and the Ethiopian army. The Ethiopian chief of defense is directly responsible for both the army and the air force. The incumbent, General Samora Yunis, is chief of the army as well as chief of defense, and the air force chief reports directly to him. By design, the ENDF is under the control of the minister of defense, but in practice, the minister of defense is responsible only for providing the budget; manpower; equipment and supplies; and strategic planning for the ENDF. As a senior member of the government, the minister of defense advises the prime minister but has no role in the employment of the force. The chief of defense, reporting directly to the prime minister (who is constitutionally the commander in chief of the armed forces), makes all decisions regarding employment of the ENDF.

The Ethiopian army is approximately 135,000 in size, while the air force has about 30,000 personnel. These figures are approximate because Ethiopia does not publish or distribute any information on the size, disposition, organization, or make-up of its armed forces. Estimates range as high as 230,000 personnel overall, but the lower figures represent the best current opinion of informed sources.[10] Both branches of service include men and women in the force. The army is very well equipped, with several hundred T-55, T-62, and T-72 tanks, including 200 new T-72 tanks, delivered in 2012. They are also sufficiently well equipped with machine guns, small arms and support vehicles, able to move them from place to place. The air force is small but capable, equipped with older Russian-made Su-27s and Czech-made L-39 trainers, along with several Russian airlift aircraft and one recently arrived C-130E. These aircraft seem to be able to provide all the support the ENDF needs to be effective.

The ENDF is one of the most effective and feared armies in Africa, owing to its discipline and experience. The Ethiopians are a proud people with a long and storied history, and the Ethiopian army reflects this. Ethiopia has a lot of deployment and combat experience. The ENDF is the 4th largest contributor to UN Peacekeeping missions. It is the largest African contributor, and virtually all of its missions are in Africa. Between peacekeeping and their combat role in the AMISOM (as well as previous adventures in Somalia), virtually every Ethiopian soldier has at least some combat experience.

## ETHIOPIAN ARMED FORCES IN THE ECONOMY

Another important factor that makes the Ethiopian military effective (and relatively inexpensive) is that Ethiopia produces most of its own combat vehicles and ammunition. Although there is no formal role of the ENDF in the Ethiopian economy for running businesses, there is a long history of military manufacturing that started in 1953 with the opening of the "Emperor Haile Selassie ammunition factory," built in cooperation with the government of Czechoslovakia. During the Derg regime (1974–1991), a very serious development program for a domestic defense industrial base was undertaken and accomplished with support from the Soviet Union and other Eastern Bloc nations. The Derg regime established factories to produce and overhaul heavy armored vehicles, tanks, trucks and many other medium and heavy defense requirements, along with ammunition factories to produce tank, artillery, machine gun and small arms ammunition, inaugurating the Bishoftu complex in 1987 specifically for those purposes.

A second domestic complex, the Debrezeit Air Force base, was built to overhaul MIG fighter jets and manufacture repair parts. The Derg regime also worked with North Korea beginning in 1985 (starting with a 6 million birr interest-free loan to be used to purchase equipment to construct a shipyard on Haleb Island, off Asab in what is now Eritrea). In the end, this project came to naught and Ethiopia never produced any ships, but the Ethiopian–North Korean military relationship continued into the EPRDF era. North Korea helped the EPRDF government by improving the complex in Debrezeit, as well as the munitions factory in Ambo (where ammunition, from small arms to artillery, is still produced). It is not known to what extent the EPRDF government is currently working with North Korea, if at all.

Following the fall of the Derg regime on May 28, 1991 the new EPRDF government inherited the Derg military-industrial complex, which included the following Ethiopian defense industry production companies:

- Hibret Machine Tools: Produces medium weapons for the Ethiopian National Defense Force. Its civilian output includes hand tools; hospital beds; aluminum saddles; and household and office furniture.
- Gafat Armament Engineering Complex: Produces a wide range of infantry equipment that meets the requirements of the Ethiopian National Defense Force.
- Homicho Ammunition Engineering Complex: Produces a wide range of ammunition ranging from light weapons to heavy mortars and artillery. It also produces various metal products that are inputs to civilian industries.
- Bishoftu Motorization Engineering Complex: Repair and overhaul center for heavy armament, tanks, and military vehicles.
- Dejen Aviation Engineering Complex (DAVEC): Center for overhauling and upgrading military aircraft.
- Nazareth Canvas and Garment Factory: Produces and supplies military uniforms, canvas, leather and strap products to the Ethiopian National Defense Force.

Currently, all military manufacturing and business operations have been put under the auspices of the Metals & Engineering Corporation (METEC), an Ethiopian military-run corporation, planned and developed to work with foreign companies as it spearheads a drive to develop industries in Ethiopia. The METEC is run by an ENDF general who formerly ran the military production facilities identified above, and was given the additional responsibility of running the METEC as it grew into a much bigger operation with responsibility for much more of the government-run industrial sector. The METEC was established in June 2010 by grouping nine businesses previously owned by the Defense Ministry, including Dejen Aviation and Gafat Armaments. Six other industries, including plastic, tractor, and vehicle spare-parts manufacturers, were transferred to the METEC from the privatization agency. The METEC now operates as many as seventy-five factories nationwide.

The METEC works with Western industrial companies, including Alstom SA, US-based solar panel manufacturer Spire Corp., and China Poly Group on engineering and manufacturing projects. By 2013, the METEC had come to dominate the Ethiopian economy and still does; it has its fingers in everything from the Grand Renaissance Dam, to arms factories, to a fertilizer factory, to ten sugar factories. Since the METEC grew out of the military industrial sector, it is still run by a General. Some of its profits are brought back to the military, while all of its revenue benefits the Ethiopian government. This has led to rumors of corruption and complaints that the METEC serves an entrenched patronage system that guarantees a large stake to the military while guaranteeing the survival of the regime. While it is likely that those charges are true, it is also true that the METEC's expanded manufacturing capabilities and sales have benefitted the people who work in the various industries and factories, as well as the overall development of Ethiopia. Importantly, the METEC is also separate and distinct from the ENDF and its operations, even though the armed forces benefit from the METEC operations.[11]

## POLICE AND LAW ENFORCEMENT

Other than Article 51 of the Ethiopian Constitution, which gives the federal government the right to establish and administer national defense and public security forces—including a federal police force and regional police forces—the document offers no guidance on the employment, authorities, or structure for law enforcement forces.

The Ethiopian Federal Police Commission (EFPC) was established by the Federal Police Proclamation (Law 720/2011). The main responsibility of the EFPC lies in preventing and investigating crimes that may fall under the jurisdiction of the federal courts. These include criminal activities that might endanger the country, such as terrorism, organized crime, and trafficking in persons and drugs. This body also provides security to institutions within federal jurisdiction like airports and highways, as well as other major installations and infrastructure centers. Additionally, it has the role to standardize police theory and practice across the country. In general, police officers have nine to twelve months of academy training before they join the force, but there is no indication of refresher courses, additional professional training, or mid-career training for the various police organizations.

Regional police commissions, in contrast, are under their own respective regional governments. Article 23 of the Federal Police Proclamation states that, "...the EFPC shall work in cooperation with and in a mutually supportive way with the Regional Police Commissions in the prevention and investigation of crimes." In addition to the two independent entities (federal and regional police commissions), Addis Ababa has its own city police and traffic police. Further, the federal police also have jurisdiction over some parts of the city because Addis is the federal capital of the country; there are many federal institutions there, where the federal police have jurisdiction and may have special units for supporting them. As examples, the Ethiopian Revenue and Customs Authority (ERCA), as well as the Federal Ethics and Anti-Corruption Commission (FEACC) run their own law enforcement programs, with the right to arrest and enforce laws.

Finally, there is the special case of the Federal Prisons Administration (FPA), established by Law 365/2003, to "...implement judicial decisions, undertake the custody, reformation and rehabilitation of prisoners whereby good governance and rule of law prevail." Unfortunately, this is not how most Ethiopians see the FPA. For most Ethiopians, the FPA does not carry out its mission but rather has been accused of ignoring judicial orders and refusing to release prisoners set free by a court of law. The FPA is generally viewed as supporting politically motivated actions against specific prisoners or groups of prisoners (such as journalists or opposition party politicians) on behalf of the ruling EPRDF. Accusations of torture—particularly against prisoners of conscience—has also been a consistent complaint in the running of Ethiopia's jails.

When Ethiopia is faced with accusations of police brutality, the government often blames a lack of professionalism within the police forces but does not take responsibility for it. A 2011 study, commissioned by the World Bank to investigate corruption in key sectors in Ethiopia, found frequent complaints against the police for petty bribes (especially among the traffic police) but also identifies abuse of power or excessive use of force as a significant complaint. Ethiopians often have an overwhelming feeling of apprehension around law enforcement officers, especially the federal police, due to their infamous and brutal approach, often marked by excessive application of force. Police harassment is commonplace and makes the "rule of law" a rare commodity in the hands of the very forces responsible to enforce it.[12] Throughout Ethiopia at every level of jurisdiction, the police are not separate from the politics.

Regular meetings between EFPC officials and the regional police commission officials are held to effect coordination and address overlapping responsibilities. There is, however, wide operational freedom exercised by the various police forces throughout Ethiopia, and each officer must use individual judgment in applying the law. In effect, the lack of guidelines and specific authorities reflects an immature and underdeveloped police sector, with little cooperation and coordination in place. Realistically, updating and improving police training, education, equipment, practices, and coordination will take significant money as well as good intentions, so it will be some time before police forces improve significantly in Ethiopia.

## NATIONAL INTELLIGENCE AND SECURITY SERVICE (NISS)

As with many countries, there is no mention in the Constitution of the requirement for (or structure of) an intelligence or security service, and there is no promulgating law. Nonetheless, the National Intelligence and Security Service (NISS) was established in 1994/95 as the Immigration and Nationality Affairs Authority. The name of the organization was changed to the NISS in 2006/07 to more accurately reflect the nature of the organization's responsibilities.[13] Initially, the director of the NISS was not a minister-level position and the director was not part of the council of ministers. That changed in July 2013 with the publication of a new proclamation which states, in part: "The National Intelligence and Security Service is re-established with a ministerial status as an autonomous federal government office having its own legal personality and the Service is accountable to the Prime Minister. The Service shall have: A Director General, appointed by the Prime Minister; Intelligence organs; Security organs; Support organs; and the Necessary Staff." Thus, at a stroke, the NISS director was elevated to ministerial status, reporting directly to the prime minister.[14]

The Ethiopian NISS has a broader mandate than most intelligence services. The institution functions as the internal intelligence service; the external intelligence service; the physical security service for the president and prime minister; the dignitary protection service; the passport and immigration service; and the airport security service. The NISS thus has the role of the following US agencies: FBI, CIA, Secret Service, Department of State Dignitary Protection Detail, Immigration and Naturalization Service, and TSA. This set of responsibilities is a complex and sometimes conflicting portfolio, and would be far too disparate to be managed as one organization in the US. However, in Ethiopia's case, the various missions have fewer personnel, smaller portfolios, and fewer issues to manage. For example, Ethiopia has only two international airports (Addis Ababa and Dire Dawa) and twenty domestic airports, thus the job of airfield and air passenger security is far easier due to the much smaller number of daily flights and passengers than in the United States. Other roles within the NISS portfolio are also relatively less complex and lower in volume, thus making the control of all those disparate jobs a more manageable task than it appears. Finally, the fact that all of these tasks are the responsibility of a single large agency (theoretically) creates one significant advantage: coordination, cooperation, and information sharing should be a much easier process without institutional boundaries. What little evidence there is suggests that this is not necessarily the case.

Most national intelligence services have little open source information about what they do and how they do it, however, the Ethiopian NISS has a website that includes detailed descriptions of its functions. The overall purpose of the institution is stated: "The objective of the National Intelligence and Security Service is to protect and safeguard the national security of the country by providing quality intelligence and reliable security services." Further, the NISS describes its specific roles and responsibilities (without being in any priority order) as follows:

- Establish and coordinate intelligence and security training, and research institutions.
- Provide security protection to the Prime Minister and President, and to Heads of State and Governments of foreign countries when visiting Ethiopia.
- Formulate National Intelligence and Security Policies and manage their implementation.
- Head and coordinate national counter-terrorism cooperation and coordination, represent the country in international and continental cooperation counter-terrorism relations.
- Lead the work of intelligence and security service inside Ethiopia and outside the country in a responsible manner.
- Provide Immigration and Nationality Service to Ethiopians and foreigners in accordance with the Immigration and Nationality Proclamation.
- Follow up threats against national economic growth and development activities, serious good governance problems, and conspiracies, and collect intelligence and evidence.
- Follow up and investigate espionage activity against the interest of the country and its people, collect information, and undertake counterespionage activity.
- Cooperate with similar foreign organizations as may be necessary, receive or give intelligence, and conduct joint operations.[15]

In addition to the NISS, the ENDF also has a military intelligence department that reports to the chief of defense. It is assumed that the ENDF shares intelligence with NISS and vice versa, but there are no details about this and it is not a public relationship. It would be expected that the ENDF intelligence department focuses on military issues, tactical and operational intelligence for the ENDF, its operations, and its possible future operations and missions. Given the tactical and operational success of the ENDF in Somalia, it seems evident that the military intelligence department is competent and effective in preparing troops and leaders for conditions in country. Further, it would be expected for the ENDF to request any and all pertinent information available to the NISS in support of their combat operations and deployments, but as is so often true with intelligence organizations, there is little open-source information on this relationship.

## ASSESSMENT

Overall, Ethiopia has extremely competent and effective armed forces. There is a complicated link between the armed forces and the METEC, a major industrial producer of military parts, supplies, and equipment. This link is indirect but appears to supply most ENDF needs at a minimum cost. A major systemic weakness throughout their security services is a lack of effective interagency coordination and cooperation, especially within and among the various police forces. This criticism applies to many other countries as well, including European and other Western countries, but the coordination in Ethiopia is rudimentary at best. Ethiopia has accepted training and courses for their various police forces and security services; however, given their extremely strong independence streak, Ethiopian institutions virtually never confer or work with outside agencies like the US FBI. The government's own different police forces seldom work together—except on difficult cases or terrorism. There is no standard interagency process.

Regarding the National Intelligence and Security Service, it is always difficult to measure the success of an intelligence agency that prefers to keep a very low profile. However, if we measure NISS success by lack of terrorist activity and compare it to neighboring countries, we can see that Ethiopia has an enviable record of low terrorist activity— a marked contrast to events in Kenya, Sudan, and even Uganda. NISS would certainly like to claim that the lack of terrorist attacks is due to their vigilance, competence, and professionalism in protecting Ethiopia; they may be right, but it is difficult to say exactly why there have been fewer attacks in Ethiopia, since NISS does not publicize its successes or failures. It could have more to do with the attackers than the target, or it could be that Ethiopia is indeed a very difficult target to hit. Nonetheless, although we know few details of how NISS goes about its mission, Ethiopia has been a safe and stable country with no successful terrorist attacks in six years, so apparently NISS has been effective in fulfilling its multiple missions.

According to Transparency International, Ethiopia ranks 103rd (in a four-way tie) out of 167 countries in corruption.[16] The extent of corruption among Ethiopian police services is somewhat less evident than that seen in neighbors or many other African countries. Corruption is mostly associated with rural police and the traffic police in Addis Ababa— none of whom are particularly well paid. The much larger problem with police forces in Ethiopia is the perception and experience of virtually all police forces being political instruments of the federal or regional governments; there appears to be no sense of accountability or concern for the average citizen. The police have not yet established organizational independence, ethical responsibility, and professional standards, but they remain essentially a tool to enforce national and regional political decisions.

As a contemporary example, the Ethiopian government has been accused of using excessive force in the Oromia and Amhara regions, where protesters have been calling for political reforms. The violence has led to over 400 deaths between November 2015 and October 2016, a hundred of them in the first week of October alone, according to human rights groups. Human rights groups have called the response ruthless, while the UN wants to send international observers to investigate. Typically, Ethiopia has denied that request, saying it alone is responsible for the security of its citizens.

The governing EPRDF still values stability over all else, but appears to be getting ever more distant from the people they rule. The government and its ministers believe that they have the best interests of the Ethiopian population in mind when they make decisions, although the people are neither informed nor consulted prior to those decisions.

The government may, in fact, be acting on behalf of the Ethiopian people in support of the common good, but their iron grip on power, denial of parliamentary representation, lack of consultation, and paternalistic assumption of support, has finally led to widespread discontent. Although the recent protests met with predictable violent repression, Ethiopia may see more of this unless the government becomes more inclusive and the people feel as though their voices are heard. More protest may engender more violence, but that violence may not stem the tide of protest. Calm may be restored, or more protests may result in more violent reactions, possibly leading to an upheaval that would threaten the current Ethiopian government. It might be wise to recall that the last two governments fell after widespread protests following a difficult drought and deadly famine.

**National Brand.** Ethiopian armed forces cannot be classified by only one brand, because the ENDF is constantly involved in two different functions: They perform as both "peacekeeper" and "defender," being posted abroad in many peacekeeping missions throughout Africa, including UN efforts in Darfur, South Sudan, Liberia, and others. The ENDF is also deployed as "defender," providing border security and preparation to defend Ethiopia from any incursions or aggressive acts on the Eritrean border in the North, as well as taking part in the AMISOM mission in Somalia against the armed group Al Shabaab. Perhaps the national brand could best be stated as "peacekeeping defenders" identifying both important roles. They also have the capacity to act as firemen, but have not performed that role since 2005, and hopefully, will not have to do so in 2017.

**Most Significant Threats.** The insurgent/terrorist group Al Shabaab poses the greatest threat to Ethiopian security all along the Somali border, while Eritrea poses a potential threat along their northern border. Ethiopia may overstate the threat from Eritrea, but brief incursions from Eritrea occur approximately once per quarter.

**Roles of the Security Forces.** The role of the ENDF has already been identified. However, the role of the various other security forces is to concentrate on internal security (especially for the NISS) and law enforcement. Unfortunately, the various police forces are underfunded, undertrained, underpaid, coordinate poorly, and too often act as an enforcement arm of the ruling EPRDF government instead of in a typical law enforcement role. The police forces do enforce the laws within their jurisdiction, and some policemen act with honesty and conviction, but too many of them are corrupt, largely due to poor pay.

**Political System.** Based upon the typology outlined in chapter 2, Ethiopia is an "institutionalized noncompetitive state." Ethiopia has well-established security institutions and distinct armed forces, intelligence services, and police. The security institutions do not influence the government's political system, although the reverse is true, in that police act to enforce the directives of the government. The police are considered untrustworthy, although the NISS and ENDF are considered trustworthy, for the most part. Decision-making is top-down and the EPRDF has ruled Ethiopia since 1991 with one prime minister (Meles) for 21 years and another since Meles's death. Although there is little outright proof, the populace assumes that there is widespread corruption in the ruling party.

**Contribution of the Security Forces to Good Governance.** The governance and capacity of the security sector for Ethiopia has both a healthy relationship and an unhealthy one. The ENDF is a capable, effective, and necessary force, and acts on behalf of Ethiopia and Ethiopians externally (in Somalia and in Peacekeeping roles), and internally by keeping the peace at the border. The ENDF in this role is very well regarded. However, there are several ways in which the ENDF does not contribute, largely by having a government monopoly on manufacturing of many products by their METEC military industrial company. Further, the police forces do not have a healthy relationship with society as a whole due to their role in enforcing government edicts, and requests (in many cases, effectively eliminating dissent).

**Trends for Security Sector Institutions.** There are encouraging trends in the Ethiopian security sector, and the current ENDF does not threaten the government of the state (the previous army, under the Derg regime from 1975 to 1991, *was* the government of the state). The constitution mandates civilian oversight of the military, and the government exercises that control, and the ENDF is not considered corrupt. Unfortunately, the trend for the various police forces has not changed, and police forces are only moderately effective and somewhat corrupt (usually due to poor pay or confiscation of their pay by their leadership), and this has been ongoing for a very long time.

## Notes

1. All opinions expressed in this chapter are my own and do not reflect official positions of either the Naval Postgraduate School or the United States government.
2. Michela Wrong, *I Didn't Do It For You: How the World Betrayed a Small African Country*, (New York: Harper Collins, 2005), 139–150.
3. Tareke, Gebru, *Ethiopian Revolution: War in the Horn of Africa* (New Haven, CT: Yale University Press, 2009), 343–349.
4. Peter Giles, "The war between Ethiopia and Eritrea," *Foreign Policy in Focus* (October 11, 2005), http://fpif.org/the_war_between_ethiopia_and_eritrea/.
5. "Observing the 2005 Ethiopia National Elections," *Carter Center Final Report*, December 2009.
6. Gebru Tareke, "The Ethiopia-Somalia War of 1977 Revisited," *The International Journal of African Historical Studies* 33, no. 3 (2000), 635–667.
7. Roger A. Lee, "The Ethiopia-Somalia War (2006–2009)" 2012, http://www.historyguy.com/ethiopia-somalia_war_2006.html.
8. Jeffrey Gettlemen, "Ethiopian Troops Said to Enter Somalia, Opening New Front Against Militants," *New York Times* (November 20, 2011).
9. Ethiopian Constitution of 1995, Article 87.
10. See, for example, Robert Beckhusen, "Ethiopia spends very little on its military, and it works, the question is how?" WarisBoring.com, https://warisboring.com/ethiopia-spends-very-little-money-on-its-military-and-it-works-1be0d725f8a9#.6xlv62l40.
11. "Ethiopian Defense Industrial Base," GlobalSecurity.org, article undated, http://www.globalsecurity.org/military/world/ethiopia/industry.htm.
12. Kalkidan Yibeltal, "Ethiopia: Policing Ethiopia - the Force vs. Service Dilemma," *Addis Standard (Addis Ababa)* (August 5, 2015), http://allafrica.com/stories/201508051502.html.
13. Aderajew Asfaw, "National Intelligence and Security Service Powers Extended" *Capital Ethiopia* (July 1, 2013).
14. Proclamation No. 804/2013: A Proclamation to Re-establish the National Intelligence and Security Service, *Federal Negarit Gazette*, No. 55, Addis Ababa (July, 23, 2013): 6961–6972.
15. Ethiopian National Intelligence and Security Service website, http://www.eth-niss.info/.

16. *Transparency International Global Corruption Index 2015,* http://www. transparency.org/cpi2015#results-table.

CHAPTER 11

# THE CASE OF CHAD

*Christopher Jasparro*

Chad defies nearly every ideal and standard of civil-military relations, good governance, and human security proposed in this volume's first two chapters. Furthermore, the country is beset by almost every threat category listed in chapter 2. However, Chad has effectively created a national brand of itself as a strong state and source of security and stability in the troubled Sahel that key external states (particularly the United States, France, and China) have bought into. Chad's ruling regime has leveraged this to obtain significant military, financial, and political assistance from external actors that it has, in turn, used to maintain traditional security and domestic power in spite of having some of the world's highest levels of human insecurity. Chad's President Idriss Déby, sometimes called a "democratic dictator," has maintained power in a system that is a classic example of a "weak state and strong regime" while obtaining international legitimacy through winning successive but severely flawed elections.[1] This chapter will apply elements of the analytical frameworks proposed in chapters 1 and 2 to help explain how Chad has turned seemingly overwhelming disadvantages into a brand of security provider, as well as some of the cracks beneath the brand and what they may portend.

## BACKGROUND

Chad, with an estimated population of 13.2 million, of which 96% are under fifteen years of age,[2] is "essentially a colonial invention"[3] with an ethnically, economically, and religiously diverse population. There are 200 official languages and dialects. In the south live settled farmers (mainly Christians and animists) while in the north live semi-settled and nomadic pastoralists (e.g., Muslim Gouranes and Arabs).[4]

From the sixteenth to the nineteenth centuries, parts of Chad fell under the suzerainty of central Sudanese kingdoms such as Kanem-Borunu, Bagirmi, and Ouaddai that owed much of their power to their location on trans-Saharan trade routes.[5] During this time, Islam entered from the north. By the late nineteenth century, local polities were in decline and riven by war, setting the scene for French conquest and colonization. In 1913 France consolidated control over what is today Chad as a military-administered part of French Equatorial Guinea. It was not demarcated as a separate colony until 1920. In 1958 Chad became an autonomous part of the French Union and received full independence in 1960.[6] Collier's four traps (see chapter 1) of geography, natural resources, conflict, and bad governance provide a useful device to characterize post-Independence Chad.

### Geography

Chad is a landlocked state encompassing 1,283,998 square km, bordered by the Central African Republic (CAR), Libya, Sudan, Cameroon, Niger, and Nigeria.[7] Currently, all its neighbors are impacted by conflict; Niger and CAR are two of the few countries that rank below Chad on the

Human Development Index (HDI).[8] N'Djamena, the capital, is situated nearly 1,600 km (1,000 miles) by road from the nearest West African ports.[9] The area around Lake Chad has, for centuries, been a focal point for trans-Saharan trade routes.[10] Most of the country is arid or semi-arid with the north dominated by the Sahara and the middle by the semi-arid Sahel. Water is not as scarce in the south, with distinct wet and dry seasons and woodland savanna. The Chari and Logone, which empty into Lake Chad, are the only significant rivers.[11]

**Natural Resources**
Chad is Africa's largest landlocked state, lacking significant resources that cater to basic human security. Limited water, vast desert, and poor soils leave only about 3% of the land suitable for farming with 35% suitable for permanent pasture.[12] This, combined with vulnerability to drought and insect plagues, leaves 80% of Chad's labor force which is engaged in agriculture extremely vulnerable to nature's vicissitudes.[13]

Chad is endowed with mineral and fossil fuel resources but conflict, poor governance, and location have, for much of its modern history, limited production. Although oil was discovered in the 1970s,[14] Chad did not become a producer until 2003 when a pipeline was able to link it to ports in West Africa.[15] Natron (soda ash) is the only mineral produced in significant quantities at about 13,000 metric tons per year.[16] Chad has deposits of gold, uranium, and other minerals that have not yet been significantly exploited.

Since 2003 Chad has become almost totally dependent upon oil. By 2013 it had fallen into a classic resource trap whereby hydrocarbon production accounted for 90% of exports, 70% of government funding, and 30% of nominal GDP, leaving it extremely vulnerable to fluctuations in international oil prices.[17]

At first, however, Chad looked like it might escape the natural resource trap as international investments, particularly loans by the World Bank, were structured to promote good governance, sound fiscal management and human development, with significant oil royalties designated for investing in education, healthcare, and other such public services. Other conditions included programs for environmental protection and capacity building. Notwithstanding significant implementation challenges and government resistance, the project was hailed as a "newly emergent model for development" for resource-curse prone states and regarded, initially, as a success.[18] However, the Chadian government soon turned emerging security threats into an opportunity for noncompliance with internationally imposed conditions. The government effectively created a resource-curse situation on the one hand, while using it to build a brand as a provider of security and stability on the other.

### Conflict

Chad has experienced civil or external conflict almost continuously since independence.[19] These conflicts have been characterized by a complex array of shifting internal and external alignments. By 1966 northern Muslim tribes were in full revolt,[20] angered by the poor rule of the southern-dominated government of François Tombalbaye. What began as a northern peasant rebellion in 1965 had a few years later morphed into a full-blown north-south civil war. The northerners received support from Libya, while France provided military support and combat troops to the southern dominated government. Factionalization among the rebels and Tombalbaye's poor relations with the military (he was overthrown in a coup in 1975) led the conflict to evolve from one of northern grievances to a multidimensional struggle for personal power that increasingly drew in foreign intervention and interference from not only France and Libya but Sudan, Nigeria, and the United States.[21]

The postcoup government led by the southern General Félix Malloum was unable to consolidate power, and in 1979 fighting broke out between the army and rebel forces led by Hissène Habré, a northern Tobou rebel leader who had briefly served as prime minister. In 1980 Libya invaded northern Chad but was driven out in 1981 by Habré's forces with substantial help from France and the US. Then Habré seized power in a 1982 coup and declared himself president. Libya invaded again in 1983, prompting France to intervene with several thousand troops and the United States to provide air and other support. Libya was finally defeated and driven out of Chad in 1987.

One of the key architects of this Libyan defeat was Idriss Déby, a former rebel who had become Habré's army chief and principal military advisor. A dispute between the two men forced Déby to take refuge in Libya, while Habré retaliated against Déby's fellow Zaghawa ethnic kinsmen. In 1990 Déby and his Patriotic Salvation Movement, with support from Libya and Sudan, drove on to N'Djamena from Sudan and overthrew the Habré regime.

Déby, however, also still faced internal and external challenges that intensified after 2005 when the constitution was amended to eliminate presidential term limits. Several political rivals launched insurgencies the same year. This opposition culminated in a February 2008 coup attempt when Sudanese-backed Chadian rebels, based in Darfur, advanced into N'Djamena and nearly toppled Déby in a vicious urban battle. The defeat of the rebels and Déby's subsequent rapprochement with Sudan left Chad free from serious internal threats for the first time in its short history.

However, even as internal conflict had largely been quashed, Chad found itself in an increasingly volatile neighborhood with continued fighting in Darfur, the Boko Haram uprising in Nigeria becoming a full-fledged insurgency, and Libya plunging into conflict in 2011. Mali experienced a coup, civil war, and a jihadist invasion the following year, as civil war broke out in CAR. Chad subsequently deployed forces in support of international and regional operations to Mali, CAR, and Nigeria.

### Bad Governance

Chad ranks low on almost every measure of governance there is. Its HDI ranking is 185 (out of 188) with 62% of its population living below the poverty line.[22] Chad has the world's second worst infant mortality at 856 deaths per 100,000 live births, a life expectancy of 49 years, and only 450 medical doctors.[23] Barely 12% of the population has access to basic sanitation, and only 50% has access to clean drinking water sources. The literacy rate is 40%.[24]

Human rights are threatened by the government's use of excessive force as well as the indiscriminate killing, looting, and property destruction conducted by armed groups such as Boko Haram.[25] According to the US State Department, security force abuse and harsh prison conditions—as well as violence and discrimination against women and children—are the most serious human rights abuses. Other abuses cited include arbitrary killings and torture by security forces; arbitrary arrest and detention; and executive influence on the judiciary.[26]

The effects of poor governance are starting to produce cracks in the regime's solidity. Although President Déby was able to win a fifth five-year term in April 2016, earning 61.5% of the vote,[27] the run-up to the elections was marred by unprecedented protests and a general strike, indicating the populace's mounting frustration. The government broke up demonstrations violently—even shutting down Facebook and other social media sites to help quell the dissent. According to one sociologist, "There has been a change of generation and of mentality which is taking place."[28]

## ARMED FORCES

Chad's military had its origins in colonial forces established by the French. From independence through the Malloum presidency (1975–1979), the military was the Forces Armées Tchadiennes (FAT), which was made up mainly of southerners, especially from the Sara ethnic group. With Habré's assumption of power in the early 1980's, the FAT was replaced by his Forces Armées du Nord (FAN), combined with a conglomeration of other rebel groups mainly from the north.[29]

Chad's present military, however, is largely a product of the 1990 coup and the ramp-up in military spending since 2006. It is dominated by Zaghawa northerners and Gourane northerners and "is as much an instrument of personal survival as of national defense."[30] Chadian security forces are primarily national forces that come under the umbrella of two ministries. The military, the National Armed Forces of Chad (ANT), reports to the Ministry of Defense, while the Gendarmerie, National Police, National Nomadic Guard (GNNT), and National Security Agency (ANS) report to the Ministry of Interior. The Ministry of Finance also operates a mobile customs brigade, and the Ministry of Agriculture has an antipoaching brigade[31] that is, however, effectively under the direct control of President Déby.[32] In 2014 Chad had a defense budget of $273 million.[33] The army has 20,000–25,000 personnel and the air force 350.[34] The remaining security forces account for another 9,500 personnel.

Chad has used its oil revenues to dramatically increase its military capability and is now "one of the most militarized countries in Africa."[35] Although the security forces are accused of being corrupt, operating with impunity, and engaging in extortion and other crimes,[36] Chad's military is nevertheless one of Africa's most capable and effective militaries. The *Wall Street Journal* has called it the "go-to army" for fighting jihadists.[37] According to French colonel Louis Pena, "A large part of the Chadian Army is well-equipped and well-trained. They charge into the rumble and have no fear. It's one of the countries and armies on which we rely very strongly."[38]

## THREATS

Chad is afflicted by nearly every man-made and natural threat imaginable. Among the man-made threats are bad governance, conflict, and insurgency, which were discussed earlier. There are terrorism threats from jihadist movements such as Al Qaeda in the Islamic Maghreb (AQIM), the Islamic State (ISIS), and Boko Haram that have escalated, following Chad's recent military interventions as well as the continuing instability in Libya. Boko Haram has launched attacks in the Nigeria-Cameroon border region and on islands in Lake Chad and recruited insurgents among the Buduma, a southern minority group, who live around the lake.[39] N'Djamena was struck for the first time in June 2015 when Boko Haram conducted suicide bombing attacks on police buildings, prompting the government to declare its first state of emergency since the 2008 coup attempt.[40]

Chad's long, porous borders and its location astride pan-Saharan land routes facilitate its status as a market or transit zone for contraband and trafficked goods such as food, cigarettes, oil, weapons, and drugs (mainly cocaine and cannabis). Some of the trafficking of weapons, drugs, and wildlife products is linked to organized crime groups, some of whom may have links to terrorist groups.[41] It is also a source, transit, and destination area for forced child labor and sexual trafficking.[42] Refugees are a major issue with Chad now hosting 450,000 from CAR, South Sudan, and Nigeria.[43]

Although Chad is a landlocked country, it has waterborne security challenges including crime, terrorism, overfishing, and environmental degradation on and around Lake Chad. Drought, extraction of lake water, damming, overfishing, and the unsustainable harvesting of juvenile fish are undercutting fish stocks.[44] The lake's surface area has shrunk from 25,000 to 2,500 square km over the past forty-five years and may vanish completely within twenty years,[45] yet by 2020 the number of people expected to rely on Lake Chad for their economic livelihoods is projected to rise from 20 million to 35 million.[46] The combination of Lake Chad's archipelagic geography and its shrinking surface area may actually increase the porosity of regional borders, facilitating cross-border transit by Boko Haram and other nonstate actors.[47]

Wildlife poaching and transnational ivory trafficking also occur. In the last fifty years, the country has lost over 90% of its elephant population,[48] particularly hard hit between 2006 and 2009 as rebel groups from Sudan accelerated the slaughter. By 2011 the elephant population in Zakouma National Park fell to 450 from 4,000 in 2006.[49]

In many respects, poaching is a microcosm of Chad's overall security situation. Since 2010 there appears to have been considerable progress on the poaching front, yet significant underlying challenges remain because this progress is only superficial. President Déby publicly committed to action against poaching, to include attending international summits and signing regional agreements. The rapprochement with Sudan eased the pressure from armed groups. Further, Chad sought external assistance on a threat that had growing resonance in the west—even turning over antipoaching operations in Zakouma to Africa Parks (a South African organization). At the same time, US Marines provided some training to wildlife rangers.

At the same time, poaching is a serious transnational problem across Central Africa to which Chad is still vulnerable. Corruption within the government and security forces is a considerable problem. Despite their improved capability, wildlife rangers are limited with what they can do, especially outside of Zakouma. There is also tension between transnational security (i.e., poaching/trafficking and biodiversity protection) and human security (subsistence farmers have collaborated with poachers to kill elephants that have been trampling their crops).[50]

Chad faces many kinds of natural disasters. In addition to droughts, Chad experiences periods of extreme flooding—the 2012 floods impacted more than 700,000 Chadians.[51] Chad is also subject to locust infestations that cause crop destruction, such as the major damage done in 2004 and 2012. Not surprisingly given its location, natural environment, low level of development, and limited governmental capacity, the country is extremely vulnerable to climate change. In 2015 it was ranked as the world's fifth most vulnerable country to climate change in the *Climate Change and Environmental Risk Atlas.*[52]

Further complicating things is Chad's extremely diverse population that has a history of ethnic conflict and "complex and fluid ethnic rivalries" that are heightened by contestation over land and water issues.[53] This is exacerbated by regime policies that have placed the Zaghawa, who comprise less than 3% of population (and sustain their own interethnic rivalries), into the majority of government positions.[54]

## FRAMEWORK ANALYSIS

Through deft diplomacy, the use of oil revenues, and international assistance to boost military capability, Chad has turned the "traps" of geography, governance, conflict, and natural resources (along with its vulnerability to a broad array of threats) into opportunities to help brand itself as an essential regional "defender" and "peacekeeper." The country has managed to forge this perception despite having armed forces that also perform more controversial regional "warfighter" and internal "fireman" and "policeman" roles.

For most of its history as an independent state, Chad's geographic situation left it vulnerable to spillover and intervention from its neighbors. The Lake Chad Basin is a convergence zone for trafficking and smuggling routes across the Sahara. To Chad's north and west are the main operating areas of AQIM. The north is also home to the turmoil of Libya, which has become ISIS' main foothold in Africa. To the southwest of Chad is where Boko Haram operates. To the east and south of Chad are Darfur and CAR respectively where conflict persists and simmers. Chad has leveraged its location amidst the Sahel's conflict to its advantage by becoming first a regional "troublemaker" and now a "defender" and "peacekeeper." Its location in the middle of all these conflicts in the Sahel and Central Africa gives it geographic value to external actors seeking to manage conflict, combat transnational terrorism, and interdict trafficking in the region. France, for instance, has chosen Chad as the headquarters for Operation Barkahne, a pan-Sahel counterterrorism operation that followed on from the Mali intervention. Brigadier General Donald Bolduc, Commander US Special Operations Command Africa, has called the Lake Chad Basin region "Ground Zero" in the battle against terrorism in Africa.[55]

Chad has used its increased military capability to subdue internal threats and, in turn, boost its military contribution to regional missions,[56] thus enabling it to transition from a *consumer* of defense and peacekeeping into a *provider*. Although Chadian troops played a controversial role in (and were removed from) the peacekeeping mission in CAR in 2013, their participation in the Mali intervention and in combating Boko Haram have been successful at the tactical and operational levels, bringing considerable regional and international diplomatic credit.[57] UN Secretary-General Ban Ki-moon, in June 2015, praised Chad "for its courageous role in the fight against Boko Haram."[58] According to one diplomat, "The Chadians are essential. They are the most capable military by a long shot, they are pretty much incomparable."[59]

In 2006 Chad's government used the intensifying insurgencies as a pretext to begin diverting significant oil revenues from development and governance to build up its military capability. Chad used conflict as a means to avoid externally imposed conditions. Among these were measures to prevent the country from falling into an oil-driven resource trap, as well as serious adherence to the governance and human security priorities discussed in chapters 1 and 2. Hence the ruling regime secured itself politically by undermining international and domestic governance, focusing on traditional security issues rather than human security ones. This, in turn, allowed the government to leverage its military capability and geography to become an internationally recognized and valuable security provider.

These developments have allowed Chad to weather international criticism for its domestic policies and the global downturn in oil prices. In 2012, IMF warnings led to the renegotiation of a loan agreement with China. In 2013 the government agreed to an IMF-monitored program to undertake fiscal reforms in exchange for the possibility of debt relief. By 2014 the drop in oil prices was leading to inflation, shortages,[60] falling exports, and predictions that account deficits would increase from 2.3% of GDP to 3.7% of GDP by 2015.[61] Despite slow progress on policy reform, in 2014 the IMF approved a disbursement of US $27 million, while the World Bank and IMF concluded that Chad qualified under the Heavily Indebted Poor Countries (HIPC) initiative for US$1 billion in debt relief.[62] Chad's willingness to take on regional jihadist groups played an important role in securing French and US support for the debt relief.[63]

There are, however, increasing indicators that Chad may not have escaped its traps and threats but merely staved them off. The regime will have difficulty maintaining its defense expenditures and coopting internal rivals if oil prices remain low and external threats remain high. Furthermore, despite the capability of Chad's security forces, they may not have sufficient capacity to sustain their current operational tempo and casualty rates—a trend exacerbated by the country's vast size, long borders, and unstable neighboring regions, along with increased targeting by jihadist groups. Domestic opposition and public disaffection, while fractured, appear to be growing, while the government has limited capability and capacity to deal with persistent and intensifying human security threats.

## Assessment

**National Brand.** Chad's external "national brand" is that of "defender" and "peacekeeper" even though its military and security forces play "fireman" and "policeman" roles internally.

**Most Significant Threats.** Chad faces every threat listed in table 2 except for cyclones. In the near term, the biggest threat Chad faces is instability in surrounding countries and in particular direct and indirect threats from transnational terrorist and criminal groups. However, in the longer term, it is the combination of aforementioned human security threats that pose the greatest threat to regime stability and the integrity of Chad as a state more generally.

**Roles of the Security Forces.** Simply put, the security forces of Chad exist to protect the ruling regime and the country's borders and territorial integrity (i.e., protect the regime from external threats). Their roles are complementary in that they all exist to protect the regime, and that all are national forces.

**Political System.** Chad's political system is one of "personal rule" with some characteristics of a "minimally institutionalized state." The country is one of the world's most corrupt and is dominated by a single individual and his close associates. Security forces are focused on protecting the regime externally and internally. Nonsecurity institutions have limited capability and capacity and are grossly underresourced.

**Contribution of the Security Forces to Good Governance.** As previously discussed, the security forces are beholden to a regime characterized by "personal rule." Resources (in particular oil revenues) have been diverted from nonsecurity state institutions to the security forces, and particularly the armed forces. There is minimal capacity to exercise basic governance functions or promote human security. Consequently, the security sector (with the exception of protecting against external aggression and terrorist attacks) exacerbates, if not promotes, poor governance.

**Trends for Security Sector Institutions.** Given the low level of governance and human security in Chad, basic progress towards the ideals espoused in this volume could easily be tracked using basic and standard measures of governance, corruption, political freedom, human development, and human rights. Polling of the public's views of security forces would also be a useful measure (indeed, the ability to conduct such polls unhindered would be a positive measure in its own right). Tracking government spending on security forces in comparison to nonsecurity institutions would also be an extremely useful measurement. Given the underresourcing of the nonsecurity sector, increases in nonsecurity spending and/or more balance between security and nonsecurity spending would be a significant signal.

Nevertheless, significant progress is unlikely to be seen in the near term. Chad's ruling regime has played what appears to be a bad hand exceedingly well, branding itself as an essential regional security player and provider. Chad's shrewd use of diplomacy and military capability have also helped it firm up relations with neighboring regimes that can also be classified as bastions of personal rule in weak and poorly institutionalized states. In 2010 Déby and Sudanese president Omar al-Bashir reached a rapprochement and stopped supporting opposition groups operating out of Darfur.[64] This not only helped reduce internal armed opposition but also secured Chad's eastern flank geopolitically. Chad's military intervention and performance against Boko Haram has helped ease tensions with Cameroon while further strengthening relations with Niger.[65] This may help position Cameroon and Niger to brand themselves like Chad in an effort to garner external support from other strong regime/weak state neighbors as they combat transnational security threats in the Sahel and Central Africa.

Despite Chad's growing geopolitical significance, the window for the regime to maintain its external brand while remaining oppressive at home may be starting to close. For instance, during her April 2016 visit to Chad, Samantha Power criticized the government's "crackdown" on press freedom during the elections and emphasized the importance of improving economic development, employment, and political inclusiveness.[66] The combination of declining oil revenues, increasing domestic discontent, and increasing jihadist threats should give the United States and other external partners more leverage to begin pushing the regime (beyond rhetoric) to start addressing domestic issues and political grievances more seriously. It is expected that this might increase Chad's durability as a partner and force for stability as it becomes more dependent upon external support and less able to buy off or repress its internal opposition.

For the immediate future, however, Chad will leverage its military capability in a high-threat regional environment to remain a state with strong branding for its external security value. Internally, the government will retain a policeman civil-military relations structure in the face of mounting human security threats and increasing yet still fragmented internal dissatisfaction. Chad will continue to play a regional "defender" and "peacekeeper" role but on softening feet of clay. The advent of serious internal instability could result in "grave consequences" for heavily dependent external partners and their regional counterterrorism strategies.[67] Even if oil revenues rebound and can be used to stave off internal opposition and bolster military capability, Chad will ultimately face a succession crisis when Déby passes from the scene. Ultimately, the country faces a choice: continue to play a bad hand and hope its luck doesn't run out, or begin to enact the reforms necessary to build a better and more durable deck of cards.

## NOTES

1. Ketil Fred Hansen, "A Democratic Dictator's Success: How Chad's President Déby Defeated the Military Opposition in Three Years (2008–2011)," *Journal of Contemporary African Studies* (September 26, 2013).
2. Jahen Selim, *Human Development Report 2015: Work for Human Development* (New York: UNDP, 2015), hdr.undp.org/en.
3. Hasdai Westbrook, "Swarms at the Border: The Dead Heart of Africa," *Guernica* (July 10, 2006), https://www.guenicamag.com/features/swarms_at_the_border/.
4. Saul Cohen, ed., "Chad," *Colombia Gazetteer of the World* (New York: Columbia University Press, 1998), 585.
5. Douglas Henry Jones, "History of Chad," *Encyclopedia Britannica*, www.britannica.com/topic/history-of-Chad.
6. Cohen, 585.
7. Ibid.
8. Selim, *Human Development Report.*
9. Jones, "History of Chad."
10. Cohen, "Chad." 585.
11. Ibid.
12. Central Intelligence Agency, "*World Factbook,*" https://www.cia.gov/library/publications/the-world-factbook/geos/cd/html.
13. Ibid.
14. Cohen, 585.
15. BBC, "Chad Country Profile," April 23, 2006, www.bbc.com/news/world-africa-13164686.
16. Philip Mobbs, "The Mineral Industry of Chad," *USGS 2013 Minerals Yearbook* (Washington, DC: US Geological Survey, 2014), 2.
17. Ibid.
18. George Mitchell, "Leveraging Project Finance for Development: The Chad-Cameroon Oilfield Development and Pipeline Project," *The Journal of Civil Society and Social Transformation* (January 2010): 14, 21.
19. Cohen, 585.
20. Ibid.
21. David Henderson, "Conflict in Chad, 1975 to Present: A Central Africa Tragedy," Master's Thesis, Marine Corps Command and Staff College Quantico, 1984.

22. Selim, *Human Development Report.*
23. "Chad Humanitarian Overview," http://reliefweb.int/report/chad/chad-humanitarian-overview-09-march-2016.
24. CIA, "World Factbook."
25. "Chad 2015/2016," *Amnesty International Annual Report*, https//www.amnesty.org/en/countries/Africa/chad/report-chad/.
26. "Human Rights and Labor, Country Reports for Human Rights Practices for Chad 2015," *US State Department Bureau of Democracy*, www.state.gov/j/drl/rls/hrrpt/humanrightsreport/#wrapper.
27. Abdur Rahman Alfa Shaban, "Idriss Déby Wins Fifth Term in Office with 61.56% of Votes, *Africa News* (April 21, 2016), http://www.africanews.com/2016/04/21/idriss-deby-wins-fifth-term-in-office-with-6156-percent-of-votes/.
28. Stephane Yas, "Chad Leader Facing Biggest Protests of his Long Rule," *Agence France-Press* (February 2, 2016), http://reliefweb.int/report/chad/chad-leader-facing-biggest-protests-his-long-rule.
29. Thomas Collelo, *Chad Country Study, Area Handbook Series* (Washington, DC: US Department of the Army, 1990), 175.
30. Adam Nossiter, "Battling Boko Haram, Chad's Strongman Pleases the West," *New York Times* (late edition East Coast; March 28, 2015), A4.
31. US State Department Bureau of Democracy, "Human Rights and Labor."
32. Joshua Hammer, "The Race to Stop Africa's Elephant Poachers," *Smithsonian Magazine* (July 2014), http://www.smithsonianmag.com/science-nature/race-stop-africas-elephant-poachers-1809.
33. "Chad Military Stats," www.nationmaster.com/country-info/profiles/Chad/Military.
34. David Chuter and Florence Gaub, *Understanding African Armies* (Paris: European Union Institute for Security Studies, 2016), 46.
35. Hansen, "A Democratic Dictator's Success," 7.
36. US State Department Bureau of Democracy, "Human Rights and Labor."
37. Yaroslav Trofimov, "For Fighting Jihadists, Chad has the Go-To Army," *Wall Street Journal* (January 21, 2016), www.wsj.com/articles/for-fighting-jihadists-chad-has-the-go-to-army-1453372372.
38. Ibid.
39. "Winning Battles, Losing Wars," *Africa Confidential* (March 15, 2015), http://www.africa-confidential.com/article/id/11091/Winning_battles%2c_losing_wars.
40. "Chad Suicide Attack Kills Many in N'Djamena," *BBC News* (June 15, 2015), www.bbc.com/news/world-africa-33133511.

41. "Chad," *2014 International Narcotics Control Strategy Report*, http://www.state.gov/j/inl/rls/nrcrpt/2014/supplemental/227752.htm.
42. "Chad," *2013 Trafficking in Persons Report*, http://www.state.gov/j/tip/rls/tiprpt/countries/2013/215437.htm.
43. Freedom House, "Freedom in the World 2015, Chad 2015," https://freedomhouse.org/report/freedom-world/2015/chad.
44. "Lake Chad Profile–World Lakes.org" (2016), www.worldlakes.org/lakedetails.asp?lakeid=8537.
45. Lake Chad Basin Commission, "Fishing in the Lake Chad Basin" (last modified 2016), www.cblt.org/en/themes/fishing-lake-chad-basin.
46. WWF, "Lake Chad Flooded Savannah" (last modified 2016), http://www.worldwildlife.org/ecoregions/at0904.
47. Scott Menner, "Boko Haram's Regional Cross-border Activities" (October 31, 2014), https://www.ctc.usma.edu/posts/boko-harams-regional-cross-border-activities.
48. Joshua Hammer, "The Race to Stop Africa's Elephant Poachers," *Smithsonian Magazine* (July 2014), http://www.smithsonianmag.com/science-nature/race-stop-africas-elephant-poachers-1809.
49. Celeste Hicks, "In Chad Elephants Make a Comeback" *Al Jazeera* (September 5, 2014), http://america.aljazeera.com/articles/2014/9/5/in-chad-elephantsmakeacomeback.html.
50. Hammer, "The Race to Stop Africa's Elephant Poachers." See also Hicks, "In Chad Elephants Make a Comeback."
51. "Chad Flood: 2012," http://reliefweb.int/disaster/fl-2012-000151-tcd.
52. Maplecroft, "Climate Change and Food Insecurity Multiplying Risks of Conflict and Civil Unrest in 32 Countries" (October 29, 2014), http://reliefweb.int/report/world/climate-change-and-food-insecurity-multiplying-risks-conflict-and-civil-unrest-32.
53. Lauren Ploch, *Instability and Humanitarian Conditions in Chad* (Washington, DC: Congressional Research Service, 2010), 3.
54. Ibid.
55. Bradley Klapper, "US Warns of links between Islamic State and Boko Haram," *Associated Press* (April 20, 2016), http://bigstory.ap.org/article/caba4db1bb964867a0aabd04171e44a3/us-warns-links-between-islamic-state-boko-haram.
56. Oxford Analytica, "Chad: Déby Regime Propped up Despite Oil Price Shock," *OxResearch Daily Brief Service* (April 30, 2015).
57. Ibid.

58. AFP, "23 Killed in Chad Suicide Bombings Blamed on Boko Haram" (June 16, 2016), https://www.yahoo.com/news/chad-capital-rocked-blasts-outside-police-headquarters-police-hq-acacademy-102829547.html?ref=gs.

59. Nossiter, "Battling Boko Haram," A4.

60. "Forgiveness, Its Own Reward," *Africa Confidential* (May 2015), http://www.africa-confidential.com/article/id/11092/Forgiveness%2c_its_own_reward.

61. Economist Intelligence Unit, "Chad Economy: Quick View–Chad Secures Debt Relief," *EIU News Wire* (June 5, 2015).

62. Economist Intelligence Unit, "Chad: Country Outlook," *EIU Views Wire* (June 1, 2015).

63. "Forgiveness, Its Own Reward," 2015.

64. Celeste Hicks, "Clay Feet: Chad's Surprising Rise and Enduring Weakness," *World Politics Review* (November 13, 2014), http://www.worldpoliticsreview.com/articles/14435/clay-feet-chad-s-surprising-rise-and-enduring-weakness.

65. "Winning Battles Losing Wars," *Africa Confidential* (March 15, 2015), http://www.africa-confidential.com/article/id/11091/Winning_battles%2c_losing_wars.

66. Klapper, "US Warns of links between Islamic State and Boko Haram."

67. Margot Shorey and Benjamin Nickles, "Chad: A Precarious Counterterrorism Partner" (April 30, 2015), https://www.ctc.usma.edu/posts/chad-a-precarious-counterterrorism–partner.

CHAPTER 12

# THE CASE OF TUNISIA

*Lawrence Cline*

Assessing the structural and organizational strengths and weaknesses
of Tunisian security organizations is particularly difficult because the
government is still in the process of establishing itself following the 2011
Jasmine Revolution. For several years, governing was performed through
a series of interim governments and ad hoc arrangements until a final
constitution was adopted (after considerable debate) in January 2014.
Simply establishing a working government unsurprisingly received the
overwhelming majority of political attention, with concern over detailed
internal security arrangements a much lower priority.

The Tunisian government, however, has been forced to pay attention
to internal security and the best ways of structuring the security sector
to address weaknesses. The continuing meltdown of Libya presented a
major security threat that metastasized into an internal threat for Tunisia,
especially with the rise of the Islamic State. Tunisia has suffered three

major terrorist attacks within a short time span. On March 18, 2015, three members of al Qaida in the Islamic Maghreb (AQIM) attacked the Bardo National Museum in Tunis, killing twenty-two and wounding fifty. On June 26, 2015, armed gunmen hit two tourist hotels in Sousse, killing thirty-eight and wounding thirty-nine. Finally, on November 24, 2015, a suicide bomber attacked a bus carrying members of the Tunisian Presidential Guard, killing twelve and wounding sixteen. Although these have been the major attacks, lower-level terrorist operations have unfortunately become common.

Before discussing the internal impact of these attacks, it is important to describe the external factors that are likely driving internal security decision-making. The first two attacks mentioned are particularly significant because the vast majority of the civilians killed were foreign tourists. This led to a marked external reaction. In response to the increased attention to the security threat in Tunisia, most Western governments issued travel advisories or warnings. The impact on tourism, which reportedly accounts for about seven percent of Tunisia's gross domestic product, has been profound. According to one report, overall tourist numbers for 2015 dropped from about five million to four million.[1] Obviously, this has created severe financial difficulties for a country that is already economically weak. These difficulties limit the extent of initiatives the government can realistically implement. In response, the Tunisian government has implemented an information campaign to stress that the country remains safe. Among other claims, "The country has introduced a number of security measures since last summer, including hiring a security consultant to draw up a handbook for tourism-related operations such as hotels and museums."[2]

The other result of the terrorist attacks may be more positive, at least in theory. This is the increased attention paid to the security requirements of Tunisia by foreign governments. The US, British, and French governments in particular have ratcheted up their security assistance, but several other Western European countries and the European Union as an organization have also implemented expanded security programs. Overall, these should be positive developments, but such foreign assistance typically comes with some caveats. Funding is almost always earmarked for specific programs, which at times are based more on the priorities of the donor country than on those of the recipient. The situation becomes even more complex when there are multiple countries or organizations providing support. Ideally, these support programs are sufficiently coordinated so that they provide an integrated package; unfortunately, in the real world the "advise and assist" programs commonly are conducted as independent efforts with little to no coordination with those of other countries.

The rest of this chapter examines the statutory bases of Tunisia's internal security system and the security organizations themselves. It must be stressed that this is somewhat a snapshot rather than a long-term narrative. The Tunisian government is very much in the institution-building stage, and it likely will have a number of false starts and organizational shifts in the coming years, especially as the regional environment becomes more malignant, as appears likely.

## THE STATUTORY BASES OF INTERNAL SECURITY

Several articles of the 2014 constitution, enacted January 26, 2014, deal with the security services, particularly the military. Article 9 states that national service is a duty according to the regulations and conditions established by the law. The military's impartiality is required by Article 18, which also states that the military is "charged with responsibility to defend the nation, its independence, and its territorial integrity." The same article requires that "the national army supports the civil authorities in accordance with the provisions set out in law." Article 17 prohibits nonstate security forces.

Article 19 of the Constitution deals with the security forces; although not specified further, this apparently is intended to cover both police and the other internal security organizations. The provisions are rather anodyne: "The national security forces are republican; they are responsible for maintaining security and public order, ensuring the protection of individuals, institutions, and property, and ensuring the enforcement of the law while ensuring that freedoms are respected, with complete impartiality."[3]

The status of legislation to actually implement these constitutional provisions remains in flux. Legislative oversight of security forces is very much a work in progress. The Tunisian People's Congress has established the Commission on Security and Defense, as well as the Organizing Committee of Management and Affairs of the Armed Forces. Thus far, there has been little public output from these bodies. In large measure, they still are determining their road maps for what their responsibilities should be. The Geneva Centre for the Democratic Control of Armed Forces (DCAF) has been conducting a series of workshops with members of these groups, resulting in the establishment of a draft plan for the drawing up of necessary laws.[4] Given the normal delays in legislation and the raft of issues facing the parliament, the actual process of passing legislation almost certainly will be a lengthy process.

The two major laws proposed to date both have been contentious. The counterterrorism law was passed on July 24, 2015. Foreign observers, particularly human rights groups, have found a number of issues with this law. As Mersch noted:

> The 2015 bill considers a terrorist organization "a group of three or more persons that has existed for any length of time and acts in concert with the aim to commit one of the terrorist acts under this law." Acts listed in the law include, among others, damage to public or private goods and infrastructure such as transport or telecommunications, punishable by up to twenty years in prison and a 100,000 dinar ($51,000) fine (Article 13). Critics of the law point out that this clause would allow the authorities to deem participants of a demonstration for social or economic demands as terrorists, if participants for example damage a police station or block transport infrastructure during the protest, even if they

have no links to terrorists. It could therefore be used to prohibit and criminalize largely peaceful social movements.[5]

Because this law was passed following major terrorist attacks, its breadth is not surprising; passing antiterrorism laws considered in the wake of attacks almost inevitably overreach. Beyond the human rights issues (which have been the major focus of critics), the breadth of this law also has a practical impact on governmental effectiveness. The more broadly such a law is drafted, the greater the likelihood that specialized counterterrorism organizations will be distracted from their core counterterrorism mission.

The second law of concern is the so-called Repression of Attacks against the Armed Forces bill. This bill provides wide-ranging protections for members of the armed forces in conducting internal security missions. Among other provisions of the bill, "Any attempt against members of the armed forces, their families or their properties could face up to 20 years of imprisonment and a fine of 100 thousands dinars for serious physical attacks, or detention for life in a case of murder."[6] A number of provisions of the law are sensible, but if viewed very expansively, it could offer members of the armed forces virtual carte blanche in their operations and could virtually eliminate effective civilian judicial oversight of the armed forces. As of February 2016, this bill had not received final approval by the parliament, but it has not been withdrawn; continued unrest in Tunisia could make its passage much more likely.

Beyond these two major laws, the actual legal structure of internal security is very difficult to establish with any precision. As Yezid Sayigh noted in 2015, "the texts of laws governing the police and Interior Ministry, which were not made available under Ben Ali, are still not publicly accessible in full."[7] Likewise, according to an international group working with the Tunisian government on security sector reform: "Despite the new constitutional right to information and the Access to Information Law of May 2011, citizens cannot easily access information on the security sector. There are no clear guidelines on which information can be released without compromising national security, judicial procedures, or privacy."[8]

These observations appear to be the same in mid-2016, with very few implementing orders and laws publicly available on the sites devoted to Tunisian laws.[9] The laws that are published in full generally are very prosaic, dealing with such issues as the civilian rank structure in ministries or which leadership positions are in charge of discipline. Somewhat interestingly, these types of published laws usually open with references to earlier Ben Ali era or even pre–Ben Ali-era laws. Although this is fairly typical in any legislation—and the newer laws supersede some provisions of the earlier measures—such continuity suggests a less-than-complete break with earlier organizational systems and structures.

Legislative oversight of the security forces appears to be patchy at best. After some police over-reaction to protestors in 2012, the National Constituent Assembly established a commission to investigate, but the commission reportedly received no cooperation from the Ministry of the Interior and collapsed without any results.[10] There have been a series of laws passed concerning human and civil rights—with additional agreements to implement international norms on human rights—but, again, their implementation is subject to question.

## THE NATIONAL SECURITY STRUCTURE

The October 2011 National Constituent Assembly elections led to a significant split within the national security structure. The prime minister, Hamadi Jebali, was from the Ennahdha Party, and the president, Moncef Marzouki, was from the Congress for the Republic (CPR). From this period until at least 2014, there were overlapping security structures at the national level.

The prime minister created a security council comprising the chief of staff, the director general of military security, and the ministers of defense, interior, and foreign affairs. A similar organization, renamed the Crisis Cell in 2014, has remained in existence since that period. Simultaneously, in the 2011 period, the president both appointed a military advisor to the president and re-activated the National Security Council (NSC). Although the membership in the NSC and Security Council was overlapping, having two centers for planning national security simultaneously under two political leaders was unlikely to provide particularly smooth planning or responses to crises. Sharan Grewal, in his excellent study of recent developments in the Tunisian military, argues that this system represented the rise of "institutional rule" of the military.[11] However accurate this assessment, two potentially competing power centers running national security policy could be fraught with complications.

More recently, the government created a separate Anti-Terror Commission in March 2016. This commission's duties reportedly include "awareness about the danger of terrorism, through the organisation of cultural and educational campaigns and programmes in which the civil society components are associated", and "to set up programmes and policies aimed to eradicate terrorism, and proposes execution mechanisms in addition to co-operation with international organisations and civil society components concerned with anti-terror fight."[12] The commission includes a representative of the president's office, together with members of the ministries of justice, interior affairs, defense, foreign affairs, finance, youth, agriculture, women, religious affairs, culture, and education. Technical experts from other security agencies also are members, as is a judge experienced in terrorism law. The commission has formally convened at least once since its formation on May 25, 2016, meeting under the direction of the prime minister.

The principal implementing agencies for internal security are the Ministry of Defense and Ministry of Interior. The Tunisian military consists of about 40,000 personnel, the bulk of them in the army. The Ministry of Interior controls both the police forces and the national guard. Police strength in particular is in a state of flux, but is probably in the 45,000 to 50,000 range. The National Guard has about 15,000 members, and it primarily operates in rural and border areas.

Addressing counterterrorism specifically, the Ministry of Interior and Ministry of Defense share responsibility. The Ministry of Interior incorporates the Antiterrorism Brigade of the national police and the National Guard Special Unit (with backup by the National Guard Commandos). These two units, both apparently rather small, reportedly have the lead for counterterrorism operations within the country, with the exception of the military exclusion zones. The military exclusion zones—under operational control of the Ministry of Defense—primarily are along the Algerian and Libyan borders. The zones appear to be focused on areas viewed as particularly threatening for infiltrations. These can be rather extensive, with one single zone around Kasserine reportedly about 100 square kilometers.[13] Operations against terrorists in these areas have increased sharply over about the last year, meaning that the military has assumed an increasing role in counterterrorism operations. According to the US Embassy Tunis, police, National Guard, and army forces have created counterterrorism task forces for the military exclusion zones, and tactical operations have shown good coordination.[14] As described in the following section, however, there may be historical reasons for some roadblocks between the military and police at higher levels.

## THE ARMED FORCES

To understand the current and future roles of the Tunisian Army, it is necessary to understand its status under the Ben Ali regime. The army was very much an apolitical organization with its corporate focus on external threats. The forces used for internal security and the maintenance of regime stability came from the Interior Ministry. As such, most of the attention of the regime was on Interior Ministry forces. One reflection of the relative importance of the various security services under Ben Ali was that the Ministry of Interior's budget was about 165 percent that of the Defense Ministry from 1992 until the fall of the regime.[15]

This difference in missions became very clear when the unrest began in December 2010. Numerous press reports from the time indicated that the military, in fact, protected the demonstrators from the police and other internal security forces. This reflected the military's sentiment at the time (it was reasonably apolitical) that its duty was to the nation rather than to the regime. This certainly was admirable, reflecting well on both lower-level leaders and the chief of staff, who refused to use the army against civilians.[16] The issue now, however, is the extent to which the resulting stresses between the police and internal security forces on the one hand, and the military on the other, have been overcome.

In contrast to its position before the Jasmine Revolution, the army assumed de facto ultimate authority immediately following the uprising. The then army chief of staff, Rachid Ammar, reportedly became the "go-to guy" for resolving governance issues.[17] Army officers were appointed as the director general of national security in the Ministry of Interior, commander of the National Guard, director general of customs, and to several governorships.

The army clearly has a more privileged position now than it did under Ben Ali. At the same time, however, there has not been a complete shift of missions from the internal security forces to the army. Even though the military has received a higher rate of increase in its budget than the police, the funding for the army still represents only 72 percent that of the internal security forces.[18] Furthermore, after the armed forces chief of staff Rachid Ammar retired, as of early 2016, no one had been appointed to assume that position, with each service having its own chief of staff. Although it is possible that this has been simply bureaucratic inefficiency, it is entirely plausible that it represents the government not wanting any single uniformed leader to gain too much power.

The army remains rather small, particularly given the security challenges with which it must deal. Conventional forces consist of three mechanized brigades, with supporting elements. There also are four "para-commando" battalions, together with a Special Forces brigade and a Sahara Special Forces brigade. The Special Forces brigade appears to be the primary army unit conducting both offensive missions against terrorist groups and providing army response to terrorist attacks. Tunisian Special Forces have received training and support from several other countries and appear to be relatively competent.

## Internal Security Forces

During the interim government period from 2011 to 2014, there were five different interior ministers, with an equivalent turnover among agency directors. This has resulted in serious issues in providing consistent leadership for the internal security units. In addition, as one report noted in 2012, "the organizational chart of the [Ministry of Interior] remains classified, which complicates the task of mapping the internal security structures controlled by it, as well as the oversight mechanisms within the ministry."[19] This appears to continue to be the case. Beyond making external assessment more difficult, it likely also complicates internal reform efforts.

The primary internal security organization under Ben Ali was the Internal State Security (sûreté intérieure de l'Etat). This was abolished (at least in theory) shortly after the new regime took power. In reality, the major organizational change was to rename it the Special Services Directorate (direction des services spécialisés). Members who were of questionable loyalty to the new government were either fired or transferred to other ministries, but many from the same missions apparently remained. Shortly after the new regime took power, it also dissolved the General Directorate for the Prevention of Terrorism (Direction générale de prévention anti-terrorisme; DPAT) and the Joint Committee on Intelligence and Borders (Comité commun des renseignements et des frontières).

During the former regime, the internal security forces (feared by the Tunisian people) suffered from a host of problems. They were poorly trained, highly corrupt, not particularly well-equipped, low paid, and encountered almost-constant political interference. Their only real success was keeping down a relatively quiescent population. In some ways, this was reflected in the strength estimates for the internal security forces under Ben Ali. Both outside observers and the Tunisian population believed that the security police numbered about 150,000. The actual figure was somewhere between 40,000 to 80,000, with many of these being part-timers or informers.[20] This meant that the new regime started with a number of problems regarding the internal security forces. In some ways, it might be fair to assess that the new government was surprised by just how weak the internal security forces actually were when it took power. This resulted in having to spend considerable time and resources to establish an internal security system that could function properly.

Some early decisions taken after the fall of the Ben Ali regime continue to impact the internal security forces. The Minister of Interior fired forty-two high-level police officials.[21] This was both understandable and probably inevitable because many of these officials were implicated in the crimes of the former regime. At the same time, however, it almost certainly left a leadership void within the police services. Along with this purge of police officials, the directors of virtually all internal security organizations were removed.[22]

At about the same time, the police internal affairs department was abolished (among other duties, this office had been responsible for internal discipline among the police forces). This was followed shortly thereafter by the rehiring of about 2,200 officers, formerly with the police and National Guard, who had been removed by the Ben Ali regime.[23] Some had been fired for their political beliefs or for being Islamist, but an undetermined number had been removed for cause. Their re-entry into the security services may not have been optimal for creating a new reliable force. One seemingly positive step also was taken: the creation of unions for members of the various internal security services. Given their previously low salaries and poor working conditions, police members certainly had reason to want unions to fight for their interests. Since the formation of the unions, however, there have been multiple reports that they have been assuming an increasingly political stance.

Overall, the strength level of the internal security forces has increased from about 50,000 in 2011 to 75,000 at the end of 2014. From December 2011 through January 2014, the government conducted a major recruiting drive for both the police and the National Guard, with somewhere between 9,000 and 12,000 becoming new members after only a month in training and two weeks of on-the-job assessment.[24] Police salaries have increased by about one-third. There also has been very rapid promotion of both earlier officers and the new recruits. In many cases, although an individual policeman has been promoted to a significantly higher rank, he continues to perform the duties of a regular patrolman. [25] This certainly has not helped in establishing a professional and experienced force.

Despite efforts at reform, major problems remain with the police. Many reports indicate continued significant corruption among the various services. According to one survey conducted in 2013, about 80 percent of Tunisians believe that the level of corruption among all government services—particularly the internal uniformed services—has actually increased since the revolution.[26] The police reportedly have routinely used violence since the revolution against protestors, with a number of civilians killed or injured.[27]

## INTELLIGENCE SERVICES

Details of the current intelligence structure are unsurprisingly scarce. Under Ben Ali, there were two primary intelligence services, both apparently more concerned with political intelligence to maintain internal control than with broader issues. These were the directorate general of special services for general intelligence and the directorate general of technical services for technical intelligence such as communications intercepts. The Directorate of State Security (DSE) coordinated these two agencies.

Shortly after the Jasmine Revolution, the new governing bodies abolished DSE—a decision understandable after the DSE's role in the maintenance of the former regime. As Bassem Bouguerra notes, "This decision was well received by ordinary Tunisians. Many security experts, on the other hand, saw it as a major mistake, since the DSE ensured the smooth functioning of the entire intelligence system by mining the torrent of intelligence data. Critics of the decision argue that the functioning of the whole system has become erratic, with no liaising entity filtering information and providing analysis."[28]

On December 16, 2014, the Tunisian government announced the formation of an intelligence fusion center directed against terrorism and organized crime.[29] Although part of the Ministry of Interior, it was to incorporate representatives of the ministries of interior, defense, finance, foreign affairs, and customs, as well as the prison administration. The formation of this center reportedly was not received favorably by leaders of the police union who argued that there were political motivations behind the personnel selections. The accuracy of this charge is impossible to determine.

In November 2014, the Directorate of Military Security was reestablished as the Agency for Intelligence and Security for Defense. It was given the mission of intelligence collection on "potential threats to the armed forces and the security of the country in general." It was removed from direct military control and provided its own budget with initial seed money of one million Tunisian dinars.[30]

Beyond the actual existence of these particular organizations, there are minimal details as to the intelligence system in Tunisia or its effectiveness. Given the problems faced by the other internal security agencies, however, it is probable that the intelligence bodies are plagued with many of the same issues. It almost certainly will be quite some time before the Tunisian government is able to implement an effective intelligence system.

## Assessment

**National Brand.** Post-Arab Spring Tunisia is still building its brand, with all its security institutions in considerable flux. Currently, its security services function primarily as "policemen" and "firemen," although they have a traditional role as "peacekeepers."

**Most Significant Threats.** Using the framework in table 2, Tunisia faces significant threats in three of the four quadrants. It is experiencing traditional internal and external threats as well as human internal threats. Many challenges face the security system in Tunisia. Perhaps the most significant is the economic weakness of the country. As already mentioned, this directly impacts the ability to fund and maintain the security organizations. More broadly, such weakness impacts the environment in which the security services must operate. As of the first quarter of 2016, the unemployment rate was 15.4 percent. According to OECD estimates, in 2010 youth who were not employed or in education or training—the most critical figure for estimating potential for internal unrest—was about 25 percent.[31] More recent figures are not as definitive, but are almost certainly even worse. In January 2016, the country faced massive public protests, predominantly economically based. These began in the city of Kasserine and soon spread nationwide. Within the first week, about fifty-nine security officers and forty protestors were injured.[32] The government responded to the protests by deploying major numbers of riot police and imposing curfews. Given the problems with quelling the unrest, it is far from clear that the newly reconstituted security forces were well prepared for these duties.

The environment along Tunisia's borders is particularly problematic. Although the attacks against foreign tourists unsurprisingly have received the most international attention, the Tunisians actually have suffered considerably greater casualties in the hinterlands along their borders, particularly on the Algerian border. In many cases, it is very difficult to determine if a particular armed clash is a result of encounters with terrorists or with members of well-established smuggling gangs; in some cases, these may in fact be overlapping categories. Whichever is the case, there have been considerable numbers killed or wounded on each side.

A further major complicating factor for the Tunisian authorities is the very significant number of Tunisian citizens who have left the country to join the Islamic State (IS). According to analysis of IS membership records by the Counter Terrorism Center, West Point, there have been 58.20 Tunisian residents per million population who have joined IS.[33] This is over double the rate for the next highest country. Such a high rate of involvement by Tunisian youth in itself is a security threat, but it becomes even more significant if one considers that at least a portion of these radicalized IS members will return to Tunisia.

**Roles of the Security Forces.** Both the armed forces and law enforcement are focusing primarily on internal security because this is the principal threat. Instruments for coordination and cooperation almost certainly remain a work in progress.

**Political System.** Tunisia does not fit neatly into any of the categories listed in table 4. Although it certainly is a "minimally institutionalized state", this is largely a function of the building of new institutions rather than being a traditional system. Clearly, the security services have a major impact on the political system, but this might be better ascribed to the overall security environment than to a series of deliberate decisions by the leaders of the armed forces and police. As noted, the Tunisian armed forces traditionally were largely apolitical, with the police and internal security forces much more intertwined with the governing structures. The relative balance among the various services and their pecking order with the new regime are still being developed.

Most countries experiencing severe internal security threats find the civilian government's role vis-à-vis the security services—whether armed forces, intelligence services, or police—to be changed, whether subtly or considerably. Tunisia will certainly not be an exception. Given the criticality of all the security services in efforts to deal with the convoluted internal security environment in Tunisia, the country's governing structure may very well find itself in the minimally institutionalized category for some time to come.

**Contribution of the Security Forces to Good Governance.** Relations between security forces and civil society remain very mixed. The army seems to be generally respected and trusted by the population, in many ways based on its response to the earlier civil uprising. The police and the internal security forces, on the other hand, have significant trust issues with the people.

**Trends for Security Sector Institutions.** Tunisia faces three simultaneous challenges. The first is simply to establish a functioning government. The second is to design and use evolving governmental institutions to provide effective internal security. The third is to accomplish both these efforts in an environment of extraordinary tensions. Each of these challenges is interwoven, with advances or setbacks in one strand affecting outcomes in the others. Although Tunisia has made some progress since 2011, it will face major problems in establishing effective internal security.

# Notes

1. Soo Kim, "Tunisia sees a million fewer tourists after terror attacks," *The Telegraph* (September 22, 2015), http://www.telegraph.co.uk/travel/destinations/africa/tunisia/articles/Tunisia-sees-a-million-less-tourists-after-terror-attacks/

2. John Hutchinson, "'Tunisia is safe': Defiant message from tourism chiefs as country struggles to attract visitors following last year's terror attacks," *The Daily Mail* (March 11, 2016), http://www.dailymail.co.uk/travel/travel_news/article-3487503/Tunisia-safe-Defiant-message-tourism-chiefs-country-struggles-attract-visitors-following-year-s-terror-attacks.html#ixzz4ACVNj5jQ

3. For a detailed examination of constitutional issues leading up to the 2014 Constitution, see Kent Roach, "Security Forces Reform for Tunisia," in Zaid Al-Ali and Richard Stacey (eds.), *Consolidating the Arab Spring: Constitutional Transition in Egypt and Tunisia*, Working Paper Series presented by International IDEA and the Center for Constitutional Transitions at NYU Law, June 2013, <http://constitutionaltransitions.org/working-paper-no7/>.

4. For details, see DCAF Tunisie, "Strategic planning for the Commission on the organization of the administration and of the affairs of armed forces (COAAAF) of the Assembly of People's Representatives (ARP)," (April 14, 2016), http://www.dcaf-tunisie.org/En/activite-partenaires/planification-strategique-pour-la-commission-de-lorganisation-de-ladministration-et-des-affaires-des-forces-armees-coaafa-de-lassemblee-des-representants-du-peuple-arp/77/10249

5. Sarah Mersch, "Tunisia's new counterterrorism law infringes on civil liberties and does not provide a framework to prevent violent extremism," *Carnegie Endowment for International Peace* (August 6, 2015), http://carnegieendowment.org/sada/?fa=60958. This report also includes other problematical provisions such as detention without trial. For other critiques of the law, see Human Rights Watch, *Tunisia: Counterterror Law Endangers Rights* (July 31, 2015), http://www.intelcenter.com/; and Middle East Monitor Tunisian anti-terrorism law: A balance between security and freedoms (June 10, 2014), https://www.middleeastmonitor.com/20140610-tunisian-anti-terrorism-law-a-balance-between-security-and-freedoms/.

6.  For details of this bill, see Heba Saleh, "Tunisian law raises fears of security state return," *Financial Times* (May 13, 2015), http://www.ft.com/cms/s/0/ac71f594-f89b-11e4-8e16-00144feab7de.html#axzz4AO4eMgkK; and Emna Guizanion, "New Law to Ban Attacks on Armed Forces Sparks Outcry," *Tunisialive* (April 22, 2015), http://www.tunisia-live.net/2015/04/22/new-law-to-ban-attacks-on-armed-forces-sparks-outcry/

7.  Yezid Sayigh, *Missed Opportunity: The Politics of Police Reform in Egypt and Tunisia* (Washington/Beirut: Carnegie Middle East Center, March 2015), 19.

8.  Geneva Centre for the Democratic Control of Armed Forces, *DCAF Assistance to Security Sector Reform in Tunisia Country Strategy 2014–2016* (Geneva: DCAF, 2014), 11.

9.  The two principal sites searched were http://www.legislation-securite.tn/fr/node/34429 and http://www.iort.gov.tn/WD120AWP/WD120Awp.exe/CONNECT/SITEIORT

10. Bassem Bouguerra, *Reforming Tunisia's Troubled Security Sector* (Washington: The Atlantic Council, October 2014), 3.

11. Sharan Grewal, *A Quiet Revolution: The Tunisian Military After Ben Ali* (Beirut: Carnegie Middle East Center, February 24, 2016), 7.

12. "Tunisia Creates National Anti-Terrorism Commission," 25 *African Defense News* (March 25, 2016), http://www.african-defense.com/defense-news/tunisia-creates-national-anti-terrorism-commission/

13. "Three Tunisian soldiers killed in a terrorist attack on the Algerian border," *Spanish News Online* (April 8, 2015), http://spanishnewsonline.blogspot.com/2015/04/three-tunisian-soldiers-killed-in.html.

14. Embassy of the United States, Tunis, Country Reports On Terrorism 2014 at http://tunisia.usembassy.gov/reports-on-tunisia/country-reports-on-terrorism-2014.html. Multiple press reports from the fighting in these areas also suggest effective coordination of the available forces.

15. Grewal, *A Quiet Revolution*, 4.

16. There is some debate as to the actions of General Rachid Ammar, the Chief of Staff. Most accounts suggest that he refused orders to fire on protestors. Grewal, however, argues that no such orders were ever issued. See Grewal, *A Quiet Revolution*, 5.

17. Grewal, *A Quiet Revolution*, 5.

18. Ibid., 9.

19. Cited in Sayigh, *Missed Opportunity*, 20.

20. Bouguerra, *Reforming Tunisia's Troubled Security Sector*, 1.

21. International Crisis Group, *Reform and Security Strategy in Tunisia, Middle East and North Africa* Report N°161 (Brussels: International Crisis Group; July 23, 2015): 4.

22. Haykel Ben Mahfoudh, *Security Sector Reform in Tunisia Three Years into the Democratic Transition*, Amman: Arab Reform Initiative (May 2014), 3.

23. International Crisis Group, *Reform and Security Strategy in Tunisia, Middle East and North Africa Report* no.161 (Brussels: International Crisis Group, July 23, 2015), 5.

24. ICG, 6.

25. ICG, 7.

26. Emily Parker, "Corruption Rife in Post-Revolutionary Tunisia, According to Survey," *Tunisialive* (July 11, 2013), http://www.tunisia-live.net/2013/0 7/11/corruption-rife-in-post-revolutionary-tunisia-according-to-survey/. Although this is a relatively early survey, more recent anecdotal evidence suggests similar concerns.

27. For example, see Amna Guellali, "To Build Trust, Tunisia's Security Forces Must Be Reformed," *Tunisialive* (August 17, 2013), http://www. tunisia-live.net/2013/08/17/to-build-trust-tunisias-secuirty-forces-must-be-reformed/. See also Sayigh, *Missed Opportunity*, 24.

28. Bouguerra, *Reforming Tunisia's Troubled Security Sector*, 2.

29. For details, see "Le pôle sécuritaire contre le terrorisme et le crime organisé opérationnel," *La Presse de Tunisie* (December 17, 2014), http://www. lapresse.tn/17012016/92813/le-pole-securitaire-contre-le-terrorisme-et-le-crime-organise-operationnel.html

30. Grewal, *A Quiet Revolution*, 11.

31. OECD, *Investing in Youth Tunisia: Strengthening the Employability of Youth during the Transition to a Green Economy*, Paris, 2015, 49.

32. Chris Stephen, "Tunisia imposes curfew as unrest grows over lack of jobs," *The Guardian* (January 22, 2016), http://www.theguardian.com/ world/2016/jan/22/tunisia-unrest-government-imposes-night-curfew-unemployment-protests-attacks

33. Brian Dodwell, Daniel Milton, and Don Rassler, *The Caliphate's Global Workforce: An Inside Look at the Islamic State's Foreign Fighter Paper Trail* (West Point, NY: Combating Terrorism Center at West Point, April 2016), 11.

CHAPTER 13

# SYNTHESIS

*Nicholas Tomb[1] and Paul Shemella*

We have introduced a new way of evaluating how African governments develop and employ their security forces—through governing security sector institutions and generating operational capacity. Examples from the case studies helped us shape the assessment tools of chapter 2; the tools, in turn, helped shape the case studies. Together, the preceding chapters have presented the reader with a wealth of information. But what is the practical effect of that information? How can government officials (supported by their societies-at-large) actually *use* this analysis to improve security governance, and generate the right amount of capacity in their security institutions? Having established a method, we decided to plug the cases back into the tools and examine the insights thus produced. This "synthesis" will begin with a discussion of common security challenges among the countries profiled here, continue with efforts to "fit" those governments into the framework, culminating with a "Level 2" assessment of Mali, presented in the format of tables 5–7. We are keenly aware that we do not live and work in these countries and that our judgments are necessarily incomplete. Nevertheless, our own "desired outcome" would be to institutionalize productive and long-term *local* dialogues (with or without Western partners) on how African governments can improve their security governance and strengthen the capacity of their security force institutions.

## COMMON SECURITY GOVERNANCE CHALLENGES

The security and governance challenges in Africa are numerous and daunting. Although defense expenditures are low compared to European and American spending, they are growing.[2] More importantly, African militaries tend have greater resources than their police counterparts. This imbalance has led to a blurring of the lines separating the three main elements of the security sector, with armies taking on a greater share of security roles than is perhaps healthy for a democratic society. In the modern era, authoritarian regimes have purposely kept their armed forces weak (selecting elite segments of the military—often outside the formal chain of command—to safeguard their power). Democratic winds (with a lot of help from the West) have begun to extinguish this legacy, but authoritarianism is alive and well in Africa. The challenge for African governments is to institutionalize real change without trampling the values that drive it.

Corruption is the single most significant challenge facing the governments we have profiled, made worse by a dearth of civilian defense expertise in Africa. When security institutions do not receive the resources they need to perform the tasks of their government-assigned roles, they are tempted to become involved in the formal economy, or even organized crime. When individual security personnel do not get paid enough, they do whatever they can get away with to support themselves and their families. Law enforcement personnel are particularly vulnerable to this temptation because they interact daily with the public. Corruption—

especially when it takes place in front of an audience—leads to the lack of public trust so vital to enforcing the law. Of the selected countries, only Tunisia and Mali earn double-digit rankings in a corruption index of 168 countries; the rest fall near the bottom.[3]

An environment of endemic corruption is a breeding ground for abuses of human rights. Under-resourced and unprofessional security forces often compensate by using a heavy-handed approach to enforcing the law. When soldiers are themselves enforcing the law, such a hand is even heavier. Political rights and civil liberties rankings are instructive here. Of the selected countries, only Tunisia stands out in terms of curbing corruption and enforcing the civil rights and liberties of its citizens.[4] More resources, including higher salaries, are needed to overcome the tendency for the guardians of society to turn on the very public they are sworn to protect.[5]

Coordination within the security sector is an enormous challenge in Africa (and, indeed, in all governments). Rivalries and disconnects are common, and the scarcity of resources overall generates self-serving behavior at the organizational level. Security institutions that lack the funding to develop needed capacity are not inclined to share information or credit. If the security sector plays a zero-sum game, traditional roles remain unfulfilled and missions are not accomplished. Government institutions outside the security sector generally receive even fewer resources, stimulating the same inward focus. Enhancing *human* security, however, requires all government institutions—and civil society organizations— to work together in a coordinated manner. Clearly defined roles and missions are sine qua non in meeting this challenge.

The governments we have profiled represent societies made up of myriad ethnic groups, each with its own language and cultural traditions. The challenge of creating a sense of national identity across and within such a population is fundamental to the provision of security—from the individual level all the way up to the national level. Ultimately, all citizens wish to be part of something larger than themselves. Traditionally, that identity has been found in the extended family, the clan, or the tribe.[6] Governments have to figure out how to make their citizens wish to belong to the nation-state as well.[7] National identity is the only basis upon which national institutions can provide the security governance and capacity all citizens need.

A careful reading of the case studies appears to reveal a lack of interest in maritime security. While it is true that three of our selected countries are landlocked, economic prosperity throughout Africa depends on seaborne trade—free of piracy, smuggling, illegal fishing, and terrorism. The collective challenge, laid out quite prominently in Africa's Integrated Maritime (AIM) strategy, is to develop a productive maritime ("blue") economy that benefits the whole continent. Meager security resources available now will have to be increased and then shared in new ways.[8] Maritime governance of disparate and competing institutions—at the confluence of numerous legal jurisdictions—poses some of the greatest challenges in security governance overall.[9]

Each democratic form of government is unique—based upon diverse geographic, historical, political, cultural, and economic circumstances. But all democracies are rooted in the rule of law. Constitutions are the starting point, but they are not enough. Laws are generated in order to mandate rules of conduct conducive to orderly and productive societies and economies. These laws must evolve with observed or expected changes in criminal behavior, and they must be enforced. Police institutions (and sometimes armed forces) provide that enforcement, but even that is not enough. Justice systems are the third leg of the legal stool that underpins any democratic system, sometimes overshadowed by law itself and the means to enforce it. The legal frameworks emerging in Africa often stand alone, ineffective without well-funded and professional security services —as well as the means to hold citizens accountable for violating the law.[10]

## NATIONAL BRANDS

The governments we have selected span the spectrum of table 1. The "warfighters" include Ethiopia and Chad, two countries that—for very different reasons—have responded to regional threats by developing the capacity to operate offensively against neighboring states. Ethiopia and Chad are also "defenders," and they both deploy peacekeeping contingents to the extent they can be characterized as "peacekeepers." With recent operations in Somalia, Kenya has become a "warfighter," as well as a "defender" and "peacekeeper." Nigeria is a "peacekeeper" (at least in theory), but it does not have the military capacity to qualify as a "defender" (dependent on its neighbors to repel Boko Haram, for instance). With the persistence of internal security threats, Nigeria has reverted to the "policeman" brand. With nascent security institutions, Tunisia must operate as a "policeman" and "fireman," providing peacekeepers where it can.

"Fireman" countries include Chad and Mali. That is to say, the armed forces of these two countries get involved in national development, disaster assistance, and just about everything else. Chad also uses its armed forces to enforce the law wherever the president wishes. This centralization and militarization of law enforcement distinguishes Chad as a "policeman" country. Mali's armed forces are sometimes cast in a support role, but they are not used systematically to enforce laws. Togo has followed the same path as Chad, where armed forces are the only institutions trusted by the government, but the country has withdrawn the primary law enforcement role from its armed forces. Policing in both is focused on regime security rather than providing public safety. From this we can surmise that Mali's and Togo's democracies will develop faster than that of Chad.

The 'troublemaker" countries on our list must start with Guinea-Bissau, a country that has become a national-level kingpin for narcotics trafficking whose reach extends all the way to Europe. The litany of destabilization activities in Central Africa since 1994 would have to qualify DRC for "troublemaker" status as well. One lesson from the DRC experience is that a large country, unstable itself, will inevitably export instability to others. The DRC is certainly large and unstable; its nine neighbors have imported much of the resulting chaos.

Our analysis has prompted us to propose two additional national brands: "security provider" and "criminal state." Chad's rebranding has made it an indispensable provider of security to the Sahel region. Guinea-Bissau's trafficking activities might have earned it the label "criminal state" in years past, but recent Western assistance programs have lifted it back to mere "troublemaker" status.[11] Both national brands are unsustainable in the medium term. The results of this part of our analysis are summarized in table 9.

## THREATS AND RISKS

As explained in chapter 2, threats and risks are not the same thing. Whether threats constitute serious risks to citizens and their property depends largely on how governments use their security forces. Table 2 lists examples of security threats common to Africa, both man-made and natural. The list is not exhaustive, but it does reveal some important teaching points. First, traditional security threats from outside the country are serious and can erupt suddenly; armed forces are the only institutions available to address them. Traditional threats from inside the country can be just as significant but often take time to develop. Police institutions are best suited to these situations, beginning at the community level, with civic-mindedness. Governments that use armed forces for enforcing the law have either extremely high crime or very weak police institutions (or both). Whichever is the case, these societies tend to have poor civil-military relations and less human security.

The second point is that human security threats—whether coming from inside or outside the country—call for whole-of-government strategic responses. Governments that assign their armed forces primary roles in responding to natural disaster, mass migration, or health insecurity dilute their vital defense functions.[12] Armed forces cannot do everything. If they try (or are directed) to do too much for too long, the mentality and skill-sets needed for their primary roles will be degraded. Other government institutions, including police institutions, should take the lead for human security, with assistance as needed from the armed forces. Intelligence institutions can have a role in both external and internal support for security forces, but—in order to insure the protection of civil rights and human rights—these functions are normally fulfilled by separate institutions. The provision of human security depends, then, on three interlocking factors: the governance of security institutions, the roles they are assigned, and how democratically they are controlled.

## POLITICAL SYSTEMS

In terms of political systems, the selected governments are an instructive group. None of the selected governments can be categorized as "collapsed states" (although Guinea-Bissau and DRC come close). As we have seen in the cases of Somalia, Eritrea, Libya, and South Sudan, states that collapse reduce security for a whole region—and sometimes farther afield (see Europe). The academic question is, then, how does the international community prevent states from regressing to that point? Or, how can "technical and financial partners" lift "collapsed states" out of chaos and total dependency? The assessment tools offered here can help at the very bottom, but they are best applied once a government achieves some degree of independence from development and humanitarian organizations.

The slow-but-steady democratic wave has not yet washed away personal rule as a method of exercising power in Africa. We believe that Chad, DRC, and Togo fall under this rubric, democratic rhetoric to the contrary (although Togo appears to be making an honest effort to transition to institutional rule). Personal rule is associated closely with firm control of security forces, albeit the wrong kind of control. Not surprisingly, the three countries in this category suffer from some of the lowest levels of human security in the world. The more powerful security institutions are politically, the less security they seem to produce. Even security forces with robust operational capacity, if they are governed badly, can produce a net loss of security at the human level.

The "minimally institutionalized states" in our grouping include Mali, Guinea, Guinea-Bissau, and Tunisia. Mali's institutional development had to be restarted, while Guinea's continues at a slow pace. Both governments are undergoing intensive security sector reform, facilitated by technical and financial partners. The reform of security sectors cannot be allowed to interfere with, or limit development of, the nonsecurity sector institutions needed to produce human security. Governments that wish to advance to more institutionalized states require a balanced set of institutions from the start.

Ethiopia is a strong and productive but "noncompetitive institutionalized state." It remains to be seen if Ethiopia can make the political transition to a competitive state (or whether it even wants to do so). The key to this transition will be the country's security institutions. At some point, the armed forces will have to be taken off a war footing, forcing the government to share resources across the spectrum of institutions more equitably. If police institutions cannot be professionalized—and corruption reduced—social discontent will mount beyond the government's ability to control it, evidenced recently in the Oromia and Amhara regions. In the longer term, Ethiopia's emphasis on traditional security will have to shift to human security.

We list two "institutionalized competitive states": Nigeria and Kenya (if things go well, Tunisia might qualify at some point). We do not mean to say that these societies are governed as well as Denmark, for instance. They are simply doing better than the others in this study, and better than most African states generally. Nigeria (with new political leadership) has finally started to roll back Boko Haram; but without substantial effort to improve human security, however, the country faces continued political risk. Kenya is still riven by tribal conflict, and Tunisia's democratic experiment rests on benign Islamist intent. All three governments have a lot of work to do. The results of this analysis are posted in table 10.

## DEMOCRATIC CONTROL

The assessment framework introduced in chapter 2 can be applied to all the selected African governments, but it comes with two caveats. First, the assignment of numbers to each desired outcome can only be useful as part of an honest discussion among experts from all sectors of government. Our intent was to make the model simple enough to be used by local officials—without the participation of foreign partners. The results of the assessment will likely yield many ideas requiring outside assistance; the resulting initiatives should be driven by Africans themselves. The second caveat is that governments should be assessed, to some degree, relative to one another. Comparing African security governance and capacity to European or American standards does not produce the best approaches to desired outcomes (and perhaps quite a lot of frustration).

There is not enough space here to illustrate how tables 5–8 might be used to evaluate security governance and capacity in all the governments we have profiled. Putting ourselves in the shoes of local experts, we attempted to flesh out the tables in a way that will help the reader understand the framework, using the government of Mali as an example.[13] Tables 11–13 are the result of that effort. For some desired outcomes, we did not have enough information to make a judgment. For others, we reached consensus on all three fields: governance, capacity, and major shortfalls. Part 2 of the Level 2 assessment, using table 8, is left to those with deep knowledge of particular Malian security institutions. We hope that our efforts give Mali's experts a head start—and all others a better idea of how to extract the most benefit from such an exercise. Given that the challenges associated with security institutions are virtually universal, we recommend that all African governments consider using the framework we have proposed.[14]

## CONCLUSION

Considering the diversity of human security threats, it is not difficult to see how *all* the institutions of government have been ushered into the security sector. Governments cannot succeed in balancing traditional security threats against resources without taking into account the resources of other institutions needed for enhancing *human* security. In other words, the traditional security sector can actually damage human security by absorbing too much funding. The framework suggested in this book can lead the analyst to a thorough assessment of security sector institutions—for both traditional and human security functions.

Africa is the second largest continent in the world, with fifty-four nations and over one billion inhabitants. As would be expected in such a large, diverse region, there is considerable variation in the professionalism and effectiveness of the continent's armed forces. The authors in this volume used a unique framework to analyze the condition of the armed forces in ten African countries and examine the state of security governance and the health of civil-military relations in their case studies. We suggest that all government officials in Africa study our framework to see if it works for them. Adjustments might be needed in some cases, but the ideas are solid.

This analysis has shown the range of professionalism that various armed forces have achieved, and the levels of trust and support that they enjoy with their citizens. It has also identified some common themes afflicting many African militaries. One key theme identified again and again is that civilian leaders fear their armed forces—and the threat to personal sovereignty that powerful militaries represent. As we saw in Togo and the DRC, the armed forces are purposefully left weak and unorganized, with only specialized units dedicated to the protection of the ruling regime receiving adequate pay, training, and equipment. At the same time—and paradoxically—we see that in many African countries the military is the strongest institution in the country.

Another theme that stands out is the unplanned growth of many militaries as rebel militias are integrated into the national armed forces at the end of violent conflict, as was the case in the DRC (and South Africa). While this may have the desired short-term effect of dealing with armed groups, ultimately such integration undermines the effectiveness and efficiency of the force, leading to problems with command-and-control and national unity. Whether or not there is a history of violent conflict, security forces—particularly police forces—should be composed of ethnic mixes that approximate the population at large. Beyond this, incorporating a significant number of women into these institutions (which some African governments have started to do) can increase their effectiveness at home and abroad.[15]

Although we have mentioned some possibilities that might lead to better scores on a government's assessment of security governance and capacity, the actual measurement of institutional effectiveness is extremely challenging. From a continental perspective, the number of governments that move toward "institutionalized competitive states" over time is an important rough measure. At the national level (as we have seen in Chad), changes in branding can indicate where a country might be headed—for better or for worse. In order to see progress at these levels, however, Africa's security institutions must increase capacity, deepen democratic control, and reduce corruption. These are the things that analysts will have to find ways to measure as we all go forward.

We have used typologies to categorize governments according to how they develop and use security forces—especially armed forces. Just as taxonomy has sharpened our understanding of living organisms, the sorting of countries can show us how they are different from each other —and how they are similar. Unlike biology, however, governments can change their classifications. This suggests they can learn from each other and make those changes more quickly. But change comes in two forms: radical and incremental. In matters of improving security governance and generating more capacity, incremental change is probably the best route to the desired outcomes we propose—a steady restructuring rather than quick transformation. African countries face many threats and challenges, but with these come opportunities. Some governments are seizing those opportunities and others are not; but the continental trend leans, however slowly, toward better security governance, as well as better governance overall. We hope the analytical framework provided in this volume will help African policymakers and practitioners strengthen that trend.

Table 9. National Brands (Use of Armed Forces).

| 1. Warfighter | Ethiopia, Chad, Kenya |
|---|---|
| 2. Defender | Kenya, Ethiopia, Chad, Mali, Togo |
| 3. Peacekeeper | Nigeria, Kenya, Ethiopia, Chad, Togo, Mali, Guinea, Tunisia |
| 4. Fireman | Chad, Mali, Tunisia |
| 5. Policeman | Chad, Nigeria, Tunisia |
| 6. Troublemaker | Guinea–Bissau, DRC |
| 7. Security Provider | Chad |
| 8. Criminal State | None from the cases profiled |

Table 10. Typology of Political Systems.

| Collapsed State | None from this sample* |
|---|---|
| Personal Rule | Chad, DRC, Togo |
| Minimally Institutionalized State | Mali, Guinea, Guinea–Bissau, Tunisia |
| Institutionalized Non-Competitive State | Ethiopia |
| Institutionalized Competitive State | Nigeria, Kenya |

Note. Libya, Somalia, and The Central African Republic arguably fall into this category.

Table 11a. Mali Level 2 Assessment (Armed Forces).

| Armed Forces | Desired Outcome | Governance Measure (1-10) | Capacity Measure (1-10) | Major Shortfalls |
|---|---|---|---|---|
| 1 | The armed forces have legal and well-defined *external* and *internal* roles. | 7 | 1 | - Chain of command (civilian and military) not clear.<br>- Unprepared for tactical operations outside borders.<br>- Heavy dependence on technical and financial partners. |
| 2 | *Internal* roles are coordinated with law enforcement and intelligence at all levels of strategy. | 6 | 5 | - Only *ad hoc* and crisis-driven cooperation. |
| 3 | Officers of the armed forces and civilian officials are given opportunities to educate each other regarding the proper use of armed forces. | 3 | 5 | - No institutions or schools for sharing of defense knowledge. |
| 4 | Armed forces institutions reflect the ethnic, gender, and tribal composition of the society at large. | 2 | 1 | - No robust policies or processes to integrate military services. |
| 5 | There is continuous legislative oversight of armed forces activities. | 1 | 2 | - Defense committee has no power, resources, expertise or incentives for oversight of armed forces. |
| 6 | The armed forces are trusted by all segments of society. | Not enough reliable information | Not enough reliable information | - Corruption<br>- Human rights abuses.<br>- Low pay.<br>- No opinion polls or other metrics. |

Table 11b. Mali Level 2 Assessment (Armed Forces) (*cont.*).

| Armed Forces | Desired Outcome | Governance Measure (1-10) | Capacity Measure (1-10) | Major Shortfalls |
|---|---|---|---|---|
| 7 | Armed forces institutions play no role in the national economy. | Not enough reliable information | Not enough reliable information | - Resource-poor institutions. |
| 8 | Decision-making by and about the armed forces is transparent. | 5 | 5 | - Transparency not proactive.<br>- No robust institutional mechanism for strategic communications. |
| 9 | Private armies and militias do not operate in the country. | 1 | 1 | - Low government security capacity.<br>- Ethnic imbalances within military. |
| 10 | Civilians exercise effective democratic control of armed forces. | 4 | 4 | - Lack of strategic vision.<br>- Lack of civilian defense expertise.<br>- Lack of resources.<br>- Corruption within security institutions. |
| Total Scores (÷10) | | 4.1 | 2.7 | - Starting from low base after 2012 military coup and defeat in the North.<br>- Professional development *ad hoc* and not institutionalized. |

Table 12a. Mali Level 2 Assessment (Law Enforcement).

| Law Enforce-ment | Desired Outcome | Governance Measure (1-10) | Capacity Measure (1-10) | Major Shortfalls |
|---|---|---|---|---|
| 1 | The internal roles for law enforcement institutions are legally and clearly defined. | 7 | 1 | - Resource-poor institutions. - Lack of professional development. |
| 2 | There are legal and operational mechanisms for allowing armed forces and intelligence units to support law enforcement institutions. | 7 | 3 | - Limited cooperation by intelligence agencies. |
| 3 | Law enforcement institutions maintain partnerships with commercial security companies. | Not enough reliable information | Not enough reliable information | - Commercial enterprises must provide all or most of their own security. |
| 4 | There is a legal framework for the use of law enforcement at all levels. | 8 | 3 | - Legal guidelines not implemented. - High levels of police corruption. |
| 5 | There is continuous legislative oversight of law enforcement activities. | 1 | 1 | - Weak justice system. - Lack of standards for selection of judges. |
| 6 | Law enforcement institutions reflect the ethnic, gender, and tribal composition of the society at large. | 1 | 1 | - Ethnic identity used deliberately for political advantage. - No integration system in place. |
| 7 | Law enforcement personnel are trusted by all segments of society. | Not enough reliable information | Not enough reliable information | - Human rights abuses. - Low pay. - No opinion polls or other metrics. |

Table 12b. Mali Level 2 Assessment (Law Enforcement) (*cont.*).

| Law Enforce -ment | Desired Outcome | Governance Measure (1-10) | Capacity Measure (1-10) | Major Shortfalls |
|---|---|---|---|---|
| 8 | Law enforcement institutions play no role in the national economy. | Not enough reliable information | Not enough reliable information | - Lack of institutional resources. |
| 9 | There is a system of judicial oversight regarding law enforcement activities. | 5 | 2 | - Lack of judicial expertise. - High rate of impunity. |
| 10 | Elected civilian officials exercise effective democratic control of law enforcement institutions. | 4 | 3 | - Less transparency than armed forces. - Weaker legal framework. - Greater opportunity for corruption. |
| Total Scores (÷10) | | 4.7 | 2.0 | - Lack of professional development. - Meager assistance from technical and financial partners. |

Table 13a. Mali Level 2 Assessment (Intelligence).

| Intelligence | Desired Outcome | Governance Measure (1-10) | Capacity Measure (1-10) | Major Shortfalls |
|---|---|---|---|---|
| 1 | Intelligence institutions and agencies, both civilian and military, have legal and well-defined roles, both internal and external. | 5 | 2 | - Lack of democratic control.<br>- Politicization of intelligence. |
| 2 | There are separate oversight mechanisms for armed forces-led intelligence services and civilian-led intelligence services. | 2 | 1 | - No legislative intelligence oversight committee.<br>- Limited information available regarding intelligence. |
| 3 | There are opportunities for civilian policy makers and intelligence officials to educate one another regarding the intelligence profession. | 2 | 1 | - No institution or school dedicated to intelligence education.<br>- Culture of secrecy. |
| 4 | There is an effective mechanism for sharing information among all intelligence institutions. | Not enough reliable information | Not enough reliable information | - Not enough transparency for decision-making.<br>- No intelligence fusion center. |
| 5 | There is a legal framework for all intelligence activities. | Not enough reliable information | Not enough reliable information | - Culture of secrecy. |
| 6 | Intelligence institutions and agencies are subject to executive oversight. | 2 | 1 | - No formal executive oversight. |
| 7 | Intelligence institutions and agencies are subject to legislative oversight. | 2 | 1 | - No formal legislative oversight. |

Table 13b. Mali Level 2 Assessment (Intelligence) *(cont.)*.

| Intelligence | Desired Outcome | Governance Measure (1-10) | Capacity Measure (1-10) | Major Shortfalls |
|---|---|---|---|---|
| 8 | There is a mechanism for judicial review of sensitive intelligence activities. | Not enough reliable information | Not enough reliable information | - Judicial review mechanism unknown and improbable. |
| 9 | There is a system for periodically declassifying intelligence information. | Not enough reliable information | Not enough reliable information | - Declassification policies and practices unknown. |
| 10 | Elected civilian officials exercise effective democratic control of all intelligence institutions and agencies. | 3 | 2 | - Largely scandal-driven. - Media/public access limited. |
| Total Scores (÷10) | | 2.8 | 1.4 | - Insufficient time to fully develop intelligence governance and capacity after 2012. |

# NOTES

1. All opinions expressed in this chapter are the author's and do not reflect official positions of either the Naval Postgraduate School or the United States government.
2. Chuter and Gaub, *Understanding African Armies*, 15.
3. "Corruption By Country/Territory," *Transparency International Corruption Perceptions Index* (2015), https://www.transparency.org/country.
4. "Freedom in the World," Freedom House, https://www.freedomhouse.org/report/freedom-world/freedom-world-2014.
5. Singapore, one of the least corrupt governments in the world, pays its key government officials a much higher salary than they deserve. This expenditure is thought to deter custodians of the public trust from engaging in corrupt activities. See "Why Singapore Has the Cleanest Government Money Can Buy," *Bloomberg View* (January 24, 2012), https://www.bloomberg.com/view/articles/2012-01-25/why-singapore-has-the-cleanest-government-money-can-buy-view.
6. For a brilliantly concise discussion of tribal dynamics, see Sebastian Junger, *Tribe* (New York: Twelve, 2016).
7. In our travels, we have been surprised at the level of patriotism displayed by most Africans toward their dysfunctional governments. Perhaps, in the lingering glow of decolonization, Africans are collectively elevating their loyalties to the national level. At the same time, Europeans appear to be *lowering* their loyalties to the national level, having experimented with globalism (see "Brexit" and the future of the European Union).
8. See 2050 Africa's Integrated Maritime Strategy" (AIM Strategy), African Union, Version 1.0, 2012. East Africa is showing significant cooperation among military and police maritime security institutions, particularly against illegal fishing.
9. Though maritime resources are negligible, African governments have institutional choices to make. The roles of navies, coast guards, and other maritime law enforcement institutions must be de-conflicted and their funds synchronized. For a comprehensive treatment of these challenges, see Paul Shemella, *Global Responses to Maritime Violence: Cooperation and Collective Action* (Stanford, CA: Stanford University Press, 2016).

10. Piracy is an interesting example. Obviously unacceptable (a so-called "universal crime"), it is not always codified as illegal in national law. The practical effect is that, on the rare occasions pirates are apprehended, they sometimes must be released. Laws must evolve as rapidly as do crimes, and maritime law is particularly slow.

11. Other "criminal states" in the world might include North Korea, Myanmar, and perhaps Russia.

12. Botswana, with no credible external threats, has chosen to use its defense forces to counter wildlife poachers—as the primary role. This exception illustrates the sharp differences among African countries regarding threats and risks.

13. Mali is both a good and a bad example of efforts to improve security governance. On one hand, there is tangible progress; on the other, external assistance (mostly from the United Nations and France) may be obscuring more serious challenges. The desired outcomes remain, but their successful implementation remains to be fully realized.

14. The development of capability and capacity in these institutions should be conducted at the organizational level in parallel, and in coordination with, the institutional assessment process.

15. South Africa operates a mostly female counterpoaching unit ("The Black Mambas"). Ethiopia has integrated women into its peacekeeping units. Ellen Johnson-Sirleaf, the president of Liberia, has set a goal of 20% female personnel in both the armed forces and the police. See Earnest Harsch, "Security Reform the Key to Protecting Women," *African Renewal, Special Edition on Women* (2012): 24.

# INDEX

# About the Authors

**Paul Shemella** retired from the Navy at the end of 1996 after a career in Special Operations. During his military service, he planned and executed counter terrorism and counter narcotics operations in Latin America, Europe, and other regions. He earned a master's degree in national security affairs at the Naval Postgraduate School and attended the Kennedy School of Government at Harvard University as a Senior Fellow in National Security. Captain Shemella joined The Center for Civil-Military Relations (CCMR) in 1998. Until 2014, he was the CCMR program manager for the 'Combating Terrorism Fellowship' program (CTFP), focusing on civil-military responses to terrorism and maritime violence. Captain Shemella was the CCMR program manager for Africa until retiring in 2015 and now serves as Lecturer Emeritus. He is the editor and principal author of two books published by Stanford University Press—*Fighting Back: What Governments Can Do About Terrorism* and *Global Responses to Maritime Violence: Cooperation and Collective Action.*

**Nicholas Tomb** is the program manager for the Africa Program at the Center for Civil-Military Relations (CCMR) at the US Naval Postgraduate School (NPS). Prior to managing the Africa Program, Mr. Tomb served as the assistant program manager for the Collaborative & Adaptive Security Initiative and the Prevention, Relief & Recovery program, and as a program coordinator for the Center for Stabilization & Reconstruction Studies, also at NPS. He is a cofounder and former president of the board of directors of Global Majority, an international, nonprofit organization that promotes nonviolent conflict resolution through education and training, networking, and advocacy. Mr. Tomb holds a master's degree in international policy studies from the Monterey Institute of International Studies (now the Middlebury Institute of International Studies), which included certificates in conflict resolution and commercial diplomacy.

**Thomas Bruneau** is a Distinguished Professor of National Security Affairs at the Naval Postgraduate School. He joined the NSA Department in 1987 after having taught in the Department of Political Science at McGill University in Montreal, Canada since 1969. Dr. Bruneau became Chairman of the Department in 1989, and continued in that position until 1995. Dr. Bruneau was the Academic Associate for the curriculum in International Security and Civil-Military Relations from its founding in 1996 until 2002. Between 1998 and 2001 he served as rapporteur of the Defense Policy Board, which provides the Secretary of Defense and his staff with independent and informed advice on questions of national security and defense policy. He became Director of the Center for Civil Military Relations in November 2000, a position he held until December 2004. Dr. Bruneau received his MA and PhD from the University of California at Berkeley.

**Paul Clarke** is an independent security expert, who has worked in collaboration with the Center for Civil-Military Relations (CCMR) at the Naval Postgraduate School in Monterey since 2009. Through CCMR he participates in combating terrorism programs throughout the world, focusing on strategy development, defense institution building and strategic communications. Dr. Clarke is also a senior defense analyst with the RAND Corporation and an adjunct professor at the Air Force Command and Staff College and the Naval War College. Dr. Clarke served as a US Air Force officer from 1987 to 2007. He had two tours at the National Security Council staff at the White House, culminating as Assistant Press Secretary for Foreign Affairs. His last deployment was to the Persian Gulf in 2006. Dr. Clarke holds a PhD in public policy from Auburn University.

**Lawrence E. Cline** completed a career as an intelligence officer and Middle East Foreign Area Officer in the US Army. His military service featured tours of duty in Egypt, Lebanon, El Salvador, and Somalia, as well as Joint Staff and Special Forces assignments. He holds an MA in international relations from Boston University and a PhD in political science from SUNY Buffalo. The author of *The Lord's Resistance Army* (Praeger, 2013), Dr. Cline has also published a number of articles on international security and internal security affairs in various academic journals. Since 2002 Dr. Cline has been a regular contract instructor for Defense Department counterterrorism programs, and in 2006 he volunteered for recall to active duty and served as an intelligence advisor in Iraq.

**Christopher Jasparro** is Associate Professor of National Security Affairs and Director of African Studies at the US Naval War College. He specializes in African and Asian transnational security issues, environmental security, cultural property protection, and security cooperation. He teaches and leads seminars and exercises on strategy development, international relations, African security affairs, and security cooperation. His audiences include mid-level and senior US and international military officers, as well as civilian officials. A former Naval Reserve officer, Dr. Jasparro is also a geographer and anthropologist with a PhD from the University of Kentucky. He has conducted field research and engaged in security cooperation activities in various African countries.

**Florina Cristiana Matei** is a lecturer as well as a program manager for the Latin America & Intelligence Programs for the Center for Civil-Military Relations (CCMR) at the United States Naval Postgraduate School (NPS). Dr. Matei is on the editorial board of several academic journals, including *the International Journal of Intelligence and CounterIntelligence.* She is coeditor of *The Routledge Handbook of Civil–Military Relations.* Dr. Matei earned an MA in international security affairs from the Naval Postgraduate School and received her PhD from the Department of War Studies at the King's College, University of London.

**Thomas R. Mockaitis** is Professor of History at DePaul University. He holds an MA and a PhD in modern British and Irish history from the University of Wisconsin-Madison. Dr. Mockaitis is the author of numerous books on terrorism and insurgency, including *Osama bin Laden: A Biography.* A renowned expert on government responses to irregular security threats, Dr. Mockaitis is coeditor of the journal *Small Wars and Insurgencies* and a frequent commentator on terrorism issues on various radio and television networks. He has lectured at military educational institutions all over the world, including the Royal Military Academy Sandhurst (UK). Dr. Mockaitis has held the Eisenhower Chair at the Royal Military Academy of the Netherlands and has been a regular faculty member of the Center for Civil-Military Relations (CCMR) since 2003.

**Bruce Sweeney** is a Military Professor and the FAO Chair in the Department of National Security Affairs at the Naval Postgraduate School, as well as an Army Foreign Area Officer for Africa. Colonel Sweeney's most recent assignment was as Defense Attaché and Senior Defense Official in Addis Ababa, Ethiopia. Prior to that assignment he was SDO/DATT in Paris, France. He has extensive overseas experience in almost every region of the world: Western Europe, Eastern Europe, Africa, the Middle East, and South Asia. Colonel Sweeney also has more than five years of command experience and served combat tours in Afghanistan and Iraq. He holds an MBA from Syracuse University and a masters of strategic studies from the US Army War College.

**Madoua Teko-Folly** is an adjunct staff member at the RAND Corporation and an assistant professor at the Defense Language Institute Foreign Language Center. He teaches French skills acquisition and cultural, political and socioeconomic related issues in sub-Saharan Africa at the US Army Command and General Staff College in Fort Leavenworth. He served as a consultant for the DDR Unit of the Bureau for Crisis Prevention and Recovery at the United Nations Development Programme, where his work focused primarily on translation and research on the disarmament, demobilization and reintegration of ex-combatants. Mr. Teko-Folly also served as a member of the Board of Directors at Global Majority (and is a current member of the International Board of Advisers). Mr. Teko-Folly earned his masters' degrees in both translation and international policy studies, with a specialization in international negotiations and conflict resolution from the Monterey Institute of International Studies.

# Rapid Communications
## in Conflict and Security

Utilizing its unique capability to combine speed of publication with high-production values, Cambria Press is proud to announce a new series, Rapid Communications in Conflict and Security (RCCS), to bring to market in a timely manner books on a range of pressing aspects of global and national conflict—from foreign policy and diplomacy to the projection of both inter- and intrastate hard power. The series is headed by general editor Dr. Geoffrey R. H. Burn, a former army officer with a doctorate in organization theory and strategy as well as thirty years of experience as the chief executive of book and journal publishing companies.

The RCCS series will provide policy makers, practitioners, analysts, and academics with in-depth analysis of fast-moving topics that require urgent yet informed debate. Wherever possible, arguments will be set within an appropriate theoretical and/or historical context—but all books will have practical application.

Since its launch in October 2015, the RCCS series has published the following books:

- *A New Strategy for Complex Warfare: Combined Effects in East Asia* by Thomas A. Drohan
- *US National Security: New Threats, Old Realities* by Paul R. Viotti
- *Security Forces in African States: Cases and Assessment* edited by Paul Shemella and Nicholas Tomb

For more information or questions on the RCCS series, please contact editor@cambriapress.com.

# PRAISE FOR THE BOOK

"Until the publishing of *Security Forces in African States: Cases and Assessment*, policy makers charged with assisting African states had no comprehensive reference describing how African states should develop and employ their security services. Now they do. Brilliantly written by security experts who know Africa, this book is a must read for security professionals, academics and students."

—Russell D. Howard,
Brigadier General (RET),
U.S. Army Special Forces and
Senior Fellow, Joint Special Operations University

\* \* \* \* \*

"A brilliant assessment of contemporary civil-military relations across Africa. The contributors to *Security Forces in African States: Cases and Assessment* create and apply a disarmingly simple yet effective assessment tool for their country studies in order to determine the state of security governance in ten politically diverse African nations. Reformers can use it to assess both civil-military relations in the context of rapid political transition and state accountability for sustaining good governance and democratic ideals."

—Chiseche Salome Mibenge,
Stanford University

\* \* \* \* \*

"Paul Shemella and his collaborators bring much needed attention to the role of security forces in African nations, examining the purpose, viability and necessity of the military in a context largely free from external threat. Readers will better understand the role of security forces, and the case studies will generate many ideas that merit further exploration."

—Jean-Phillipe Peltier,
Colonel, US Air Force and
Former Director of USAFA International Programs

\* \* \* \* \*

"An important and highly cohesive volume, providing a comprehensive approach to assessing the role of the security sector in a variety of African states. The individual chapters, using an invaluable analytic framework developed by the editors, offer illuminating national assessments as a foundation for determining next steps in reform. Highly recommended for practitioners and scholars alike."

—Phil Williams,
Wesley W. Posvar Chair, and Director,
Matthew B. Ridgway Center for International Security Studies,
University of Pittsburgh

\* \* \* \* \*

www.ingramcontent.com/pod-product-compliance
Lightning Source LLC
Chambersburg PA
CBHW031412270326
41929CB00010BA/1430